No Success Like Failure

No Success Like Failure

The American Love of Self-Destruction,
Self-Aggrandizement
and Breaking Even

by Ivan Solotaroff

The Sheep Meadow Press
Riverdale-on-Hudson, New York

"In the Land of the Fischer King" and "Sympathy for the Devil" originally appeared in *Esquire*. Portions of *"Once a Man, Twice a Child"* originally appeared in *Entertainment Weekly*. The remaining stories originally appeared in the *Village Voice*.

Published by the Sheep Meadow Press
Post Office Box 1345, Riverdale-on-Hudson, New York 10471.

Designed and Typeset by the Sheep Meadow Press.

Distributed by the Sheep Meadow Press.

This book meets the guidelines for permanence and durability of the Committee on Production Guidelines for Book Longevity of the Council on Library Resources.

Library of Congress Cataloging-in-Publication Data

Solotaroff, Ivan
        No success like failure: the American love of self-destruction, self-aggrandizement and breaking even / by Ivan Solotaroff
                p.   cm.
        ISBN 1-878818-32-5 (cloth) – ISBN 1-878818-31-7 (paper)
        1. United States–Civilization–1970-   2. United States–Social conditions–1980-   I. Title.
        E169.12.S66 1994
        973.9–dc20   94-2092
                                                                            CIP

TABLE OF CONTENTS

ACKNOWLEDGMENTS

The professional good will of many people went into these pieces. Jonathon Z. Larsen, new then as editor-in-chief of the *Village Voice*, published my first feature, on Charlie Barnett, after it had languished "in the well" for some four months. Stanley Moss of Sheep Meadow was more than gracious in taking this manuscript after it lost its moorings at two other houses. I'd particularly like to acknowledge David Hirshey and Will Blythe of *Esquire*, as well as the magazine's former editor-in-chief, Terry McDonell.

Linda Sanders first gave me the idea of writing journalism, as did my father, Ted, who insisted that any writer should at least be able to pay the rent with it. My brother, Paul, with his bottomless knowledge of popular culture, suggested a good number of these pieces. My wife, Janet Byrne, read every word I wrote, dozens of times, and tens of thousands eventually thrown out.

For support, ranging from massive to inchoate, in alphabetical order: Peter Alson, Max Apple, Deborah Baker, Andre Behr, Marianne Butler, Aldem Byrnes, Michael Caruso, Rachel Clarke, Jose Cucci, Hy and Sandy Enzer, Jim Fitzgerald, John Gaffney, Amitav Ghosh, Jimmy Glenn, Joel Griffiths, Virginia Heiserman, Andy Hsiao, Susan Kamel, Deborah Karl, Jeff Klein, Kenny Kleinpeter, Pete Kuhns, James Lasdun, Paul Lazar, Louis London, Melody London, Gary Lynch, Jim Mairs, Bob Massie, Albert Mobilio, Jane Moss, Charles and Wendy Murphy, Irene Naumola, Geoffrey O'Brien, Neil Ortenberg, Eric Perret, Carmela Perri, Daniel Pintschbeck, Chris Raymond, Lisa Ross, Greg Sandow, Irene Skolnick, Michael Solomon, Jason Solotaroff, Isaac Solotaroff, Elaine Stillerman, Ed Swift, Peter Tanzer, Bill Tonelli, Tom Verlaine, Marcus Viscidi, Mark Warren, Alan Wells, Linda and Alicia Whitaker, Mark Yoffie, and Marcie (whose last name I never quite caught).

Most important, I'd like to acknowledge my subjects, who gave, freely or unwittingly, of their time and honesty and suffered the inevitable betrayal.

For my mother, Lynn Solotaroff.
Rest in peace.

The Dreamer Deceiver
The Reno Trial of Judas Priest

By the banks of the Truckee River, under a nearly full moon, a tall, vaguely Hispanic-looking man with beautiful shoulder-length black hair, a foot-long beard, and a plump, perfectly relaxed body comes over to tell me that Satan is walking proud. He introduces himself as Jacob, slips a small U.S. Army pack off his shoulder and tells me he just missed the midnight bus out of town.

"Satan's walking proud through the cities," he quickly amends himself, taking a deep whiff of grass and river. "That's why I'll only work migrant, out in the country. I know the joy of the mountain cat's full belly," he says, fixing me with an aggressively devout smile, "and I know the pain of the deer that's in there."

It's my third night in Reno, and I've come down to this river that snakes through the center of town for some fresh air before turning in. I was hoping to spare myself that 24-hour passion play of the casinos, but there's no escaping it here: Heaven and Hell are married on every other street corner in Reno. Two blocks down, across from the Washoe County District Courthouse, where I've been spending my days watching the Judas Priest "subliminals" trial, a storefront window advertises summer cut rates for their QUICKEST MARRIAGES IN RENO. Three blocks up, the Truckee used to glisten as it crossed under the Virginia Street Bridge—from all the wedding bands thrown in after the quickie divorces. And Jacob, though his voice is warm and clear as a bell, has blue-green eyes that flash from one extreme conviction to another with a scary rapidity. I've gotten used to people like him by now, picking me out of a neonlit crowd on Sierra Street to announce Apocalypse to, spilling out of the casinos at two a.m. on a 90-degree Saturday night and offering to mow my lawn for $3. Still, this guy's frightening.

"I'm just here to cover the Judas Priest trial," I tell him.

"Three times," he says angrily, "thou shalt betray me ere the cock crows."

While I consider the wisdom of reminding Jacob that his quote concerns Peter, not Judas (Iscariot), he continues: "Oh, I'll go to the cities. Salt Lake, Sacramento, Vegas. But I tiptoe through town. Satan's walking proud."

Pointing to the hotels' 20-story skyline a block up, I begin to tiptoe away from Jacob. "He's walking proud up there," I say.

"No, that's Mammon," he says matter-of-factly, as though I've mistaken a crow for a raven. "Robbing, cheating, beating people up in the middle of the night's no good," I hear him say from 10 paces off. "It'll come back to you, sooner than you think. Good and evil. Life and death. Gain and loss. The mountain cat's joy"—he begins shouting—"and the deer's pain. No pain, no gain. People who want something for nothing will lose their souls to Satan."

•

Reno, depending on how your cards are flopping, might or might not be a town for Satan, but it is a town for losers. You see your first half-dozen before reaching the end of your plane's disembark ramp, grim old ladies in bright holiday dresses, feeding the 25-cent slot machines at three quarters a pull. Downtown, the slots are mostly "progressive," with red six-, seven-, even eight-figure jackpot numbers progressing faster than the eye can move on large digital displays above your head. Though it's impossible not to see that these jackpot numbers are spelling nothing but the losses of millions of people, this is a fleeting awareness if you harbor the slightest conviction that life owes you anything. Within hours of landing in this three-square-mile city that, for no immediately discernible reason, sits in the middle of the Sierra Nevada mountain-desert range, you've learned to feel indignant, hopeful, and a little out of control every time you put a quarter in a pay phone.

By various estimates, 50 to 70 percent of the people living in Reno and Sparks, the adjacent bedroom community, have moved here within the last 10 years, helping to make Nevada the fastest-growing state in America in the 1980s. The migration pattern—families that have failed elsewhere and come here for a last chance—becomes clear quickly enough. To sit quietly for more than five minutes in most public places in Reno, be it a diner counter, casino lobby, or poolside at a $25-a-night motel, is to invite the person to your right or left to tell you his troubles. And, however dubious their confessions seem at first—the morose mechanical engineer who tells you, over third helpings of prime rib at the $10.95 buffet, how he was tortured out of his mind in Vietnam, the pretty jazz dancer who came out west with her gun-toting boyfriend from the Pine Barrens and became a 21 dealer—the statistics are there to back them up: Nevadans, "the last of the free thinkers," have among the five highest rates per capita of marriage, cancer, heart disease, AIDS, alcoholism, prostitution, second mortgages, cocaine use by adults, divorce, churches, teenage covens, legal handguns and rifles, illegal handguns, murder, death-penalty cases, incarceration, child abuse, rape, single white mothers, teenage pregnancies, abortion, and successful suicides by white males ages 15 to 24.

Two "progressions" of that last statistic—Raymond Belknap, 18, by a sawed-off shotgun blast to the chin in a Sparks churchyard on December 23, 1985, and his best friend, Jay Vance, 20, who managed only to blow away the bottom half of his face—have led to what a Vegas bookmaker called the "biggest crapshoot" in Reno's history: A multimillion-dollar product-liability suit brought by three local lawyers against CBS Records and the British heavy metal band Judas Priest. Seven "subliminal commands" (audible only by the unconscious)—all saying "Do it"—were allegedly embedded on a song on Judas Priest's 1978 release, *Stained Class*, the album that was on Ray Belknap's turntable the afternoon he and Jay formed their suicide pact. Coupled with four alleged "backmasked lyrics" (audible only when playing the record in reverse) on three other songs: the exhortations, "Try suicide,"

"Suicide is in," "Sing my evil spirit," and "Fuck the Lord, fuck [or suck] all of you"—the *Do it*s, say the lawyers, created a compulsion that led to the wrongful death of Ray Belknap and to the personal injury of Jay Vance. (Jay died of a methadone overdose three years after his suicide attempt.) The Belknaps are asking for $1.2 million, the Vance family for $5 million. "If you're going to hurt someone," one of plaintiffs' lawyers tells me, only half-joking, "you're better off killing them. It's a lot cheaper."

The suit was first brought in 1986 after Jay, in a letter to Ray's mother, Aunetta Roberson, wrote: "I believe that alcohol and heavy metal music such as Judas Priest led us to be mesmerized." Initially citing the content of the *Stained Class* songs "Heroes End" ("But you, you have to die to be a hero/It's a shame in life/You make it better dead") and "Beyond the Realms of Death" ("Keep your world of all its sin/It's not fit for living in"), the suit seemed dead in the water after the California District Court of Appeals ruled that the lyrics of Ozzy Osbourne's "Suicide Solution"— which had been cited in a similar suicide/product-liability suit— were protected by the First Amendment. Two copy-cat suits, for example—another California heavy-metal suicide and an Edison, New Jersey suit brought by the family of a 13-year-old who stabbed his mother 70 times and then flayed her face before killing himself—were dropped shortly after the Osbourne decision.

The Reno suit made its bizarre beeline into the unconscious a year and a half later, when six Sparks metalheads, hired by plaintiffs' lawyers to decipher the lyrics of the *Stained Class* album, reported concurrent nightmares of going on killing sprees with semiautomatic weapons in neighborhood shopping malls. On the advice of Dr. Wilson Bryan Key, the godfather of the "subliminal exposé" (his books, *Subliminal Seduction*, *The Clam-Plate Orgy*, *Media Sexploitation*, etc., have sold over 4 million copies), plaintiffs' lawyers hired Bill Nickloff, a self-taught audio engineer who had achieved wealth and some local fame through the personalized subliminal self-help tapes he'd been marketing through his Sacramento firm, Secret Sounds, Inc. Examining a CD of *Stained Class* with his original "backwards engineering" process—by which he claims the audio signal of a piece of recorded music can be deconstructed into its component 24 tracks on his Mac II personal computer—Nickloff discovered the "smoking gun": seven subliminal *Do it*s in the first and second choruses of the song "Better By You, Better Than Me."

Though he is never called to testify, Key is the genius loci of this suit. A 65-year-old Henry Miller look-alike with a MENSA belt buckle, huge forearms, and a young wife he is able to put to sleep with a posthypnotic suggestion, he lives 20 miles from Reno, off a highway running through surreal, sage-scented moonscape that yields the most exotic roadkill I've ever seen. We lose 15 minutes when I pull out my pack of Camels (and he tells me the subliminal history of the camel and the pyramid and palm trees it's standing in front of), but he's quick to point out that the issue of subliminals and the adverse (and actionable) effects of music are not without precedent. The Billie Holiday ballad "Gloomy Sunday," for example, was banned from the radio in 1942 when several war widows killed themselves after listening. And the foreman of a jury in Pennsylvania cited subliminals as a mitigating factor in the 1989 guilty verdict for Steven Mignogna, a 19-year-old metalhead who murdered two 10-year-olds after listening to AC/DC, Ozzy Osbourne, Motley Crue, and Judas Priest for 12 hours in the cab of his pickup. Mignogna, who was defended by the Bishop of Sardinia (then in Pittsburgh for medical reasons), was given two consecutive life sentences rather than the death penalty the State asked for. Key served as an expert witness in that trial.

Key and Nickloff eventually concluded that the *Do it*s had been uttered by a different voice than lead singer Rob Halford's. Nickloff also speculated that they had been "punched into" (or layered beneath) the swirling chords of a Lesley Guitar, a backward cymbal crash, a tom-tom beat, and the prolonged exhalations of Halford's falsetto rendition of the lyric

> *Better by you, better than me-ee-uh! [Do it!]*
> *You can tell 'em what I want it to be-ee-uhh [Do it!]*
> *You can say what I can only see-ee-uhh [Do it!"]*

Nickloff also felt that enhancements of the *Do it*s had been spread across 11 of the 24 tracks by a second machine, perhaps a COMB filter. He couldn't prove this, however, simply by testing the CD.

Thus began a three-year hunt for the 24-track master tapes, not only of "Better By You" but of every other Judas Priest song, album, and rehearsal and live tape in CBS's possession. The song left a long paper trail, and discovery of the 24-track proved far easier than other Judas Priest masters. The album's only number not written by band members, it was recorded after CBS's New York a&r men, who felt none of the album's original eight songs had hit potential, proposed a list of "adds." The list itself became a major piece of evidence, as the only songs highlighted for serious consideration by the a&r men were the Manson "Family" favorites, "Helter Skelter," "Revolution #9," and "I Am the Walrus"—the last two of which promoted endless fascination with backwards lyrics.

CBS located the master of "Better By You" in September 1988; they delivered a safety copy to Nickloff three months later—an "18-minute-like gap" that became plaintiffs' second "smoking gun": CBS, they alleged, had used the three months of studio time to cover up the embedded *Do it*s. Nickloff asked for the original master, then refused to examine it when it arrived. The tape's outer coating of zinc oxide, he said, had begun to flake (suspiciously, he thought), and he wouldn't accept responsibility for it.

A series of motions and court orders regarding CBS's cooperation in the search for other masters followed, leading to two and a half years of immensely mistrustful exchanges between plaintiff and defense lawyers. It degenerated into one of the ugliest, most contentious suits since *Jarndyce* v. *Jarndyce*: public accusations of complicity and conspiracy; shouting matches at prehearing depositions; detectives (including a former Scotland Yard man) digging into the silt of CBS corporate policy and procedure and the Oedipal dramas of plaintiffs' families. It culminated in a 14-day trial that featured some exquisite dramatizations of humility, rage, bathos, incredulity, and condescension; Rob Halford's a capella singing from the witness stand; enough repeated playings of his *ee-uh*! heavy breathings to make the court stenographer cover her face in shame; strident attacks, by CBS lawyers, on the existence of a Freudian unconscious and the work of Karl Meninger; a Manichaean courtroom divided between local born-agains and metalheads, and, on the last day of trial, disclosures of the professional lives of plaintiffs' two principal lawyers, Ken McKenna and Vivian Lynch.

•

Courtroom melodrama isn't something that bothers Ken McKenna. A likable, unabashed media animal ("My phone hasn't stopped ringing since 1986," he tells me), he's responsible for the enormous publicity the suit has earned. The inevitable epithets— "tort twister," "slip-and-slide man," "ambulance chaser"—bring a bemused, faintly proud smile to McKenna's face, and he's not one to linger on the moral or emotional aspects of his cases. Not until closing statement time. Then he suddenly becomes pure corn, extremely fond of homespun similes, homilies ("I guess the lesson to be learned from all this," etc.), and the words "gosh," "sorta," and "heck." When the subject of his work comes up, his pudgy, angelic face (at 38, McKenna still looks like his high school yearbook photo) takes on a devilish grin.

"I was born to sue," he says in the two-family house in downtown Reno he practices out of. "I didn't know who or why or where or what I was till I discovered contingency law."

At 8 a.m., sprightly during the first of several interviews he has scheduled for this Saturday morning, he looks like he's just stepped off a budget cruise liner: blue shorts, salmon Polo shirt, a big smile on his well-scrubbed face, a solid gold Mickey Mouse watch on his right wrist. Stacked next to his *Catalogue of Expert Witnesses* are heaps of anti-heavy-metal pamphlets. While McKenna faxes a client, I leaf through one with an R. Crumb-like cartoon on the cover, *Stairway to Hell: The Well-Planned Destruction of Teens*. An epigram from Boethius—"Music is a part of us, and either enobles or degrades our behavior"—prefaces a chapter on backmasked lyrics that focuses on the alleged backward content of Led Zeppelin's "Stairway to Heaven" ("It's just a spring-clean for the May Queen" = "I live for Satan. He will give you six, six, six," etc.). Italicized in the first paragraph of text is the premise driving the ultra-right's fascination with backmasking: *Induction into the Worldwide Church of Satan is predicated on the ability to say the Lord's Prayer backwards!*

McKenna (who represents the Belknaps) and Lynch (who represents the estate of Jay Vance) deny identification with these anti-metal fanatics, but that Southern California-based fringe (known as the "Orange Curtain," from their support base in Orange County) is very much behind the suit. Two of plaintiffs' expert witnesses, Dr. Robert Demski, medical director of a San Antonio hospice for troubled adolescents, and Darlyne Pettinicchio, a Fullerton, California, probation officer, were recommended by Tipper Gore's Parents Music Resource Center. Though their testimony—that Judas Priest's music induces self-destructive behavior by glorifying Satan—was not allowed on record (*Stained Class*'s lyric content not being at issue), the metal link to the suicide would probably have not been made without them. It was through attendance at one of Pettinicchio's seminars, or the reading of an anti-metal "police training manual" prepared by Demski, that one of the detectives handling the shootings knew to advise Ray Belknap's mother to hang on to the *Stained Class* LP on his turntable.

"You can borrow that stuff if you want to," McKenna says, putting a heavy, distancing accent on the word stuff. Walking me out to his porch after the interview, though, he can't resist telling me that Led Zeppelin's Robert Plant "did, in fact, buy Aleister Crowley's mansion." (He's not far off: Jimmy Page, Zeppelin's guitarist, bought the Loch Ness estate, Boleskine House). I stop to look at an ornately framed photograph of the wreckage of a twin-engine plane in a copse of pine trees, given pride of place in McKenna's front office. His head nodding with a connoisseur's delight, McKenna admires the details of a splintered wing, caught in a bough some 20 feet from the plane, and the molten metal of the demolished cockpit and fuselage. That devilish smile comes to his face as he tells me, "That's $2.2 million you're looking at."

Vivian Lynch, unlike McKenna, is a "lawyer's lawyer." A middleaged woman who speaks in perfectly constructed declarative sentences, she has a sober, battered look on her face, and pretty, penetrating blue eyes that become a rapid flutter of mascara and sky-blue eyeshadow whenever she concentrates on a point of law, cross-examines a witness, or addresses the court. Holder of the highest bar exam scores in Michigan and Nevada history, among the defense team she's knows as "the dragon lady," and three of their expert witnesses tell me how unnerving it is to be cross-examined by her. On both state and national amicus curiae committees, much of her legal work for the last two decades has been the drafting of other attorneys' motions for the Supreme Court in Carson City. She entered the suit at the beginning of defense's constitutional challenges in 1987, and has singlehandedly defeated every motion to dismiss, quash, and relocate that Reno and New York counsel for CBS have come up with.

Unlike McKenna, Lynch has no taste for publicity. She once left the suit for months when she felt that his media hijinks, particularly an interview given to the *National Enquirer*, had crossed over into the jury-prejudicial. She also seems entirely unmotivated by Mammon: A supporter of Tipper Gore, she's "in this for my children," two of whom were "extreme metalheads." When she pulls up to her office for our interview, one side of her pickup's flatbed is stacked with Diet Coke empties, and the passenger seat of the cab has a three-foot stack of legal paper. When a local Holy Roller, overhearing us discuss the suit in a restaurant, comes over with his two young daughters to testify that the "owner of a major U.S. record company belongs to the Worldwide Church of Satan," and that his best friend's brother jumped off the high bridge in Santa Barbara because of that company's music, Lynch hears him out patiently, then gives her address so he can send his compilation tape of backward lyrics.

"I think that man's insane," I say when he shepherds his two daughters from the restaurant.

"I don't," says Lynch, draining her third iced tea. "I think he's tripping. Didn't you see how dilated his pupils were?"

Even if McKenna and Lynch can prove the existence of subliminals on "Better By You" to Judge Jerry Carr Whitehead (both sides agreed to forgo a jury), they still have to show those subliminals were the "proximate cause" of the suicide pact. CBS, arguing that Ray Belknap and Jay Vance tried to kill themselves because they were miserable, investigated the home lives of the boys, focusing on Ray's mother, Aunetta Roberson (three husbands by the time Ray killed himself), the religious conflict in Jay's life (his mother, Phyllis, is a born-again Christian, and Jay converted on several occasions), the alcoholic and allegedly abusive tendencies of both boys' step- and adoptive fathers, and the bleak work prospects and fantasy-ridden lives of the pair once they'd dropped out of high school. The circumstantial evidence they uncovered is enormous.

By McKenna's and Lynch's own lights, however, the families of Ray and Jay were enviable. McKenna's first case out of law school was the Murder One appeal of his brother Pat, for the slaying of a fellow prisoner while awaiting sentencing on a multiple-murder conviction. And though McKenna seems an extremely peaceable man (and is remarkably polite and gentle with hostile witnesses), he has no trouble improvising the most dramatic moment of the trial: a soliloquy of a father's rationalizing thoughts as he beats his son ("I didn't mean to hit him so hard"; "he was provoking me"; "I barely touched him") that has the entire court's heads bowed for over a minute. True to form, he prefaces the speech by placing a two-by-three-foot blowup of Ray Belknap's tenth-grade yearbook photo on an easel facing the court.

"Following the defense's logic," says Lynch, "I should have killed myself 10 times over." The eldest of three abused children, she and two younger sisters were taken from her parents when she was three years old. Institutionalized in a Long Island orphanage, after being sexually abused by another relative, at 14 Lynch moved her two sisters to Detroit, found a studio with a single Murphy bed, and went to work to support them. She entered Wayne State Law School on scholarship at the age of 19, held down a full-time job as a secretary (she can still take shorthand at 240 words per minute), and saved money by memorizing her textbooks and selling them back before classes started. She had three children of her own before her marriage ended with a divorce suit on grounds of abuse: "It took me a lifetime," she tells me, "to learn that this wasn't the way it's supposed to be lived." The divorce came through in 1972, four years after she had come home from a day of practicing law in New York, turned on the evening news, and saw her house being fired on by tanks with 9mm anti-personnel weapons during the Detroit riots. Six months pregnant, she returned to Detroit and was bayoneted in the back as she tried to enter her house.

In the 17 years since she moved to Reno, Lynch has raised seven children, her own and four from troubled households in her neighborhood. "The histories of the Vance and Belknap families," she tells me without batting an eyelash, "are certainly no different in kind or degree than what you'll find across America. I can say this for sure: They grew up like most of the kids around here."

•

On South Virginia Street, you can lose a roll of quarters as you wait for your take-out order at El Pollo Loco or the Two Brothers from Verona House of Fine Dining, and the billboards are as likely to read: DIVORCE? WANNA MARRY? or HAVE YOU BEEN ABUSED?—followed by seven-digit numbers—as to announce Dolly Parton at the Sands, or next Saturday's fight card at Harrah's. Otherwise, South Virginia is a typical ten-mile burger strip leading out of town: small businesses, chain restaurants, mini-golf courses, teenage boys screeching their tires on Saturday night till they find a girl or a fight, and the occasional mammoth concrete structure, like the Reno-Sparks Convention Center, where Ray and Jay saw Judas Priest on their 1983 *Screaming for Vengeance* tour. It was a big tour for the band (the album was their first to hit platinum), and it meant a lot to the boys: Ray stole the six-foot tour poster—his stepbrother, Tom Roach, described it as a "mythic drawing, sort of a tank with a bull's face, horns, y'know, missiles, guns"—and taped it above his bed for a year.

I drive to the Peppermill Casino, halfway out of town on South Virginia, to meet Scott Schlingheyde, a high school friend of Ray. A striking 21-year-old with long, immaculately blow-dried blond hair, he's on parole after two years in the Carson City penitentiary (for selling crank, a methamphetamine), and has arranged this meeting place because he doesn't want anyone to know he's "back in town." It seems like teenage vainglory: I can hear the Megadeth tape blasting in his yellow 1979 Le Mans from a block away.

Still, it's sadly easy to forget Scott's age when we sit in the hotel bar: He seems far more like some hardened and prospectless *maqui*—come down from some Philippine hill town to talk to a very foreign reporter—than any American teenager I've met. The only clues are his gape-mouthed appreciation of a 40-pound striper in the bar's fish-tank, and a fit of uncontrollable giggling when I ask if it's true Ray and Jay played Cowboys 'n' Indians with live ammo. "Yeah," he says finally, squelching his giggles by downing half a bottle of Bud, "that sounds like Ray." When he speaks of guns, prison, child abuse, and suicide, he sounds like he's talking last night's ballgame.

"Ray and Jay weren't all-out crazy, out-and-out violent people," he says. "They did pretty much normal, crazy shit. We talked about suicide, all the time, but it was just tough-guy talk, normal weapons talk. They had normal problems. Maybe Ray had more than most."

Scott stonewalls when I ask what problems: "He shelved that shit the moment he got out of the house, and I wasn't allowed in there. Only Jay was. Those two were as close as you can get. I do remember one time, though, we went up to shoot my brother's gun and Ray had to go get some clothes, 'cause he couldn't go home. I think we ripped some beers on the way up."

"What did you do at your brother's house?"

"We did some crank, and shot some bottles."

"Did Ray and Jay do a lot of drugs?"

"Anything that came their way. Anything they could afford. Mostly, drank a lot of beer. Beer was the only thing we could buy, underage, and it's easier to steal than booze."

"Did you guys steal most of the things you had?"

"No, no," Scott shakes his head emphatically. "We bought our own cigarettes and music and beer. Mom bought the jeans and T-shirts. We never thought much about food."

On the day of his autopsy, Ray, 6'2", weighed 141 pounds, and the only thing in his stomach was a stick of chewing gum. He wore blue jeans over sweat pants, a gray MIAMI DOLPHINS SUPER BOWL '85 T-shirt with sawed-off sleeves and vents cut out, brown construction boots, white tube socks, and a belt with a buckle shaped like a cannabis leaf. He had one tattoo, a green RB on his upper right arm (unlike Jay, who had many on his arms and upper body), and 25 small lacerations on his fists, from playing "knuckles" with Jay—punching each other's knuckles to see whose bled first. Tom Roach testified that their stepfather, Jesse Roberson, would often take Ray to the garage, lock the door, and whip him with his belt until Ray could get the garage door unlocked and scamper to his room, but no indication of that or any beating showed up on the autopsy.

"Growing up," Scott tells me, "Ray didn't really have friends. He didn't like anyone, and he didn't like himself. He really hated his red hair."

The only person Ray ever took to was Jay, whom he met in sixth grade. Jay, who had been left back twice, had BMOC status with his extra years, and his immediate love for Ray was an unending source of pride. Ray was never at ease with girls, unlike Jay, who would often find two girls waiting at his door when he came home from work. A pretty redheaded girl named Carol fell madly in love with Ray in tenth grade, and he left home for a week to live with her, but he could always be counted on to ditch her to spend the night with Jay. Their parents were gratified when the boys "showed their first sign of domesticity," shortly after leaving high school: buying a pair of pit bull pups. Both dogs became ferocious after the shootings, and had to be put down.

Jesse worked at a Sparks auto-parts shop for $20/day plus commissions. Aunetta has worked for the past five years as a 21 dealer in a Reno casino for $35/night and tips. Ray, who was good with his hands (he made a shelf for targets he and Jay would take up to the hills with them), loved construction work. In his two years at Reed High, he flunked all but two classes: Shop I and Shop II. On his last application form, he wrote that he'd worked on a building site in Truckee, California, beginning as a day-laborer at

$5.50 an hour and ending, a month later, as a $10.75-an-hour framer, but there's no reason to believe this is true. His next job was at minimum wage, in a used furniture store. After three weeks, he stole $454 from his boss's desk and left Nevada for the first time, on a bus to Oklahoma, to see his real father. A week later, however, he was back in Sparks, facing trial. He received a suspended sentence and, after much counseling, a generous probation that allowed him to leave the state and live with his father, on condition that he behave himself. It's not known what happened to Ray in Oklahoma, but he was back in Nevada 10 weeks later, working the graveyard shift at a Sparks print shop. The job—feeding massive paper reams into a cutter—paid 10 cents above minimum wage. Two weeks before he killed himself, he was fired for refusing to work overtime when the morning man called in sick.

Ray liked to think of himself as a karate master and was very fond of his weapons: a sawed-off 12-gauge shotgun, a 12-gauge pump gun, a .22, a BB gun, a blowgun, and a two-foot-long, hard-rubber "whipstick," whose purpose, as Tom Roach later testified, was simple: "It hurt when he hit you with it." Both he and Jay were good shots, and when not stalking Tom Roach with BB guns through the house—for listening to "mellow" bands like Def Leppard and Night Ranger—would often spend weekends in the Sierras with their .22s, hunting quail, which Ray loved to eat spit-roasted. On work-days, they went to a cave in the Sparks city limits, where they could "nail whole families of bats to the wall with air-rifle shot," as Jay later testified. Ten days before the suicide, police came to Ray's house on Richards Way to investigate a charge of animal torture: Ray had apparently shot the neighbor's cat with his blowgun.

Other than the occasional trip to the mall or a night of playing "terrorize the town" on South Virginia, Ray's only regular activity was up in his room with Jay, "listening to Priest" and fantasizing about becoming a mercenary. They loved Priest, Jay said later, because they got power from the music—"amps" was his word—and because their connection with Priest was more intimate than with bands like Iron Maiden, whose "'Kill 'em all, let God sort 'em out' sort of lyrics," Jay said, "left us cold." If they had a credo to live by, it was "Ride Hard, Die Fast." In the hospital after the shootings, Jay used an index finger to draw the words LIFE SUCKS, when detectives asked why they had shot themselves.

Of the thousands of details that surface in the Judas Priest trial, two of the few that defense and plaintiff don't dispute is that Ray and Jay loved Judas Priest more than any other band (in a deposition taken shortly before his death by methadone overdose in 1988, Jay said he "would have done anything those guys asked me to do"), and that the two boys were inseparable. Several friends testify that when they met Jay after the shooting, the first thing he would ask was if they blamed him for Ray's death.

"I ran into Jay at a gas station one day," Scott tells me. "But I didn't know who he was till he started talking, 'cause he didn't really have a face or anything. I couldn't understand him either, because his tongue was gone. I was angry at him, though. There's nothing in this world so hard you gotta shoot yourself over it," he says, clenching his fists slowly, as though offering himself as proof. "Nothing."

"What did you say to Jay at the gas station?"

"Nothing. Just walked away. I never saw him again."

•

Growing up, Jay wanted to be a hunting or a fishing guide. Several early backpacking trips had a huge effect on him—in the Desolation Wilderness of northern Nevada, and, on visits to a favorite uncle up in Oregon, along the Pacific Coast Trail. He took up gardening work in junior high school and, never one to let reality get in the way of self-mystique, told his school psychiatrist he had a few landscaping companies and many investments in pieces of heavy equipment. As he began to realize he'd never make it through Reed High, his fantasy of enrolling in the Lassen Gunsmith College in Susanville evaporated; at the New Frontier drug program he lasted half of, trying to cure himself of a crank addiction, six months before the shooting, he spoke indifferently of becoming either a mercenary or janitor. He studied typing and applied science after the shooting, and had plans to become either

a physical therapist, or, once his tongue was rebuilt, a suicide hot-
line operator.

Something went very wrong in Jay's life in the first and second
grades. One school psychiatrist called it "extreme hyperactivity,"
another diagnosed him for Attention Deficit Disorder; he repeated
both years. His mother refused to give him the nervous-system stim-
ulant Ritalin, though it was strongly recommended by every doctor
who examined Jay. "Those kids on Ritalin," she says, "were
zombies." She agreed to see the district psychiatrist after Jay tied a
belt around his head and began pulling his hair out one day in
second grade, but refused to see the man when he came to examine
Jay in the home environment. Driving home after being expelled for
violent behavior in the third grade, Jay became enraged when his
mother wouldn't listen to his version, and wrapped his hands
around her neck. Two years later, he went after her with a hammer,
and with a pistol a few years later. From the age of 10 until he
dropped out of high school in the first weeks of his junior year, he
spent his school hours in the Special Ed Room with paraplegics,
Down's Syndrome kids, and the severely impaired (he remembered
befriending one speechless boy who had swallowed a bottle of
bleach at the age of three). He tested low on every proficiency and
I.Q. test—his greatest problems being with hand-eye coordination—
but Jay was hardly stupid. From the sharp, direct responses he gave
in depositions after the shootings, one can see a quick-minded, intu-
itive, thoroughly ineducable kid who never had a chance in school.

From the age of 15, when he discovered Judas Priest, Jay had an
album or song for every mood and period of his life: *Unleashed in
the East*, when he wanted to get amped; *Hellbent for Leather*, to
party; *Screaming for Vengeance*, when he left school and for nine
months lived-in as a baby-sitter for an older woman. Both he and
Ray loved the early album, *Sin After Sin*, with its cover: a black
figure with no face. He said they listened to the songs "Epitaph"
and "Dreamer Deceiver" when they needed to cry:

> *Saw a figure floating*
> *Beneath the willow tree.*

Asked us if we were happy.
We said we didn't know.
Took us by the hands, and up we go!
We followed the dreamer deceiver."

"Jay recited those lyrics like scripture," says Phyllis Vance, who agrees to see me once I swear I'm not from "one of those smut magazines like *Enquirer*, or *Rolling Stone*." "Me and Tony [Jay's adoptive father] would be watching TV in the living room and he'd be listening to Judas Priest in his bedroom, so loud that— *through his earphones*—we couldn't hear the TV. And if I'd go in and tell him to turn it down, he'd point that finger at me, just like Rob Halford, and scream, 'ON YOUR KNEES AND WORSHIP ME IF YOU PLEASE!' After he was born-again, in 1983, he sold all 13 of their albums to Recycled Records. He stopped doing drugs for a while too. It's like I always say: Either you worship Jesus Christ or you worship Judas Priest."

Jay later said it was Priest's music that turned him, temporarily, into a white supremacist. His high school guidance counselor, Susan Reed, sent him to the infirmary in his sophomore year when the swastikas and Judas Priest logo he'd drawn with black magic marker on his left arm had caused a serious infection.

•

The 23rd of December, 1985, a freezing, overcast day, began for the Belknaps with a family trip to the Happy Looker hair salon in the shopping mall off Richards Way. Ray's four-year-old half-sister, Christie Lynn, was getting her first haircut; Ray went home to get a camera, and on the way back to the Happy Looker decided the time had come, after years of wearing his long hair back in a bandanna covered with Priest logos, to have it cut into a manageable buzz—especially while his mother was paying.

Ray was in a good mood. He'd lost his first paycheck in three weeks over a few games of pool at a local tavern the night before, and all but one installment of the $454 he'd stolen from his former boss was still owed, but he had enough money to buy Christmas presents for everyone. Not one to stand on ceremony, he opened the records he'd bought (including the hard-to-find *Stained Class* LP he'd bought for Jay) when he got home from the Happy Looker. Rolling a joint, he thought about Jay's plan to get the paycheck back from the contractor he'd lost it to: "I was going to stomp on him in the back of his knee, and then crunch his knee to the concrete, karate chop him in the back of the neck, and he would pretty much be helpless at that moment," Jay later testified, "'cause I know karate."

The day had begun for Jay shortly after noon. In a deposition given under hypnosis two years later, he remembered that he "woke up, saw my death, and looked around." He cleared his eyes, had a piss, took a glass of chocolate milk from the kitchen to the bathroom, and drank the milk slowly as he sat under a hot shower for a half-hour. Then he put the glass on the toilet seat and washed his newly buzzed-cut hair.

He'd stayed too long in the bathroom, and missed his ride to the print shop, where he worked the second shift as an apprentice. His mother had left a note in the kitchen: She was at her sister's house, and wanted Jay to call if he needed another ride. Jay, however, couldn't find or remember his aunt's number. Perhaps he didn't want to: He hated his 12-hour shifts, which left him so filthy it took up to three hours to scrub the print-ink off his forearms.

Ray was baby-sitting Christie Lynn and a few of her friends all afternoon, but he had time to pick up Jay in his mother's car, then stop back at the Happy Looker to get his hair recut to look more like Jay's. They drove back to the ranch-house on Richards Way and, in Ray's room, put on *Unleashed in the East* and *The Best of Judas Priest*. After a spat over the two joints of "scrub-bud" they were smoking (Jay was angry Ray "stoled the pot from a friend of mine"), they got to work on their first six-pack of Budweisers. They left the room an hour later, Ray to tell his sister and her little friends he was going to bust their fucking heads if they didn't stop running around and slamming doors, Jay to get some more beer from the fridge in the garage. In the dining room, he ran into Ray's pregnant, un-wed half-sister, Rita Skulason, who was yelling at Ray to stop messing with the kids. She scowled at Jay as he came in holding the beers. Rita hated Jay, which bothered him (he was used to girls fawning over him), but today he didn't care: He was feeling good, having come to the decision that he would no longer be a printer's apprentice. He told Rita that if his mother called, she should say he'd already left the house and was walking to work. Rita couldn't wait for Phyllis' call. She knew it was the only way to get Jay out of the house.

Ray had a big smile when Jay got back to the bedroom with the beer. He'd also made a big decision—not to wait until the 25th to give Jay his present. Reaching behind his stereo for the *Stained Class* album, he put the disc on the turntable and gave the jacket to Jay, saying, "Merry Christmas, brother." As the opening lyric of "Exciter" played: "To find this day/We'll surely fall," Ray and Jay stood up and hugged and punched each other, then started dancing around the room, playing air-guitar and punching the walls.

They listened to both sides two or three times (depending on which of Jay's depositions you read) before going back out to the garage for more beer. Rita was still sitting at the dining room table. She later testified Jay came over and fondled her breast, but Jay denied that: "Rita wasn't the kind of girl you could do that to. She'd bust you in the mouth." Perhaps they were a little drunk: When Ray killed himself, two hours later, his blood-alcohol was a hundredth of a point below legal intoxication. They might have already considered suicide: Jay asked Rita if she would name her baby after Ray if anything happened to him. "Not unless it's a goddamn redhead," she said.

Half an hour after they returned to Ray's room, Jay's parents were at the Belknap's front door, to drive Jay to work. They were too late. "I was rocking out," Jay later said. Phyllis tried to reason with him, asking, "How are you going to buy your cigarettes if you don't have any money?" but she and Tony were out the door a minute later, Jay a foot behind them, screaming, "LEAVE ME ALONE!"

It's not clear how many more times they listened to *Stained Class*, or which song was on when Jay told Ray, "Let's see what's next." In one deposition, Jay said the lyric, "Keep your world of all its sin/It's not fit for living in," finally led them to understand the message they had been "struggling all afternoon to understand": "The answer to this life is death."

Ray seemed to understand immediately and said "Yeah," offering his knuckles. They rapped fists together until it was too painful, then began to trash the bedroom, smashing and slashing everything except Ray's records, mirror, bed, and two burlap sacks, stencilled 50 KG—MEXICO, that hung over his guns in the corner of the room. The kids down the hall started crying, and Rita Skulason made an emergency phone call to their mother, who immediately left her 21 table at the casino and drove home. They were still going strong when she pulled into the driveway, ran to the bedroom door, and began calling Ray's name. Jay wedged a two-by-four against the jamb as Ray grabbed a pair of shells and his favorite weapon, the sawed-off twelve-gauge, and opened his bedroom window and crawled out.

By the time Jay had followed out the window, Ray was already 20 feet down the alley behind his house, a few feet shy of the six-foot concrete wall of the yard of the Community First Church of God. Jay yelled at him to wait, and the two scaled the wall together. At 5:10 p.m. on the third shortest day of the year it was already pitch-black in the churchyard, and Jay had no idea where they were. A neighborhood dog had begun to bark, and they were worried about the police coming. Neither was old enough to be outdoors with a loaded gun within the city limits. It was well below freezing, and both boys were wearing only jeans and T-shirts.

Ray gave Jay a shell, then stepped onto a small, rickety carousel in the corner of the churchyard and loaded up. He looked terrified as he heard the gun cock. In depositions taken a few months later, Jay remembered saying, "Just hurry up" to Ray; in his later testimony, he also remembered Ray beginning to spin around on the carousel, chanting "Do it, do it" for four or five circles. In his first hypnotic deposition, taken almost three years later, Jay remembered that his last words to his friend were "Just do it."

As the years went by, Jay's memory put him further from Ray's suicide. In all but one of his later depositions, he testified he had his back turned when Ray pulled the trigger. In the year after the shootings, he could remember seeing Ray kill himself only in a recurrent nightmare—inaccurately: In the dream, he would see fire coming out of the back of Ray's head—a memory, plaintiffs lawyers claim, not of the shootings, but of the *Stained Class* album cover, which shows an android's silver head pierced by a laser-like beam that flares up as it exits the skull.

Two days after the shootings, however, Jay told detectives he watched Ray stop the carousel and plant the gun on the ground between his feet. The coroner's report located the entrance wound in the exact center of Ray's chin, confirming Jay's memory that Ray had the gun barrel "so tight under his chin his voice was clipped when he said, 'I sure fucked up my life.'" He reached down for the trigger and squeezed it with no hesitation. The shot imploded inside his skull, causing no exit wound and little disfigurement. It sprayed the carousel, the gun, and a square yard of ground in front of the carousel, however, with "an incredible amount of blood."

Jay remembers "shaking real bad" as he picked up the gun from the ground, uncocked it, and put the shell Ray had given him into the chamber. "I didn't know what to do," he said. "I thought somebody was going to stop me." He told police he only went through with his half of the pact because he was afraid of being accused of Ray's murder. When he tried to put the gun end into his mouth the blood on it made him gag, so he put it under his chin, then stood next to the carousel for an uncertain amount of time, thinking about "my mom, and people I cared about." He eventually heard the siren of a police car responding to a call from a neighborhood woman about the first shot—which, by the police dispatcher's log, puts him standing frozen with the gun held under his chin for over five minutes. When he heard the siren he tried to steady the gun; its barrel, trigger, and nose felt greasy from the blood, however, and Jay's hand-to-eye coordination failed him one last time as he slowly worked his hand down the barrel for the trigger. The shot took off his chin and mouth and nose, missing his eyes and brain as it exited just above his high cheekbones.

He remembered a tremendous weight leaving him as he dropped to his knees and fell face-first to the ground, then a long numbness, followed by a stinging sensation, as though someone had slapped him. "Then somebody [a paramedic] turned me over on my back ... and checked out my blood," and he "fought with that person to get back" onto his stomach, though he never could remember why he did. As he was tied to a stretcher and placed into the ambulance, choking on blood and fragments of his face, he was given an emergency tracheotomy, and he remembered the strange sensation of having his throat cut into and feeling no pain. He had no idea that his teeth and tongue and palate were gone, and he couldn't understand why the simple sentence, "I don't want to die" wouldn't come out when he tried to say it to the paramedic.

•

The buffets broadcast from the hotel marquees get cheaper, the entertainers get older, and the hold 'em games go from $1-3-5 to $3-5-10 as you drive from Reno to Sparks. A suburban sprawl crawling up the northeastern ridge of the Sierras, Sparks extends higher and seemingly at random with each year into the canyons and mountain hillocks: endless streets of one-story houses with one willow or evergreen on each lawn, a car or two in each driveway, and one four-wheel-drive vehicle, RV, or big boat in front of every other house. Most of the four-wheelers, RVs and even the boats have gun racks in the back windows.

Four doors down from Ray's old house on Richards Way, I find the yard of the Community First Church of God. A 20-square-foot patch of grass surrounded by six feet of cinderblock (interrupted only by a chain fence on the east wall), it looks more like a prison yard. Formerly a playground for Sunday school kids, it has a spooky, cloistered feel to it. The peeling, whitewashed cross on the church roof is visible between two immense weeping willows overhanging a brace of swings; only one swing is still on its chain. Two feet from the sawed-off stump of a third willow is the small foot-pump carousel Ray was sitting on when he shot himself.

The worst of Jay's endless nightmares after the shootings were filled with Christian symbolism of slaughtered animals and stained glass. There is no such glass visible from the yard where the boys shot themselves, but there are three cheap panels of stained glass on the front of the church that would give anyone nightmares. The last bears a striking resemblance to the *Stained Class* album cover: a faceless, purple and mauve Christ Ascending that has the head of Christ being penetrated by one of the metal rods connecting the glass.

Jay lay in the hospital for three months, receiving daily injections of morphine and listening, he later testified, to *Stained Class*, playing over and over in his head. When he couldn't take it anymore, he got a friend to make a tape of the album and played it for weeks, trying, he said, "to get the music out of my head" and "to bury my grief for Ray." Once he got accustomed to his morphine dosages, his feelings of guilt kept him from falling asleep. "It's so weird," he said, "saying goodbye to someone."

The extent of the reconstructive surgery was enormous. Doctors at Stanford University Hospital began with the only piece of facial skin remaining, a flap of forehead, attaching skin extenders to pull it gradually down and across the area, leaving the greatest bulk in the center, to become a nose. The skin grew hair and had to be shaved daily. After two years, a surgeon began working on a pair of lips from skin taken from the smooth crease under the knee, and Jay was halfway toward his third and final chin—bone fragments from the back of his right shoulder blade—when he died. A third of his tongue remained, but he'd lost his gag reflex when the back of his palette exploded, and he drooled and swallowed his tongue. He had only one tooth, and he ate by using his thumb as a second incisor. When he went to watch McKenna and Lynch work on an unrelated trial, he was ejected from the courtroom for upsetting the jury; when the six-year-old daughter of another lawyer saw him on an elevator, she screamed for a few seconds and then fainted.

Jay was in constant agony for the last three years of his life: Coupled with the initial trauma, the skin extenders pulling on the flap of forehead caused massive swelling and chronic infection. He survived numerous addictions to prescribed Percodan and Xanax, and often said that he hadn't known what a "real drug addiction was like" when he checked into the New Frontier program for crank abuse in July of 1985. The Percodan and Xanax were nothing, however, compared to his abuse of cocaine, which he began injecting into his arm to ease the pain. (Though he'd always hated needles, he no longer had a nose to snort the coke through.) He was up to two grams a day before he overcame the addiction with weekly nerve-block injections—two-inch needles in the base of his neck. To qualify for Tony's insurance (to pay for what he called his "$400,000 face") he stayed with his parents. Incredibly, his love life didn't slow down: He turned down two offers of marriage, and an old girlfriend—who came to live with the Vances after her step-father booted her out of the house on her 18th birthday—bore a child of Jay's a year before he died. "I told them I didn't want them monkeying around in the bedroom," Phyllis recalls. "Jay said I forgot to mention the garage, the front lawn, the backyard ..."

Despite being placed on suicide watch in Washoe Medical Center on Thanksgiving Day, 1988 (Jay got enormously depressed every year around the holiday season), he died of a methadone overdose on December 2, a few hours before he was due to return home. The death was listed a suicide, but it isn't clear how he got enough of the drug, not only to kill himself, but to reduce his brain matter to a substance the Washoe District Coroner described as "gelatine." Phyllis Vance is convinced it was the hospital's malprac-tice: "Jay felt he had everything to live for. He used to say that he was literally reborn after the accident."

Jay put his mother in the hospital on two occasions after the shootings—both, she tells me, during seizures of cocaine toxicity and withdrawal agony: He split her lip the first time; the second time he fractured her nose. "But we were never closer than after the accident," Phyllis Vance tells me over Diet Cokes in her back-yard, where we've come because she won't let me or Tony smoke in the house. "Jay'd wake up screaming in blind terror in the middle of the night, and I'd be lying right there beside him. It was literally blind terror. His face was so swollen he couldn't see anything except his dream, the same one, night after night: Ray blowing the back of his head off and the fire coming out."

Tony, sitting beside her, lights a Marlboro and nods his head. I ask if he'd like to respond to reports that Jay's was a violent home. "I remember one time," he answers with a flat, emotionless voice, "when Jay came back from California with his eyes all glassy. I told him, 'Show me your eyes,' and he wouldn't. So I went into his room to punish him. He said, 'Daddy, I'm too old for you to be spanking me.' So, I haul off and belt him, two or three times, with my fist. I don't know if it did any good," he says, "'cause I never did it again."

Tony is a Blackfoot-Cherokee from Kentucky, a quiet, handsome man with jet-black hair, broad shoulders, and huge hands that have a slight but constant tremor. He never seems at ease, either in his backyard or in the courtroom, where defense lawyers continually refer to his alcoholism and gambling, and repeatedly cite the evening Phyllis pulled a gun on him to stop him from gambling his overtime pay. The tremor in his hands becomes more pronounced when he tells me he didn't drink until the Oakland GM plant he drove a forklift for closed down in 1979, and that he didn't gamble until they moved to Nevada. "And that gun thing only happened," Phyllis explains, "because Tony was used to gambling with his overtime money, which is only fair. After the accident, though, we needed all of it for Jay."

Phyllis is a short, stocky, enraged-seeming woman with a high, strident voice and piercing stare. Though she's not an easy person to get along with, after an hour of talking in her backyard I'm able to see her for what she is: a powerful, angry woman who, five years later, finally knows why her son shot himself. She now works for a Christian organization, counseling suicidal teenagers. "The one thing I'll never be able to get over, though," she says, truly mystified, "is that he did it in a churchyard, without even knowing where he was. Piece by piece, though, you put it all together, and you can finally stop asking yourself, 'Why? Why?' It was the subliminals." I nod my head and try to concentrate on what Phyllis is telling me, but my eye keeps wandering across her yard. But for a few tons of concrete Tony laid down for Jay's pit bull to run in, it looks exactly like the churchyard of the First Community: a 20-foot patch of grass bordered by a six-foot wall, two big weeping willows overhanging a brace of swings that has only one chain swing left. A few feet from where we sit is the sawed-off stump of a third willow.

When we go back into her living room, there's a repeat episode of "Geraldo" about covens on the 25-inch TV, and Tony sits down to watch. "We've seen this one already, Tony," Phyllis says, turning the volume down so she can listen to a long message on her answering machine. It's from a young woman in Hidden Valley, near Carson City, calling about the suicidal condition of a 15-year-old girl she and Phyllis are counseling. "She *had* returned to Christ, Phyllis," says the young woman. "But I have to say she seems very desperate now."

•

By the last week of the trial, the horde of metalheads protesting outside the courthouse has dwindled to a few aging stoners with goatees and Motorhead and *Houses of the Holy* T-shirts and one 90-pound girl wearing white pumps, a white bustier, and jeans with a copper zipper that goes from front to back. Their tinny cries of "Let the music live" are drowned by the right-to-life pamphleteering of a slack-jawed scarecrow of a man named Andy Anderson, who's been running for lieutenant governor of Nevada for three decades. "I still haven't found the right man to share the ticket with," he tells me.

Of the 75 media people who had come here from seven countries, the three networks, four cable channels, and the major newsweeklies and dailies, only four rather cynical stringers for the wire services and local papers, some local TV and radio people, and a documentary team from New York have lasted the first week of the trial, which has become extremely technical. Three-quarters of the testimony given is from "expert witnesses"—psychologists, audiologists, and computer experts—many of whom seem to have confused their testimony for Oscar-acceptance speeches. "We had a suicide shrink here last week," one stringer says, "who thanked everyone in the Yellow Pages for his long career. He was so deadly the bailiff was talking about putting speed bumps by the exit."

The 83-seat courtroom, no more than half-filled till the last day of trial, is noticeably devoid of metalheads, whose attendance was successfully dissuaded by Judge Whitehead's strict dress-code order after the second day of trial. Other than Phyllis Vance (who comes every day, accompanied by a visionary-looking black-haired man dressed in impeccable linen), there are very few magic Christians here, born-again or otherwise: a fascinated 15-year-old girl with strawberry blonde bangs, who sits behind me telling her rosary; the man whose friend's brother jumped off the Santa Barbara bridge; and one very anxious elderly woman, wearing the same emerald pants and midnight-blue shirt every day, who seems poised to rise and object to every question posed by defense's lawyers. (On the last day of the trial, she finally stands to say, "Please stop this! I have 25 children that I work with downtown and someone has to care for them. Someone has to stop this." As she's led out, she pleads with Judge Whitehead, "Oh, please put me on the stand, Your Honor. I'm an electronics expert.") The empty jury room, formerly needed to handle overflow press, has been given over to defense's entourage for recess breaks: U.S. and U.K. management people, producers and recording engineers, a few CBS corporate types, two very jolly 275-pound security toughs from Tempe, Arizona, Rick and Nick, who have the entire defense team addressing each other with "Hey dude," and the four forty-something members of Judas Priest, the band one recent critic called the "doyens of heavy metal."

After a first decade of opening shows for the likes of AC/DC, UFO, and Ratt, Priest has been on a roll since their 1980 release, *British Steel*, which earned them a hardcore metal following. Like Spinal Tap (the parody metal band based largely on Priest) they've been accused of glomming from every trend imaginable: the guitar pyrotechnics, dry-ice smoke, mythic-medieval themes, and onstage monsters of Deep Purple, Black Sabbath, and Jethro Tull; Kiss's two-tiered stage sets and multi-layered leather costumes; and the hell-oriented themes that bands like Venom, Mercyful Fate, Scorpions, and Megadeth hit gold with by reaching the various covens and Satanic wannabees in the U.S. and Europe. Led by lead singer Rob Halford (who began as a theater apprentice in Birmingham and only switched to metal, he tells me, when he realized he'd "stay in the limelight longer that way"), they have worked their way into the heart of heavy metal: show biz. First they shed their 1970s kimonos, velvet robes, and buckskin boots for leather, studs, spurs, and choke collars; then they began riding onstage on Harley-Davidson two-tone Low Riders; by 1985, the tour included whips, industrial-grade smoke machines, fire pits, flamethrowers and a 15-foot robot that shot stadium-length laser beams and lifted the two guitarists, Ken Downing and Glenn Tipton, 20 feet into the air during lead breaks.

Skip Herman, "Morning Mutant" deejay of Reno's metal station, made friends with the band in the early days of the trial and began hanging out with them in the mountains near Lake Tahoe, where Priest has rented a suite of deluxe cottages. Over and above a mutual love for music, he and Priest share a guiding passion: golf. "They talk about the trial for the first two or three holes," he says, "then maybe a little music, girls, a lot of old times. Ian [Hill, the bassist] and Glenn talk about their kids. From there to the clubhouse, though, it's nothing but setting up a good, steady tripod with your legs, and establishing that perfect pendulum for your swing." Skip invites me to his radio station to hear a slew of reverse-direction lyrics he's found, his favorite being Diana Ross's "Touch Me in the Morning," on which I clearly make out the chant: "Death to all. He is the one. Satan is love." I ask him to play Zeppelin's "Stairway to Heaven" in reverse. Every word of the "I live for Satan" chant is perfectly audible.

•

"It'll be another 10 years before I'll even be able to spell subliminals," Ken Downing says as he signs autographs on the way into the courtroom on the last Monday of trial. Rob Halford and Tipton, however, don't see the joke. "It's terribly wrong, you know," says Tipton, "for my family to have to turn on the tube, see this poor kid with his face blown off, and have the finger pointing, 'Judas Priest did this.' I have a lot of guitar work to do, but you can't go around to court every day, sit down behind your lawyers, have the knife twisted in your gut for eight hours, then go home and pick up your axe."

"These people act like we drink a gallon of blood and hang upside down from crucifixes before we go onstage," Rob Halford says. "We're performers, have been for two decades. Do the show and wear the costumes our audience expect us to." Halford is a complex man: extremely polite and soft-spoken, with a thick working-class Birmingham accent and bright, caricatural droopy eyes, he has a dry, caustic wit that makes everything he says, sees, and hears seem in doubt, in contempt, and in quotes. The trial, he admits, "is good publicity," then quickly adds. "It's been murder on my creativity as an ar-r-tist, though. I can't wait for it all to end. I'm going to explode when this next tour begins. Legal proceedings are so-o frustrating."

He's the only band member who seems to pay attention to the proceedings: grinning widely at the clipped King's English spoken with enormous largesse by half of defense's witnesses, several of whom are Australian; at the boastful testimony of a Dr. Bruce Tannenbaum (Jay's psychiatrist in his last two years) that he is "the only white man ever to have endured the Native American fire-sweat ceremony"; as an advocate for subliminal self-help, who claims his tapes have been documented to promote hair-growth, enlarge breast size, cure homosexuality, and "to've turned a local college's worst football season in its history into a division contender" (a wide receiver from the team is also called, to verify). Halford seems in awe of a Toronto psychologist who's called in by defense to recite the entire "Jabberwocky" section of *Through the Looking Glass* backward (he's finally instructed by Judge Whitehead to stop), and deeply touched by the testimony of five friends of Ray and Jay, who contradict reams of evidence as to their whereabouts on December 23, 1985. One glassy-eyed kid, whose testimony places Ray in his pickup an hour after the suicide, is asked by Whitehead to show his eyes to the court, then quickly dismissed from the stand.

Whitehead's eyes betray nothing. An austere Mormon with a quiet but pronounced sense of his own dignity, he seems like a man who has grimly determined he will catch more flies with honey than vinegar. Whether sustaining or overruling an objection, he delivers his rulings with exactly the same measured deference, consideration, and inaudibility. (Several times a day he is asked by defense lawyers to repeat his ruling.) His courtroom has a statewide reputation for running by the book and to the minute. Entering each morning at precisely 8:45, he says, "Thank you, please be seated," and clears his throat away from the microphone. But for an occasional question from the bench and visible winces when witnesses refer to the "backmasked lyric" "F— the Lord" as "Fuck the Lord" (after 11 days of trial, Whitehead still listens to that section of tape with his face averted from the court), he sits impassively till 5 p.m., then whispers the day to a close without the slightest clue as to what he's seen, heard, or thought.

After Lynch files a Motion in Limine (asking to be awarded the decision outright, on the basis of CBS's lack of cooperation in producing evidence) and a Motion for Sanctions (money), the first three days feature endless declarations of the utter impossibility of "punching" anything into mixed-down two-track or 24-track tape, then of CBS's hopeless task of locating those tapes—probably the first two times in American legal history an arts corporation has argued for its lack of control of the matrix of production. Two mornings and afternoons are devoted to some very unconvincing testimony as to the scarcity of both types of backward lyrics: phonetic reversals (lyrics that form a sensible fragment when played in reverse) and backward-recorded reversals (words recorded forward, then added to the mix in reverse direction). After eight court-hours of testimony (by men who engineered and/or produced such records as *Electric Ladyland*, *The Wall*, the first four Zeppelin albums, and *Her Satanic Majesty's Request*, which has an entire song in reverse), a 32-year-old engineer/producer named Andrew Jackson (called to testify because he served as assistant engineer on the "Better By You" recording session, 13 years ago) is asked if he knows of any back-masked lyrics in the rock industry.

"Yes I do," he says with a Cockney accent so thick Judge Whitehead asks him to deliver his testimony while facing him. "In fact, just last month I produced a band had a song with the lyric, 'And I need someone to lie on/And I need someone to rely on.' Played in reverse that becomes 'Here's me/Here I am/What we have lost/I am the messenger of love.'" The singer, Jackson testifies, memorized the backward phrase, with all its reversals of sibilants and plosives, then sang it on a track that was used—backward—as a forward-running vocal overdub.

"And do you know of any instances of backward-recorded lyrics in the rock industry?" he was asked as CBS lawyers covered their faces.

"Why, yes, I do," Jackson says. "A Pink Floyd song I worked on has a lyric: 'Dear Punter. Congratulations. You have found the secret message. Please send answers to Pink Floyd, care of the Funny Farm, Chalford, St. Giles.'"

I get to hear the alleged *Do it*s when court adjourns to a 24-track studio across town on one of the last days of the trial. Two stringers have harrowed grimaces as we enter a darkened room that, through a two-inch plate-glass window, looks onto the engineering console the court is reconvening in. "We were in Carson City last month to report on a death-penalty execution," one explains. "It was set up just like this."

From the four-foot UREI Studio Monitors in our room I hear the title cut's first chorus, played—to Whitehead's consternation—forward first:

> *Long ago, when man was king,*
> *This heart must beat, on stained class*
> *Time must end before sixteen*
> *So now he's just a stained class thing.*

It's followed by the reverse of the next line, "Faithless continuum into the abyss"—the alleged "Sing my evil spirit." It is a creepy sound, inhumanly high-pitched and strangely clipped and emphatic: "S-s-eeg maheevoh s-s-speeree."

Whitehead asks to hear the reverse of "White Hot, Red Heat"—because it confirms the "message" of the song when played forward, the "desecration" of "The Lord's Prayer":

> *Thy father's son*
> *Thy kingdom come*

Electric ecstasy
Deliver us from all the fuss ...

I only hear what sounds like an evil dolphin chanting, "F-f-f-fuck thlor-r-r-r', S-ss-suck-ck tolleyuse-se-se."

"Better By You, Better Than Me" is the kind of Priest song Jay said he and Ray most loved: "a steady, galloping rhythm ... only changing for the chorus, [when] the beat would get more dramatic or more intensified." After the screeching lyric:

Tell her what I'm like within
I can't find the words, my mind is dim

the first chorus comes, with its prolonged *ee-uh* exhalations. I don't hear anything that sounds like *Do it,* but there is an extra, syncopated beat falling after the third beat of each measure, a disco-like mesh of noise that has nothing to do with the musical or lyrical content of the song. It does sound—if not "punched in"—added on.

As the song moves into the second chorus with the lyric:

Guess I'll learn to fight and kill
Tell her not to wait until
They find my blood upon her windowsill

The extra beat seems to land with greater emphasis, more elaborated and groan-like with each *ee-uh* sound, until I hear the words *Do it*—as a kind of antiphonal chant—falling, with relative clarity, on the last rendition of "You can tell her what I want it to be." Far less clear is Halford's rendition of the lyric itself. In his screeching desperation, it sounds far more like "You can tell her what I wanted to be." All I can think of is Ray sitting on the carousel, saying, "I sure fucked up my life."

•

The issue of backward masking seems resolved forever on the last day of testimony. Halford, absent from court all morning, arrives late in the afternoon with a large, black double-deck and a cassette.

Put on the stand, he says that he's spent the morning in the recording studio, spooling *Stained Class* backward, and would like to play what he's found for the court. Ever the showman, he asks if he can play the tape forward, sing the lyric once, play that "back-masked stuff," then sing that.

Lynch objects furiously to the tape's admission, and to Halford's request to perform for the court. Whitehead agrees there's no need for Halford to sing again, then cracks his first smile of the suit. "I want to hear this though."

"Some of these aren't entirely grammatical," Halford deadpans apologetically. "But I don't think 'Sing my evil spirit' would"—

"Objection," says Lynch.

"Sustained," says Whitehead.

A blast of heavy bass and Tipton's 32nd-note trill accompanies the fragment, "strategic force/they will not," from "Invader." Its reverse is the insane-sounding but entirely audible screech: "It's so fishy, personally I'll owe it." When Halford plays, "They won't take our love away," from the same song, the backward, "Hey look, Ma, my chair's broken," has the courtroom howling. Lynch and McKenna are livid.

After a week of suspending disbelief, I lose it when Halford plays his last discovery, in which the rather Mighty Mouse-ish chorus of "Exciter":

> *Stand by for Exciter*
> *Salvation is his task*

comes out backward with the emphatic, high-pitched

> *I-I-I as-sked her for a peppermint-t-t*
> *I-I-I asked for her to GET one."*

The band is exultant after Halford's performance. Up in their Reno counsel's offices, Ken Downing and Ian Hill are talking of issuing a Greatest Hits album, *Judas Priest: The Subliminal Years*. Their American manager is on the phone booking Tipton's family on a morning flight to the Grand Canyon, and Halford, giving an interview to the New York documentary team, is saying, "I've never known such a lull in me bloody sex-life. I don't think I've had an erection since we've got here."

I ride down with Ian and Ken to the bar in Harrah's, where both they and their drink orders are well-known by the maitre 'd. The two original members of the band (they dropped out of their secondary school in Birmingham in the same year), and the only two that don't seem compelled to shower plaintiffs' every statement with scornful smiles, they watch the proceedings with a mixture of curiosity and incomprehension till the late hours of afternoon, when they both look ready for a long nap and a stiff drink. Over second Bloody Marys, I tell Downing I've noticed that his ears seem to prick up every time Ray and Jay are mentioned. A 38-year-old man with a shoulder-length permanent, deeply receding hairline, a slight paunch, and a tendency to repeat the words "You know?" when he tries to explain anything, he seems fascinated when I say I've been to the churchyard where the shootings happened.

"Will you take me?" he asks, then grimaces. "Maybe that'd be in bad taste, eh? I've got strange feelings about those kids. It's not guilt, you know, but I do feel haunted when I hear about their lives, because they were the same as mine. I hated my parents, you know, terribly. These kids just didn't get to live long enough to put all that past them."

"So you made up with your parents eventually?"

"Oh, I talk to my Mum all the time."

"Is your father dead?"

"No, he's alive. But I don't talk to him. I don't hate him anymore, though, you know? I don't feel that I really matured till I stopped carrying that anger around with me, and that wasn't till a year or so ago. The music was the only real release, till then. I do feel angry, though, when they play all that backward surf music and talk about the harm we did these kids, 'cause I think our music was the best thing they had, you know? I remember citing sophisticated stuff verbatim to *my* folks—like they say Jay did—Jimi

Hendrix lyrics, like, and they'd look at me, like, 'Where's all that coming from?' You know? My parents aren't clever people, you know? They're just normal people."

Halford and Tipton, finished with their interview, arrive with the security guys, Rick and Nick. On our way into the three-star restaurant, Rick is arguing with Nick about Nevada's other major court case—the libel suit brought by the Las Vegas Stardust Hotel against the animal rights group, PETA. "Some dude slaps an orangutan around a little," says Rick, "and they ask for $800,000,000."

I don't remember much of that dinner, but I'll never forget the next morning's hangover. Between repeated calls for "one more bottle of this Chateau Neuf-de ... POP!, Captain Bong," to our Filipino headwaiter, Halford, who sat at the head, regaled the table with recitations from his favorite Mafia movies, then led a backward-sounding finger-chorus by everyone at the table on our Diamond Optic crystal wineglasses. Rick and Nick ordered the Chateaubriand for Two, apiece, and the argument began raging again when Nick told Rick he must have plaintiff and defendant confused in the Vegas case. "It would have to have been the animal rights guy who slapped the orangutan. It's the Stardust that's suing."

Ken, who sat to my left, ordered a second appetizer instead of an entree—"I'm worried about fitting my stage clothes," he confided— and told me how he hated secondary school. "I was all thumbs in Woodworking Shop. Metalworking, which is a biggie in Birmingham [several members worked for British Steel before joining], was even worse. The only thing I liked was Chess Club. I got to beat up on those kids with the perfectly pressed uniforms. And Cooking."

"Why Cooking?"

"'Cause you got to watch the girls bend over. I went to work as a cook after I left school, and I loved it, you know? Still do. I mean, how many people do you know, even at this age, who can bake an egg? You know?"

Sometime between the third bottle of Moët and the warmed Grand Marnier, I remember a silver plate with an $800 check hitting the table. "Happy Verdict, Captain Bong" was written on the back.

•

Judge Whitehead's decision on both the suit and Vivian Lynch's Motion in Limine and motion for sanctions was handed down two weeks after the end of the trial. An impressive document, it runs 68 pages, stopping en route to cite Sir Edward Coke's 17th century interpretation of the Magna Carta and Thomas Paine's and James Madison's arguments for the right to trial.

After criticizing CBS's actions in the discovery process, he awarded plaintiffs' lawyers $40,000. Finding (1) that the 24-track of "Better By You" submitted by CBS was authentic and unaltered, he declared (2) that there were several *Do it*s; (3) that they were subliminals; (4) but they were placed on the record unintentionally; (5) and that lack of intent establishes lack of liability under invasion of privacy theory; (6) that plaintiffs established a sufficient foundation for the effectiveness of subliminal stimuli, and that the decedents did perceive these; (7) but that plaintiffs failed to prove these stimuli were sufficient to explain conduct of this magnitude; and (following a lengthy disclaimer of any intent to demean the Vance and Belknap families) (8) that a number of other factors existed to explain the boys' behavior.

Whitehead's other findings concerned backmasked messages, which he rejected out of hand. Though he had "grave concerns" over their possible use if perceived by the unconscious, he found no reason to believe they could be so perceived. And though he indicated his displeasure with heavy metal, several times, he closed by thanking the members of Judas Priest for their courtesy during the trial.

Vivian Lynch felt Whitehead was wrong in construing this as an invasion of privacy case. "This is product liability. If somebody explodes in a Pinto, you don't have to prove Ford intended that to happen."

McKenna was more succinct: "Hey man," he tells me, "I'll take the $40,000."

Throw Out Your Gold Teeth
The Loneliness of the Trick-Bike Rider

Jonathon Gold, 14 years old and 90 percent perfect from the top of the key, is shooting series jumpshots in the playground on Houston Street and 6th Avenue in the Village. It's an ugly afternoon, 95 degrees and 90 percent humidity for the sixth straight day, but Jonathon is sweating only slightly, keeping a measured, machine-like pace, taking small sips from a litre bottle of Evian water as if it's fine motor oil that keeps him running. Twenty years ago, he would have been called *dedicated*, and he probably wouldn't have been the only ballplayer on this court.

Near the gate at the Sixth Avenue exit, Pete Kearney, the only other kid out here, is trying to induce Hyperspastic Infinity Rolls on his silver General freestyle bike: Picking up speed, he brakes suddenly to get the bike up over the front wheel, *a pointe*, then puts his left foot on a small peg extending from the front axle and swings the back wheel up and out behind him—hard enough, hopefully, to get a full 360-degree twist over the front wheel. When the trick works, which it rarely does, both Pete and the bike keep weaving in a kind of heavy metal pirouette, what freestylers call "tight circles," picking up centrifugals until the trick gets "spastic," and the bike and rider become a blur.

I recognize Pete from this month's issue of *Freestyling*, where a pair of electric-colored, fish-eye-lens photos identify him in midair with the captions, "This dude is quite the streetmonger!" and "Become one with G-turns!" But in this playground (the trick riders' main stomping grounds in the city) he looks like a mirage—

brought in on some weird bend of light from Rodondo Beach, c. 1972: not a drop of sweat on him, his dirty blond hair freshly sheared to 1/16th of an inch, his limbs covered with colored pads. Where the pads end, the gashes and scars and the striated discolorations of old and fresh bruises begin. Ranked among the top five amateur freestylers in the country, Pete is also *dedicated*. At the height of a sport peopled by preteens, teens, and the occasional madman, however, Pete, who is 20, aggressively sane, and studying business administration at a California state college, is looking at early retirement. Until last week he was "factory," a rider on a team sponsored by the General company, but he had a fight with the captain and quit.

"When you get caught in a trick," he tells me, absentmindedly picking skin out of a deep gouge above his right eye, "you can't afford to panic, go back on it and change your mind, or you'll get hurt. You have to fall into the trick, either bail or ride out."

I get the feeling Pete is depressed about the factory spot he lost, but he denies it emphatically. "Freestyling," he tells me, "is all street." I ask after his blackened eye and the wrong turn his nose takes below the bridge.

"No, that was the Banks," he says, "not a trick."

"The Banks?"

"That incline to the wall under the Brooklyn Bridge. I was going to blast the wall ..."

"Blast the wall?"

"Carve it," he says impatiently. "But I lost it halfway up, I didn't get the air I needed and blasted my face instead. The nose"—he points like it belongs to someone else—"I broke on a ramp in L.A. But that was months ago."

Pete goes off on a date-and-place litany of his black-and-blue marks, putting them all safely in the past. Most are from riding ramps, quarter- and half-pipe curves made of plywood and two-by-fours, which the hardcore riders flush against a wall so they can continue climbing—up to 15 feet—before they spin in midair and "ride out" back down to the ground. A seven-foot ramp, Pete tells me, costs $200 and lasts until the cops tear it down. He invites me to come out to watch him ride one in Staten Island tomorrow, warning me with a look of great distaste, "There'll probably be a few skateboarders there. This isn't kid stuff, you know," he says, looking me in the eye for the first time since we met. "It's a sport. This is work."

A blur named Dwayne whizzes by, brakes, and goes vertical. He comes out of the trick to scratch Pete's crewcut. "You look terrible," he says.

"Thanks. The Banks," says Pete. "I quit General."

•

The word's gone out there's media in the playground, and the freestylers come tooling in on their small, expensive bikes—about 20, half of them dressed identically in blue jeans, blue T-shirts, and high-top New Balance sneakers reinforced with duct tape. They seem a little suspicious of me—a working adult with no visible technology about his person—until I drop words like *spastic* and *bail*. Then their ears prick up for a half-second and they slouch acceptingly over their handlebars. A few tell me they took a "repulsive" math final yesterday. None of them seem to feel they passed it. "Look at G.I. Joe," one of them tells Pete, noogying his scalp.

"I quit General," Pete greets them, then goes off to work on a trick. On the back of his sawed-off T-shirt is the ad copy for General—IF FREESTYLING WAS OUTLAWED ONLY OUTLAWS WOULD RIDE—which, as the afternoon drags slowly on, seems more and more like wishful thinking: These are fairly clean-cut kids, squared off in tight circles across the playground, each in his own dead-serious, workmanlike battle with what they call The Limit, both of one's own/the group's capacity on two wheels and of one's fear. Peak riding ages seem to be 16 and 17: The younger kids have trouble controlling their bikes, and the older ones are clearly more afraid. There's a pecking order at work, but it seems to change from minute to minute; Pete's semi-professional status doesn't seem to mean anything, but his tight G-turns cause a subtle shift throughout the playground from bravado tricks to more technical ones. And when Dwayne goes off on a Cherry Picker, all the Elbow Rolls and Boomerangs and Noury Handstands go on hold: Climbing over the handlebars, he eases into a crouch above the front wheel, rises slowly until he's standing on the bars, then rows his arms through the air to keep it going. In the collective hush that falls over the playground as they stop to see how far he'll take it— out the gate onto Sixth, where he somehow makes a right and heads uptown—I start humming the lyrics of a song I haven't heard for 10 years:

> *Who are these children*
> *Who scheme and run wild?*
> *Who speak with their wings*
> *And the way that they smile?*

Seeing Dwayne's pack on his back, his empty Hit cookie bag on the ground, I realize he's taking off and run out to ask if he's coming to Staten Island tomorrow to ride ramps. He's already halfway up the block, threading through the trees, completely in control. Pedestrians are darting out of his way.

"No," he yells back, fighting for balance as his voice throws him off slightly. "My girl won't like it."

"You sure?"

"You don't know my girl," he says. "She's mean."

"Why don't you hang around awhile?"

"Gotta go now," he says, disappearing in the leaves. "She'll beat me up."

•

At the dock in Staten Island, I waste a miserly impulse, worrying how much I'll have to slip Freddy, our ex-biker/speedfreak cabbie to take three bikes in the trunk of his modified Rambler station wagon. I haven't understood yet how deep 25 cents and a 40-minute ferry ride takes you into the bowels of America, where people understand about things like bikes. At the last light in St. George, with one smooth motion Freddy puts the pedal to the metal, fingers his AC/DC T-shirt over the last two ridges of his gut, throws a Heart tape into the deck, cranks it up to 11, fingers a Marlboro from one of several packs on the dashboard, fires it up, adjusts his mirror to see if he's dusted Chris Bos (a 19-year-old freestyler following us on a scooter), then turns to say something evil to me and Raul Mendes, a biker crammed between us in the front seat. Between the music and Raul—who's been filling me in on the plots and most gruesome moments of various *Friday the 13th* sequels since I met him yesterday—I miss what Freddy says, and point to my ear.

"I said: *That little faggot*," he lowers the volume an indiscernible notch, "*is topping that shitcan all the fuck up.*"

I look out the back window, smelling rubber, WD-40, and steaks burning in the backyards we're whizzing past. Chris, gaining steadily on the Rambler, sees me looking back at him and pops a wheelie for good measure. Freddy loves it, and blasts the music, so that we can all share:

> You got me down, down, Down on my kne-e-e-es.
> Ooooh, Barracuda.

A gang of fifth-graders with amazingly filthy mouths and heavy accents are skateboarding in Tysen's Park down the island. The smallest, an adorable looking nine-year-old with thick plastic glasses, sees us unloading and skates up. "Kill a bikuh, save a gehbidge can," he yells, scraping to a halt with a sharp pivot. "Mothafuckin' freestyluhs."

A Cherokee Turbo Diesel pickup with a huge ramp in the back pulls past and stops 10 feet in front of us. Tex, the pony-tailed Hardcore skater at the wheel, guns the motor so we can taste his hydrocarbons. His friend Eric, spotting Chris Bos, cranks open the window to tell him he's really just a New Wave moron. "Skateshit," Chris screams, unleashing his bike from his scooter. Though he's barely looked at them, he tells me that their ramp—our ostensible reason for coming out here—is five percent more vertical than a bike ramp, and too dangerous to ride. "Doesn't matter," he assures me. "Bikers don't need that stuff"—which he illustrates by charging a picnic table and somehow mounting it, then flying off toward a park bench, where he jams his front wheel into the seat.

Our other ostensible reason for coming out here, a four-foot

concrete retaining wall with a 45-degree slope on both sides, is stenciled with a huge NO BIKE RIDING sign and a three-by-ten-foot red
heart that has the promise JIMMY & DONNA 1/16/84–4'EVER
spraypainted inside. I sit down among the skateboarding 10-year-
olds, feeling 1000 light years from home, and start taking notes. The
little one with the glasses comes over to read what I'm writing.

"It wahn't fawevvuh," he says helpfully. "He faw-effed huh."

"He what?"

"He faw-effed huh," he says. "Find huh," the kids scream in
unison, "feel huh, fuck huh, fawget huh!"

"Whyn't you fuckin' brats watch your fuckin' mouths," advises a
teenage mother sitting nearby. "I got a small kid here, you little"—
the last of her words lost in a roar of Spanish as Raul yells something ugly on his way up the wall. At the top of the incline he pulls
hard on the bars and blasts four feet of air, landing on the other
side with a thud and a boast/neologism culled from his beloved
Friday the 13th movies: "I Jason the wall."

•

At twilight, the metal kids come out, sitting immobile and silent on
the edge of the park, beautiful and dangerous-looking in their tight
jeans and stiff shoes and leather jackets and feather cuts, far too
cool to bother with anything like conversation. They don't give a
fuck about anybody or anything, but they seem to respect the
freestylers: It might be a clean-living sub-cult, but it's got wheels.
As Pete passes by, one lets two words pass his lips: "Pete Kearney."

"How you doing?" says Pete. "I quit General."

A group of local bikers have come down—hearing that a
reporter's come from "off-Island"—and are waiting on the blast-
line for a go at the wall. They're full of contempt for Tex and Eric,
who are performing some amazing skating tricks on their ramp. I
ask Raul, the clan elder at 21, if he knows these kids.

"I think I do, I think that I"—he raps as he cuts them off by
heading for the wall before them—"that maybe I, just might be I,
be better than them." Halfway up the incline he brakes and slides
down backwards, however. The others have been doing likewise
after watching Chris take a nasty fall; Pete, the only one still

blasting, is having a hard time of it. Again and again he lands on the far side with a bellow of "Damn!"—the closest he'll come to cursing—louder and angrier each time. "I crashed into that wall the other day, and I cannot get that fact out of my ... head!"

I'm tempted to ask why he doesn't just give it up, but I realize he's made his commitment to this wall, and, for a little while longer, to his freestyling life. "This time," he says, cutting off the newcomers as he goes for it again, his face clenched in an object lesson in How to Deal With Fear: Get Furious. At the top of the incline, he jerks the bars up angrily, and with his mouth open like a ski-flier's, blasts a good six or seven feet of air, enough for a triumphant Sideways Lookdown and to resume his seat so he can land safely on the other side and ride out.

There's a begrudging hush of respect from Eric and Tex and the 10-year-olds as he rides by. I seize the chance to taunt them.

"So what?" says the little one. "He's factory."

"Not any more," I finally silence the brat. "He quit General."

●

Coming off the ferry at midnight, I take a ride on Raul's bars and listen to his rather complicated life-story and employment history as we cruise toward the Seaport by way of the Brooklyn Bridge. Approaching the Banks, where he wants to show me his ramp technique, we surprise a man in a dark silk suit, leaning against one of the huge supporting pillars of the bridge. A young woman wearing heels and a dark skirt suit is kneeling in front of him, performing fellatio, and she screams when she looks up and sees us riding past. "Fuck her face," Raul advises as she runs toward the water, drawing a look of anger, then a wink from the man. "Keep riding," the man says menacingly, and we do.

"What I really like," Raul tells me as we head toward the Seaport and its two ramps, "is titty-fucking. Especially them big Dominican titties. I like Puerto Rican titties too." On he goes, his strange, neutral voice behind me sounding like the Stage Manager's of "Our Town" as he tells me of other sexual proclivi-ties and the restaurants he's worked in as a prep-cook. As I add it up, it dawns on me that Raul's a good five years older than the 21 he claims to be—and probably ten years older than most of the kids he rides with everyday.

There's been a huge wreck on the East Side Drive, and the Seaport is swarming with police. We make a left and head toward the last possible ramp—in Chris Bos' apartment, which is in a building of expensive co-ops on West Broadway. His room is at the end of a dark, 3,000-foot loft filled with his mother's paintings, enormous canvases that glow menacingly in the dark and give off a heavy musk of fresh oil paint. A note on Chris' door reminds him to call his Dad. "P.S." it reads, "IT'S TOO LATE FOR THE RAMP."

"Doesn't matter," Chris shrugs his shoulders. "I'm tired anyway." His bedroom is wired: two TVs, personal and lap-top computers, a massive console of tape decks, a CD player, and a small VCR library of freestyling tapes he's shot himself or bought from the ads in the back of *Freestyling*. Ten feet out from one wall is a seven-foot-high quarter-pipe ramp, leading up to the top of a home-made double-decker bed. "This's how I go to sleep," he says, mounting his bike. He rides it straight up, then bails out at the top, landing with his arms crossed behind his head on his pillow, his bike lying next to him like a trusted family dog. He smiles obliviously when his mother yells out, "I said, no ramps, Chris," and to say good night to his friends.

•

Outside, the heat still hasn't broken, and though it's still only June, the streets have that superreal quality of an endless New York summer. Standing on Raul's pegs at the head of our diminished convoy of freestylers, listening to his ongoing monologue, I remember the chorus of the song I was singing yesterday:

> *Throw out your gold teeth,*
> *and see how they roll.*
> *The answer they reveal,*
> *Life is unreal.*

"I see everything that happens," Raul is saying, "riding my bike. I saw it when those people were burning on the Williamsburg

Bridge, when that manhole cover exploded in Midtown, 57th and Eighth. People got fucked up. I seen it when the cops busted 20 whores on the Bowery, loaded their asses into schoolbuses. I was in Times Square the other night too ..."

I ask Raul how long he's been riding. "I rode all the time for years. Night and day. When I finished school, I went into the military. I wanted to move up a class of vehicle, become a helicopter pilot. They put me somewhere in Carolina, though, I don't know. They kept me there—jerking me day in and day out—giving orders to everyone but me."

"What did you do?"

"Only thing I could do. Worked my way out. I couldn't wait to get back and get a job and get on the streets again."

"What do you like most about freestyling?"

"Like I was telling you, riding around, seeing everything that happens. Like I was telling you, I was in Times Square the other night, watching *Poltergeist II*. I walked out of the movie, it was late at night and everything was crazy like in the movie. This guy walking next to me is holding a knife, a ten-inch chef's knife. I know, 'cause I work with them."

"Sounds pretty scary."

"Yeah, but I didn't even think about what I was looking at. I was still in the movie. And next thing I know, this cop, thinks he Rambo and shit, got a gun to this guy's neck, and he's saying, 'Drop it, or I will baaa-lowww you fucking brains out.' I couldn't believe it."

"What did you do?"

"Got on my bike and rode out," he says as we pull up in front of the playground on Houston and Sixth. Raul says he's going to ride awhile before going home to sleep tonight. "Only one thing to do," he repeats. "Got on my bike and rode out."

King of the Park
Cracking Up With Charlie Barnett

On the third step of the entrance to the Palace Hotel on the Bowery and Third Street I catch an unmistakable whiff of aging vomit; halfway up the steep concrete stairs I step on a purple jumbo vial and shatter it, then tiptoe through a small, multicolored minefield of empty vials up to the front door, which is decorated with a wreath of plastic holly and some black magic marker graffiti reading "DON'T SMOKE CWACK." The tiny lobby looks like a cage: Straight ahead is a fenced-in reception desk papered with admonitions for transients and "ticket men," nonpaying emigres from the men's shelter next door. A steel-mesh door to the left leads to a long, narrow hallway of rooms, another to the right opens onto the "dayroom," a huge holding pen of a rec room, smelling of Lysol and hissing with the static of a TV tuned to an empty station. Five or six desperate-looking men are sleeping as far away from the TV as possible. I ask the stubby-bearded desk clerk if he's seen Charlie Barnett, and he tells me he's never heard of him. Turning to go, I ask how much the rooms are. "Six dollars, 50 cents tax," he says. "But you don't want to stay here."

It's been a long morning already, making the rounds of comedy clubs like Catch a Rising Star and the Improv for news of Charlie, hearing one How the Mighty Have Fallen comment after another. There was a time when Charlie had carte blanche in these places, dropping in at midnight after a day of street shows, stealing the prime spots from the scheduled acts, moving on to another club for more. Nobody was surprised when he made it, a little over four years ago, and abandoned the clubs for the West Coast and stardom; there's a polite but noticeable relish of his low profile since coming back. "Two years ago, la dolce vita," said Sylvia, the day manager at the Comedy Cellar. "Now he's back out on the street—Third and Avenue A, the Palace Hotel. Poor Charlie."

Out on the street is where Charlie always was, performing on Bleecker and Thompson, behind the newspaper kiosk on Sixth Avenue and Third, Washington Square Park, any semi-enclosed spot where he could set up shop, start yelling, and get a crowd. His half-hour shows—an entirely original, filthy, spontaneous-seeming comedy—were revved up by pyrotechnical, viciously funny exchanges with his audience: winos, druggies, tourists, local professionals, professional loiterers. One afternoon in 1980 a William Morris agent in the Village named Greg Mullins "discovered" Charlie—performing for about 300 people in Washington Square Park—and booked him into clubs across the country. He also got Charlie an audition for "Saturday Night Live" during the crossover from the original cast to the next generation, which he made good on, getting called back a number of times for further tests. Jean Doumanian, the show's producer at the time, remembers Charlie and his talent affectionately, but not the details, and nobody at the current show goes back far enough to comment. The "inside story," sworn to by someone close to both Charlie and the show, is that he lasted through final auditions on the strength of his own material, then lost the spot to Eddie Murphy when it was learned Charlie wasn't literate enough to read the cue cards.

His "break" came in 1984, when the casting agent of *D.C. Cab* saw him passing the hat in Washington Square Park, filmed a performance in the Comedy Cellar, and sent director Joel Schumacher a tape. Schumacher, looking for performers with a "raw, spontaneous edge," says he "fell in love with Charlie at first sight," and cast him opposite Gary Busey, Mr. T, and Adam Baldwin. Within weeks after the shoot, Charlie was bicoastal, shuttling between New York and his condo on Sunset Boulevard, with week- and night-long stopovers at clubs in Miami, Chicago, Las Vegas. He aced his next shot at the big time, a spot on an episode of "Miami Vice," playing a police snitch called the Noogie: The character proved popular enough for 10 more episodes over the next three years and served as a springboard for three low-budget films, a dozen HBO comedy specials, and an episode of "T.J. Hooker." Every two or three months he'd be back in Washington Square Park, talking about blacks who made it ("In L.A. they got big-lipped, blue-black Alabama porchmonkey Negroes lying in the sun trying to tan their asses white"), how Abe Lincoln nodded out on his monument while waiting for Mr. T to deliver his one line of the evening without fucking it up, and how rewarding it is to work your ass off and finally get what you always wanted: Enough Cocaine To Last the Night.

Though he was funnier than ever, over the next few years it became clear something wasn't right with Charlie: Longer and longer pauses began to crop up in his formerly seamless shows, Charlie staring at his audiences as though they were made of ether, coming down to the park looking like he'd fallen out of bed, performing for 15 minutes then taking off. Mullins remembers this period with exasperation. "You'd get to the office and your first problem was a Charlie Barnett problem: Charlie's cancelled a date, Charlie's missed the plane, Charlie's in the office for a check that's not due for another few weeks. On 'Miami Vice' they loved his character, his performances. But Charlie could bring confusion to any set he walked onto. And then there were the drugs. Finally, a year and a half ago, I had to cut it off with Charlie. He just got to be too much to deal with."

A little over a year ago Charlie dropped out of sight: no more movies, TV, or street shows. A few months back a friend saw him performing in Washington Square Park, badly, and said Charlie looked completely cracked out.

•

A black Econoline van with Jersey plates is backing up to the curb in front of the Palace. Four mid-thirties leather boys step out, rough and ready, wearing mascara, eyeliner. I watch them unload a stack of well-traveled Marshalls into CBGB next door, grateful for their hardcore, harmless presence, only gradually becoming aware of a finger poking gently into my arm from above. A heavily bearded man in a beat-up, pea-green corduroy jacket is standing on the first step of the Palace stairs, smiling warmly as he tells me in a bizarre, rapid-fire Negril-cum-Bowery patois not to worry, he's got what I want, we'll go for a walk, just call him Bigger, everyone does. Does he know Charlie? Of course he knows Charlie, Charlie's a funny man, personal friend. As we turn onto Third Street, stopping at the Men's Shelter so he can talk shop with three guys named Stretch, Frenchie, and One-Eyed Shorty (everyone here seems to go by monikers), I understand Bigger's trying to sell me something, but I can't figure out what it is. He sounds more like an advance man for the Palace than any card-carrying crack dealer.

"Some very respectables come here," he says as we complete our first lap around the block, never losing his salesman's smile. "The suit, the tie, the stockbroker, the chemical engineer, people like yourself. Journalists. But they cannot compete with the people who live here. In the dayroom, when we past the drug, having lunch, watching TV, you see our quality of people—singers, entertainers, civil engineers, people like yourself. Journalists. Those people who come to the Palace in their limousines, go to the Prince Town University, they cannot compete with men like I, who spend 75, 80 per cent of life on the street. You learn too much on the street. Is the biggest college there is."

As we turn onto Second Avenue again I lean against the fence penning in a vacant lot to catch my breath, while Bigger says hello to a few colleagues speeding around the block. All are selling crack, Bigger tells me, except for a short man in his 50s named Hook, selling $75 "Perry Ellis" shirts for $3 apiece, and a good-looking African kid in stonewashed jacket and jeans, 16, 17 years old, who looks like he's just begun the program. "Now I feel secure," he says, appraising a K-57 switchblade he closes and opens in his hands.

Bigger's face is without its smile for the first time as he watches the knife go by. "Everything good and bad must come to an end," he says. "Thirty, 40 per cent of them get out from under the crack, the rehab program. The John Belushi, the entertainer, Charlie, 90 per cent need something to hype them onto the stage, keep them going long after the stage is finished. They come to see me, they know it is an event. Something is going to happen."

Two huge gray rats are scavenging by the fence. I point them out to Bigger with a nod of my head, and he just smiles. "Charlie once must have had a lot of money. On a personal note though," he says, turning around. "I have been completely honest with you. How come you no give me two, three dollar?" I give him some money, and ask when I might find Charlie. "You just miss him by an hour," he says. "But he will be back."

I ask Bigger why he thinks someone like Charlie would throw it all away. "The same reason as we all," he says. "Because he is addicted."

•

A twilight congregation of 50 or so stands under an elm tree near the arch in Washington Square Park, blowing into their hands for warmth, laughing and screaming. In the center of their circle sits Charlie, his tiny butt propped on the top of a wire wastebasket, talking about how hard it is to fuck a prostitute in your room at the Palace when you're cracked out of your mind. He's picked up a few decibels, and the staccato cadence and full-bodied gestures of a Southern Baptist preacher; he sounds like a man testifying, but proud, unrepentant, with an "And I only am escaped alone to tell thee" delivery.

"I had me a fine room there," he's yelling. "Finest room $6.50 can buy. And a stack o' rubbers"—he raises the imaginary stack in his left palm, Exhibit A. "I was prepared to meet the virus. And I had me a stem," he lifts his right hand, "and $50 of what goes in it. And I had me a beautiful black woman. And she was willing, brothers and sisters. She was fuckin' desperate."

Charlie lowers his right fist and inhales for a long time, closing his eyes. He looks like he's seeing something horrible when he opens them again. "When you smoking crack," he says with a lowering voice, "you get paranoid. Like a motherfucker. I'd be checking out the woman, the rubbers, then back at the bitch. And she be saying, 'C'mon Charlie, I wanna get down.' And I get mad. Furious. 'Soon's I finish,'" he inhales, glowering, his eyes growing wide until he looks furious, dangerous. "'Soon's I finish,'" he inhales again, "'I am gonna fuck the shit out your black ass. Just as soon as I finish.'" He inhales once more, then looks at his left hand. "I'm so paranoid now I put on all the rubbers. Sixteen of them."

Everyone starts howling as Charlie mimes it, each one more difficult to force on. "Even my rubbers was paranoid!" he screams. "By the time the last one's on, they're yelling, 'No Charlie! Please! Don't make us go in there! Let's go in that bathroom and massss-tuhbate.'"

Two elegant men with matching double-breasted suits, gold wire-rims, and Grace Jones coifs fall to their knees on this last joke, pleading, "Oh shit, oh shit." Charlie checks them out, rising from the garbage can. "Jesus!" he screams. "There's two of you motherfuckers. The rhinestone asshole twins. But I like my man's hair," he points to one, strutting the width of his circle like a five-foot-four Jake LaMotta, making eye contact with anyone who'll dare. "Looks like a fuckin' shoebrush."

As he settles back into the garbage can to do his imitation of a crackhead vet pirouetting paranoically down the Bowery in his wheelchair, a six-foot-six, 250-pound wino spills out of the crowd to join the fun, coughing up ugly fluids, roaring like a hippo. He gets an ovation from the crowd—seemingly the only response he's had in months—and decides to stay. Charlie borrows a dollar from someone in the crowd, announcing, "The only way to handle bullshit like this is to go matador." Holding the bill up to the man's eyes, Charlie says, "Here Papa. Here Papa," until the man lunges for the bill, repeatedly, as Charlie leads him out of the circle.

"How many you people like my show?" he asks, returning the dollar; he gets a huge round. "Good. Because now I collect for real. I want you to pay me! I don't drink, I don't steal, and I've been off drugs for ... excuse me, what time is it?"

The last time I saw Charlie, I realize as he passes with his monogrammed leather baseball cap in his hand, was in this spot, over a year ago. I've forgotten how small and fragile he is, how childlike his features are, how lean and pre-adolescent his body looks. All his clothes seem outsized, like he's still a few months shy of growing into them: cuffed Levis, always clean and ironed, plain blue T-shirt, unlaced Avias, and his cap, which he always wears backward when he's not passing it around. He looks more like a well-scrubbed Little Leaguer heading for a full day at the playground than a 34-year-old man who's spent the night in an SRO.

•

"Sure, I'll talk to you," Charlie says while signing autographs, confirming an amorous Columbia Grammar student's suspicions that it was him she saw on "T.J. Hooker" and all those episodes of "Miami Vice." Once the fans are gone, he counts the coins and bills in his hat. He isn't pleased. "I had me a lot of money once," he commiserates with himself. "So you want to talk about drugs, right?"

Struck dumb by his directness, I ask after his resumé, and he reels off a list of performances: his movies, a ton of cable specials, a film he wrote and starred in called *Terms of Enrollment: Charlie Barnett's Guide to Higher Education*, a role in *Nobody's Fool*, the list goes on. I ask if he made a lot of money for *D.C. Cab.* "Yep, and a $1.2 million contract for three more movies. Plus points and all that bullshit. Fucked that up. Plus 10 'Miami Vice' episodes ..."

"What was it like working with ...?"

"Don't like him. Don Johnson? He doesn't like me either. I had a fistfight with him, right on the set, first few days. 'Cause I stole the episode. It was called 'Cool Runnin'. I stole it. They were talking about how this black guy's great, and the man just started fuckin' with me, saying 'You been on this show for a week and you think it's yours.' And so I said, 'Fuck you,' and we got into it."

"Did you get in any good shots?"

"Nah, it turned into a wrassle. The Teamsters grabbed us and dragged us off. He called me and apologized. I just did another 'Vice,' a year ago."

I tell him I can't connect all that with doing street shows for chump change. He shakes his head, telling me that isn't the problem. "I made $200 one show last Saturday and I woke up on a bench in Tompkins Square Park next morning. I did even better that day, and I was standing in the food line Monday morning. I'm trying to handle these drugs."

A woman who looks faintly familiar to Charlie comes over to talk. A friend of a friend, she tells him about the strange time she's had since coming to New York. She doesn't seem like she's begging, but when Charlie reaches into his hat for a $5 bill—a substantial fraction of what's in there—she doesn't refuse. "Listen," he tells me, "I gotta walk. Let's do this tomorrow or something." I watch him walk the woman to the corner and say goodbye to her, patting her shoulder and making a couple of jokes before he turns around and heads east, toward the Bowery, walking faster and faster till he's out of sight.

•

The next day comes but Charlie doesn't, nor the next or the day after. Saturday, a gorgeous day, brings a mob to the park, and an almost medieval array of performers sets up shop in the center of the fountain: Joey Joey, a unicyclist/sword-swallower; mimes; a martial arts juggler; a six-five Senegalese transsexual in green body paint, imitating the Statue of Liberty; a pornographic magician; the Calypso Tumblers, flipping and flying over each other and making a ton of money. By Wednesday it's cold and rainy again, and the main attraction in the park is a squad of bright-eyed, bearded men in yellow T-shirts talking in relay about the Power of Darkness Within You. They seem powerful and learned until a homeless Hispanic woman comes over and refutes their arguments with the simple reduction, "I'd marry a pit bull before any of you godless excuses for men."

Late that afternoon, I witness something nasty: a black man in his thirties, leaning awkwardly over a chess table in the corner of the park, an intense, vacant look on his face as a patrolman with a size-18 neck frisks his torso, arms, and legs from behind. Finding nothing, the cop snarls some unacknowledged words to the wise and takes off, and the man sits down at the empty table to gather his wits and papers. I recognize him suddenly: Alex, a weak but iron-willed chess player who used to be here constantly, falling into lost positions almost every game, finding one saving move after another till his opponent finally dropped. It's been a while since I've seen him, and the change is baffling. Six months ago he was a gentle, solvent professional who didn't seem a day over 25.

A few tables over, a hustler named Livermore, who's dying of AIDS, has stopped his chess clock to watch the proceedings. "Damn," he says, starting his clock as Alex takes off fast across the park, "Alex is gone." I ask where he's gone to and Livermore, flashing his opponent a How-stupid-can-this-white-man-be? grin, says, "East. See? The man has gone east on important business. What I hear," he concludes, sacrificing a rook with an angry flourish, "business is booming."

•

At twilight I find Charlie sitting by the fountain, wrapped up in a white polyester-filled ski coat, watching a comic named Albert try to perform while a THC-crazed kid from Westchester aims karate kicks at his head from six feet off. An enormous man with a skull like a cinderblock is also lecturing the crowd about the $36 million the Defense Department owes him for stealing the sun from him, and Albert has given up telling jokes for the moment. Charlie greets me warmly, putting his arm around my shoulder, and together we watch Albert's show disintegrate. "It's getting cold," he says. "People gotta go to work tomorrow. I hate to do this—"

Charlie walks 20 yards away, drops his coat on the ground, and starts screaming, "Showtime. Showtime, motherfuckers." Minutes later, he has every cogent person in the park in his corner and the show begins, Charlie down on his knees, pounding the bricks and screaming, "I hate that bitch. I hate that bitch. Robin, Bitch, Ass, Fuckin' Givens wants $20 million for eight months of marriage and I know for a fact the Champ didn't get to fuck her ass but four times. That's $5 million a fuck. I know a woman on 3rd Street who'll do it for $20. Yo, Mike," he whispers, "*spend* the extra buck on the rubber—it's worth it. And I knew," he raises a fist in solidarity. "I knew … she married my man for his money. Think about it. Would a bitch that fine fuck a gorilla for free?"

And on he goes, one racist, sexist, homophobic joke after another, each laced with some rage or foolery so extreme he can get away with it. Charlie is always acting something out, something childish and familiar; whether he's making fools of the audience or himself, he's making you an accomplice. If the joke doesn't get you, the anger or panic on his face will: getting Japanese tourists to laugh about their big cameras and tiny dicks, "token-sucking niggers" to agree they've never worked a day in their lives, Puerto Rican men to laugh about how they're born with knives in their hands and live 4,000 to a room, "butt-slamming homos" to demonstrate the way they walk when they're cruising for "a ma-a-an," a woman in the first row to agree that she smells like a barnyard once a month and sounds like a small rodeo when she's coming.

Thirty minutes later, Charlie's feeling good, with a hat full of money and a gaggle of admirers around him, easing the bridge from showtime to reality. His girlfriend, Marcie, a 27-year-old cellist working on her second master's in music, has returned from visiting relatives in Germany, and he's living happily and—this week—drug-free out in some obscure part of New Jersey with her again. He's been offered a movie about sea monsters set to film in Florida over the winter, and is booking himself into the New York clubs for the month ahead, the weather dropping too rapidly for him to be able to count on street shows for a living anymore.

I go over to watch Marcie sing soprano with Jodi and men named Zeus and Chicken George, an a cappella group called The Village All Stars that seems to change personnel every month. It's been a while since I've heard good four-part harmony, and I've forgotten how beautiful it can be, how much meaning it'll lend even the most insidious tripe:

> In the words of a broken heart,
> It's just Emotion,
> Taking me over ...

A few feet away, Charlie is settling accounts with some neighborhood creditors—the shish kebab man, the hot dog man, a guy who lent him $5 last week—everyone who asks, seemingly, but for one grinning, self-conscious man who seems amazed that Charlie's yelling at him to go fuck himself, to go fuck his mama, to go fuck the three guys who fucked his mama last night. "You just remember that next time you come to me," the man says with a smile.

"I hate those motherfuckers," Charlie tells me, leading us to a bench nearby. Realizing this is my formal interview, I get the tape running and ask my first question:

What motherfuckers?

"Motherfucking drug dealers. They want me to kill myself," Charlie answers. "They always smiling, saying, 'Hey, Charlie, how many? You got my money?' Nah, I can't do it. It's a fuckin' nightmare. Heroin, you get to nod out of reality. Cocaine, you hear the least little sound. Lots of guys you see are doing the speedball, they say it'll slow you down, you won't go back and buy coke right away. And I say, 'Wait a minute, me and you both go running back to the drug spot, you buy the speedball, all I'm buying's cocaine, how much is it slowing you down?' It's just, I'm the one making the money, and they're figuring, they get me into heroin, I buy 10 bags a day."

So on a day you're smoking crack, a typical day ...

"In the life of Charlie as Crackhead. Let's see, I do a show. I walk that way [he points east]. Toward Third Street. When I disappear, just like that, then I'm going to get high. Over by the Palace, the Men's Shelter. Tons of fuckin' crack. Five-dollar vials. Get a stem, light it up, suck it in, blow it out. 'Come on. Poh'lice. 'Sgetouttahere. Keep the stem on.'"

So how much will you do at a time?

"The whole thing."

Which whole thing?

"Whichever whole thing there is."

Somebody I don't get a good look at passes by, telling Charlie he shot his girl; from the look on Charlie's face, I get the feeling the guy isn't joking. When Marcie comes over in between songs and nestles into Charlie's shoulder, I ask if he's funny at home. "No way," she says, "the lazy fuck just sleeps all day." She slaps his face and goes back to her quartet. On cue, a six-foot, blackhaired woman who doesn't look more than 85 pounds drifts over to say she loved the show. He says he's being interviewed, explaining, "That's an old-fashioned junkie," as she wanders off. Then he identifies what some of our neighbors are on. Half are drugs I've never heard of. I ask what the crack high's like.

"Paranoia," he says. "I was high now, I couldn't sit here, I'd be looking 'round, thinking everyone's trying to get in my pocket."

When was the last time you smoked?

"Seven days ago. I still haven't recovered. It got to a point, recently, where I couldn't even—not that I wasn't funny, but I'd only do $10 shows. Soon as I could get $10 in the hat I'd end it."

Why do you do it?

"I don't know. I've spent hundreds of thousands of dollars on a high I cannot stand. Drugs make me work my ass off. I got good at being funny 'cause I needed the money to get high."

Do you think you're punishing yourself for something?

"Probably so. 'You got a low self-esteem/if you like to beam/ and it ain't what it seem/'cause you're chasing a dream/down Third Street/the Devil's beat.'"

Sounds like a rap song.

"Me and Marcie wrote it together. It's called 'Third Street.'"

He takes out a dog-eared, typewritten copy of the lyrics and starts reading:

> *... This drug is a drug*
> *that will kill your ambition*
> *but ya jus' won't listen*
> *coz ya can't stop dissin'*
> *and you're always in position*
> *for goin' on a mission*
> *it's an everyday tradition*
> *on Third Street.*

I get the feeling Charlie's self-conscious about reading, and I look down, nodding to his faltering beat, surprised at how lame his rap is, how little snap is in his bravado. Charlie's a consummate clown, and this would seem a simple enough persona. By the last page his voice is almost inaudible, incredibly plaintive, and I look up. His eyes are closed and I realize he's no longer reciting, that he never really was:

> *I jus' gotta get high*
> *and I don't know why*
> *I wanna take away the pain*
> *but then it's back again*
> *I'm just sick and tired a bein' sick and tired*
> *   a bein' sick and tired*
> *a bein' sick and tired*
> *a bein' greedy and needy and seedy.*
> *I'm finished with the filth and the crime*
> *crack crack crackin' it up all the time*
> *crawling through the gutter and slowly dyin'*
> *cryin'*
> *sighin'*
> *Jus' can't stop buyin'*
> *on Third Street,*
> *the Devil's beat.*

I wait out a long moment before responding: *Sounds pretty dreadful.*

"It is. Right from the start. I want to stop. I've been running good and bad with it, going to NA [Narcotics Anonymous] meetings. One day I'll smoke, then I'll stop for a week, then I'll do it for a month. Pure paranoia. If your hand was here, I'd watch my bag. I don't trust nobody."

I look at his hands, which are enormous: huge, spatulate fingers, each fingernail as wide as two of mine. "I've got these E.T. fingers," he shrugs. "I was born with an enlarged heart, then I got rheumatic fever when I was a year old."

Where were you living then?

"Well, I was born in Boston; when I got that they said I was in North Carolina."

Charlie talks a little of his past, sketchily, and with a tenderness that belies the content of what he's saying. His mother, he says, "was fucked up, stepdaddies and booze." His one memory of his real father takes the form of a joke, and not one of his better ones: "My daddy cracked up in the Korean War. By the time I was a year old he'd told enough of the neighbors he was Jesus they put him in the nuthouse for five years. When he came out, he didn't say he was Jesus anymore. He said he was God—which was fine, 'cause that made me Jesus."

He doesn't have any jokes to tell about his childhood in North Carolina, just bitter, impressionistic memories of being largely uncared for by relatives, of the stigma of his semi-orphanage and complete poverty. "They used to never promote me in school. I used to always get whuppings. The kids used to beat up on us afterward, and it was an embarrassment to play with the Barnett boys. My older brother and me, the black sheep on the street. My mother dumped us off down there when she was drunk, and I didn't see her for 11 years."

When he finally returned to his mother, she was "still drunk" and he was practically illiterate, which in the Boston of the early '60s meant an effective end to his education. (After the "Saturday Night Live" auditions he taught himself to read.) He remembers adolescence as a series of reform schools in Massachusetts, which taught him only "how to fight, to stay alive, and what drugs did what for your head." He went through withdrawal for the first time at 16, shivering in a one-room, padlocked shed at the edge of the school compound called the Discipline Cottage.

"Comedy," he says, "came much later, as a kind of gift I never knew I had. I learned I could make people laugh, that I loved to do that, and that after a while I could make a living at it. I never thought of making it, I never thought of auditioning for anything. Everything I ever got came from someone seeing me on the street and wanting me."

Joel Schumacher, his director on *D.C. Cab*, remembers an "incredible need to succeed in Charlie, and a shyness and inno- cence that I formed an immediate attachment to. He was like a kid who'd fallen asleep dreaming up one of his street shows and then woken up on a Hollywood set. A lot of people got very interested in Charlie very quickly, making him all kinds of offers. It confused him, brought on all sorts of conflicts and doubts. I felt a little culpable, and wondered if I wouldn't have done better to have left him in the park, where at least he knew the turf. He's such a complicated, fragile person, and a true original. Over the years he's paid the price for being so. Even when everything was going so well, there was a kind of Judy Garland, John Belushi side to Charlie, very angry, self-destructive, very much the same anguish, finally the same response. In our little Marie Antoinette era, we say, 'Just Say No to Drugs.' What does that mean to someone like Charlie? 'Just say no to a lifetime of anger?'"

Greg Mullins says that Charlie's is "the saddest case I've ever seen, and I've been in the business 14 years. I remember one night, during one of Charlie's drug-free periods, I took a colleague to a show that just wasn't working. He was clearly uncomfortable onstage, unfunny, not like himself at all. My friend said, 'Greg, how do we get him back on drugs?' It's a cruel story, but it illustrates the point: Charlie's humor comes from his life, and his life's been a cruel one."

"I've had a fucked-up life," Charlie nods. "My life *is* fucked up. I'm an angry man, and I'm an angry comic. I'm funniest when I'm mad. But you have to be on, and you've got to be quick. My brand of humor, you can't be—shit, what's that word?" Charlie racks his brain for a buzz-word from his N.A. meetings, then gives up. "The audience will take over. You have to be so bold they'll just accept you, so they say, Fuck it, we have to, 'cause he's too fuckin' crazy for us to reason with him. I say all that vulgarity—sex, all that shit. People will—I get hecklers. They don't like what I say and speak on it. So I dog 'em. You can't be laid back worth a fuck. Some women get angry during the shows, 'cause that's where a lot of my anger comes from, and that's where it goes. I used to have a hell of a temper, used to always beat up on women.

"It's funny though, my father died this summer, and I went to see my mother, first time in years. When I was a year old, she was drunk, and sent me away for 11 years. When I came home, she was drunk, and when I saw her this summer she was drunk. Only now, I was a junkie, and I had to forgive her a lot of shit. We both just started crying. I'm a fuckin' junkie. All she ever did was drink."

"Charlie," Marcie told me later, "has lots of sides to him: his image side, which is really up for grabs, day-to-day. He's got a very 'personal' side—the 'Fuck it, I might just as well be honest' side—which isn't really him either. He's got what he calls his 'nigger' side, which is very proud, and pretty cutting. And there's the real Charlie, that only people like One-Eyed Shorty know, bums, crackheads, addicts, winos. That's how Charlie knows himself: King of the Park. Lots of times, we wouldn't have enough money to eat, and Charlie'd give them half of it, 'cause they had nothing. It comes from knowing what it's like. And sometimes we'd be walking through the park at 7 a.m. after a night of partying, without a dime and hungry, and he'd yell, 'O.K., I'm collecting for yesterday's show,' and they'd pay up—a quarter, 50 cents. Doesn't sound like much, but at times like that it can be a lot of money."

The Village All Stars are retiring for the night. There's no one left in the park to sing for but the Rastas, selling drugs by the chess tables, and they're here for the night. Charlie really wants to go, rushing Marcie, saying a quick goodbye to me. Last week this time, he was eastbound once the show was over, and it's clear he's still programmed that way, strongly, only what he wants now is to get home while he still can. When the five of them head up Fifth Avenue, Charlie's a few steps ahead and looking back over his shoulder, impatient at their dawdling and singing, which he keeps telling them is "completely homeless."

•

The Comic Strip, on 82nd Street & Second Avenue, is a welcome anachronism among the nouveau quiche cafes and boutiques of the Upper East Side, a place you'd sooner expect to pop up in some Jack Webb vehicle of the '50s. Inside is the warm comfort of old wood, old beers like Schaeffer and Rinegold, and old jokes; the clientele at the dimly lit bar (ex-comics, mostly, and comics waiting to go on), arguing about George Bush, seem like they might as well be talking about Duke Snider or Abe Beame. I find Charlie, glum and angry, sitting with Marcie in a graffiti-scarred oak booth opposite the bar. He's been given the best spot, at 1 a.m., but there are four comics on before him, and he says he doesn't want to be here tonight, he doesn't want to be anywhere tonight.

It's been a few months since I first met Charlie, and I've gotten a powerful secondhand taste of what "running good and bad" with a major league drug habit is like, the good time spent largely recuperating, the bad in tremendous isolation, in a place where I can't follow him. Charlie is remorselessly candid about his life (it's the source of his comedy, and he doesn't seem to know how to be any other way), but piecing it together from what he says is puzzle work. Events he describes in a deeply historical tone have a way of having taken place two days before, and his mood swings are baffling and sudden: One afternoon, I'll find him performing in the fountain at Washington Square at the top of his form, wearing his sleeveless CHOOSE LIFE T-shirt, doing a perfect moonwalk as he explains he's just trying to get the shit off his shoes, and then witness one of his $10 corner shows and quick getaways later that week. The end of it all seems to be the mood I find him in now, depressed, hostile, confused, utterly disgusted.

Still, things are looking up. There's a tentative two-week offer from a big club in Fort Lauderdale, coinciding nicely with the sea monsters he'll be co-starring with nearby. Charlie, a professional, knows how to take the good in the same stride as the worst of it. Though he's feeling like shit, he's all business tonight, hustling agents who've come to see him, talking shop with club-owner Richie Tinken, a big man in the comedy field and someone in a position to do him some good.

He settles back in the booth and tells me about life in L.A., how he got sick of the condo swimming pool after a month, then retired each afternoon to the sauna in his apartment, sweating the drugs out. After a cold shower he'd walk down Sunset Strip past the Chateau Marmont (the luxury hotel where John Belushi and Janis Joplin OD'ed) to the Comedy Store, or hitch a ride down to Venice Beach to do "a street show near the bodybuilders and the fake hippies with the tie-dyed T-shirts and incense." I ask Charlie how the clubs in

L.A. compare to New York. "Same shit," he says, "nice places."

The Comic Strip's eight-by-10-foot stage is only a few inches above audience level, so well-lit it's practically glowing in the dark, 200-seat room surrounding it. It's a full house tonight, 98 per cent white: aging jocks from the boroughs in threes and fours, awkward, half-drunk couples, flocks of tourists. A lot of the women look like they've been dragged here, and it is a fairly macho scene. The beginning of a 10-man, all-night bachelor party has a lock on the two first-row tables; the groom, a kind of Spuds MacKenzie on two legs, has an audible head start in the booze department and pride of place under the microphone. He's been heckling the shit out of the last two comics.

Limited to 15 minutes, Charlie hits the stage running, and by his second joke is walking up and down in front of the first-row tables, asking the two black couples in back to smile so he can see them, giving high-fives to Bachelor #1, yelling "How the hell are you, fuckin' A, how's the wife, how's my kids? Heckle me and I'll bust your fuckin' ass," then stepping onto a second-row table to ask a stony-faced middle-aged woman where she's from.

"From St. Louis," she says.

"And do the women there masturbate?" Charlie asks politely.

Apparently they don't, or would rather not say, and this enrages Charlie. "You lying bitch," he yells, walking to the stage and flopping on his back. "What the fuck is this?" He puts a finger to his groin and starts convulsing up and down the stage until the woman, who can't believe what she's looking at, snickers under her hand a little. Charlie keeps it up, his mouth open and gagging and salivating, his eyes going white, and finally the woman starts roaring, louder than the bachelors in front of her. When Charlie finishes, he leans back on an elbow, looking like he's just gone through electroshock. "Now do you remember?" he asks, nodding his head. He keeps it nodding until, finally, she nods with him.

"I thought you would," he says. "Fucking bitch."

•

After his set, I offer Charlie and Marcie a ride to Port Authority in the cab I take downtown. Coming into Times Square, wall-to-wall crowds at 3 a.m., I ask Charlie, who's been quiet the whole ride, if he'd ever perform in a place like this. "I do perform here, all the time," he says. "That corner over there."

I take a long look at the furtive congregations forming and unforming on the "Meat Market," the corner of 42nd and Eighth; it's been said over $1 million changes hands on this corner every day. To me, it's like watching a beehive, only more alien, dozens of people moving back and forth, no one seeming to leave. To Charlie, it's just another crowd: "Huge audiences," he says, looking out the window with me. "Any time of the night. Drag queens, dealers, pimps, hookers, winos, crackheads, heroin addicts. They pay real well. You'd be amazed how well they pay here. Good place to work on your heckler lines, any new material. I learn how to time my routines here."

I've never heard Charlie talk about *material* before, or *timing* or *routines*. I've been laughing at the same jokes for months now, but I've never thought once about his craft. I ask if there are any other comedians he likes, and he says, "Richie" really softly, with incredible tenderness. "And Lenny."

"Why on earth," I ask, "would men like that destroy themselves with drugs?"

Charlie turns to Marcie and says he wants to go for a bite before getting on the bus to Jersey. I wonder if he hasn't heard me, or if he's just impervious to such questions. "Because they're addicts," he finally says, looking lost in thought as he steps out of the cab and eyes the crowd. "What more reason do you need?"

The Regulars
1900 Years in Yankee Stadium

There's an evil-looking man with a pencil mustache in the last row of Yankee Stadium's rightfield bleachers, leaning back against a 50-foot-high CITIBANK IS YOUR BANK sign. Immaculate in his tan fedora, sky-blue leisure suit, glowing white T-shirt, and white patent-leather loafers, he snorts the end of a joint through a gold roach-clip as the California Angels take the field for the bottom of the second inning, then begins to twist his arms and hands and fingers in suave convulsions, his mouth stretching into unnatural shapes as he trains his magnetizing gaze on Angels' rightfielder Chili Davis, pacing the well-lit grass of right field 90 feet below. I've been watching this man for months now, casting his limp-wristed spell on every American League rightfielder not born in the Dominican Republic, and I have learned to fear his power. Midway through this late-August Yankee homestand, I feel a tingle in the back of my skull every time he starts conjuring.

Teena, a paper-thin Hispanic woman known among the Regulars as the Secretary of Da Fence, sees the effect he's having on me, and yells up at him to Cut That Voodoo Bullshit Out. "He isn't no Yankee fan," she assures me, tucking a loose blond curl back into her impromptu Mohawk. "Bullshit Voodoo Man. I show you what's a Yankee fan."

Teena gathers the wealth of gold chains on her neck, and her yellow ashtray eyes cross as she looks down to exhibit the ornaments to me: six variations of the Yankee logo in 14 or 16 karats; a small, diamond-studded baseball and bat, accompanying the word YANKEES; the brightest is a solid-gold 31, for Yankee all-star right-fielder Dave Winfield.

"I show you the biggest Yankee fan there is," she says, taking my hand and leading me down to Row A to meet Chico, a happy 300-pounder in a cobalt-blue Yankee jacket with a home-made 31 sewn on the back. "You Ain't Nothin' But a Hound Dog" is blasting on the P.A., and Chico's rocking out an imaginary bass guitar, all ten fingers moving in spidery patterns. "He's been in the papers lots," says Teena. "Hasn't you, Chico?"

"Bellevue," Chico agrees, keeping good time on the bass. "New York hometown paper. Intensive care. Times Square. Fifteen years." At Teena's prodding, he reaches in the pocket of his Yankee jacket for a half-dozen Polaroids of himself and an equally large woman having sex in a living room furnished entirely in red velvet.

"Motherfucking co'sucker, Chili Davis, *marecon*," Chico screams suddenly. He takes his Polaroids back and pivots on his heel with surprising agility to rock the entire stadium, yelling "Chili Willi fuck you silly" until the inning begins.

•

In 1973 Rick Goldfarb was my classmate at the Bronx High School of Science, a studious, awkward kid no one knew much about, except that he had a good head for numbers and a job selling beer at the Stadium. Over the years he's kept a CPA practice going on Allerton Avenue in the South Bronx, from January to April 15; from April 16 through October he sells beer in the third-base box seats—for the first four innings; from the fifth on, he's "Cousin Brewski," the sweetest and loudest guy out here.

"How are you? How are you? How are you?" he greets me from ten rows away. "I'll tell you everything you wanna know about the Regulars. They're the best fans out here. Class. They know everything you wanna know. Teena's got it all: the batting averages, all the ERA's, all the Won and the Lost. Bob the Captain knows every word of the 'Gang Bang Song,' the 'Get the Fuck Out Song,' 'Syphilis,' the 'Alibi Song,' all the fabulous songs. And over there's Melle Mel.

A big rap star [of Grandmaster Flash], one of the originals."

Rick's mouth widens into a horse grin as Melle begins leading the Regulars in a rendition of "Camptown Races," lyrics modified to honor Chili Davis' alleged anal-passive tendencies. "Famous? Melle?" Rick asks himself rhetorically. "Oh-h, is he famous! Sees everything going on out here, too. The others tend to drift a little. Frank's out here every day, brings candy"—

Rick excuses himself to go to the first row to join the second verse:

> *Chili takes it up the ass,*
> *Doo-da, doo-da*
> *Chili takes it up the ass,*
> *Oh, da-doo, da-day,*

then climbs back up the concrete steps, saying "Where was I? Where was I? Where was I? Frank brings candy for the kids, Turkish Taffy sometimes. He's got a heart of gold out here, do anything for anyone. If he knows you. We got business students from Clark University, summer interns from *The Nation*. There's Buttonhead, sells all the different buttons—RED SOX SUCK, TIGERS SUCK, A'S SUCK, METS SUCK, STEINBRENNER SUCKS. And there's Yankee Joints, sells what he sells. They're here when it's 100 degrees, when it's 40. They brought in a huge plate of Spanish rice last week, chicken with chick peas, stuffed cabbages, all those greens with the good olive oil dripping off. Just one big heart of gold, getting old."

I ask Rick how many years these people have been coming here, a question that brings out the accountant. "Figure, say 100, 115 individuals, total," he calculates, surveying the 12 rows in front of us. "Then, maybe 20, say 17 years apiece, average. So you're looking at what, maybe 1900 years out here. But those are just numbers," he says, waving an index finger. "You gotta figure in the human factor."

•

The Yankees, 2-8 in their last ten games, come into the fifth inning down by a familiar four-run count. Frank and his friend Ike are already ingesting their time-honored slump-remedy: Many Jumbo Beers. It only takes Don Mattingly's lead-off single to left to make them crazed. After the obligatory four notes of the *Hallelujah Chorus* sound from the Stadium organ (echoed by Frank and Ike's "O! the Mets suck!"), they get the first 12 rows up and pointing at Chili Davis:

> *U, G, L, Y,*
> *You ain't go no alibi.*
> *You uglay.*
> *You uglay.*
>
> *P, A, P, A,*
> *We all know your papa's gay.*
> *He's homo.*
> *He's homo.*
>
> *M, A, M, A,*
> *We know how he got that way.*
> *Your mama.*
> *She uglay.*

The entire bleachers looking on, Melle Mel decides to create some game-changing noise. Flipping his night-game shades up, tightening the doo-rag on his head, he spies a newcomer in a Hawaiian shirt. "BOOK HIM," he commands, and the Regulars obey by nah-nah-nah-ing the "Hawaii Five-O" melody in the man's face until, with a longing look at the blue seats of the loge level, he's up on his bench and surfing it.

"If the Yankees are the best team in the world," Melle yells above the roar of a 4 train passing ten feet behind the bleachers, "say Yo-o." Hundreds agreeing—and #31 himself stepping up to the plate, 375 feet away—Melle has a moment worthy of the Great Cause. "Let me hear it, one time, for my man, Mr. Da-a-a-ve Winfield." "Dave, Dave, Dave," a huge crowd chants as Winfield looks at a strike. They're still chanting "Dave" as Winfield whiffs on a second pitch, looks at a third strike, then lopes indifferently back to the dugout.

"That's the greatest number of all about this sport," Rick explains when I mention that Winfield's strike-out doesn't seem to bother anyone. "You fail two out of every three times, 66 percent of your professional life, and out here you're God's gift."

•

Statisticians of the great American game would do well to analyze Ali Ramirez, a tall, white-haired man who brings a cowbell to the games in a bowling-ball bag. A serious student of the game, Ali won't ring his bell until he feels a Yankee hit. For the last few weeks I've been getting goose-bumps every time Ali stands and unsheathes his bell; with the Yankees down now by four runs and two outs, no one on in the bottom of the sixth, I suddenly understand why: I've been hearing this bell in the distance my entire life, behind Phil Rizzuto's hypnotizing psalmodies on WPIX, and I've learned to expect a *Holy Cow* (Rizzuto's unfailing ejaculation for Yankee home runs), or at least a single, every time Ali rings the bell.

As Jack Clark steps up to the plate, Ali hammers out an eightbeat salsa rhythm, which is echoed by a drumming on the free seats by the Regulars that I can feel, 10 rows up, through my tail-bone. He follows with a 16-count, then ends with a steady beat that gets a deafening "Ay-oh" chant. It's broken by an unmistakable crack of Clark's bat, and a flurry of kids heading to the empty rightfield grandstands, where Clark's 370-foot homer soon lands 20 rows deep.

"The Gods have spoken," yells Melle Mel, up on his seat and salaaming. "Prai-ai-se A-A-Ali!" Almost everyone in the bleachers obeys, a moving sight—350 people bowing in a wave to this quiet man wearing a barber's shirt, cradling his bell and drumstick, already evaluating Don Slaught's stance at the plate.

Apparently it's rally-time, for Ali rings out another eight-count. Before he can start his sixteens, another long-ball crack gets the entire bleachers on its feet. I look up in the klieg-lit sky over right field and see a baseball coming at me, then under my seat for my first-baseman's glove to catch it, then back up in time to see the ball falling in the trough penning the bleachers apart from the rest of the stadium—50 feet from Clark's homer, and 15 feet to the left of the man with the bell.

Ali, ignoring the pleas of the Regulars, zips up his bowling ball bag as Gary Ward strikes out to end the inning. The timeless nature of baseball wafts over me like car exhaust as it dawns on me that I haven't had a first-basemen's glove for 20 years. Twenty rows up, the Voodoo Man is striking an Edith Piaf pose against the Citibank sign after his exertions.

•

By the seventh inning, timelessness has given way to insoluble tedium, and I organize a small press conference in the top rows with some of the Regulars: Bob Greco, machinist from Bergen County, Captain of the Bleachers; Frank Herrera, a college baseball umpire with a major stutter, who talks endlessly about whom he's willing to beat up for the Yankees; and a strange man named Big Bird, who seems to have an obsession with Australia: Tonight he's telling me about the difficulties of sending videos of the 1978 World Series to Melbourne. "He was there six weeks, six years ago," Bob explains. "Still fuckin' talkin' about it."

The Yankees seem to have fallen into the lull. Though they ended the sixth down only two runs, the Angels have pounded relief pitchers Dave Candelaria and Mike Shields for four runs. For Bob, Frank, and Big Bird, however, watching a routine single drop in the hole between Ward and Winfield for extra bases, it's clearly not an important failure. "If you came here every day, you'd just get used to it," Bob says as Teena climbs the steps to tell me to tell the world that every Yankee reliever makes her puke. "And you would grow to like it out here. You would see how it's like the family unit. You yell a bunch of shit, fifty people yell out with you. Get into a fight, you got a hundred backers. Plus, you can see everything from out here. Call balls and strikes. You can see inside the dugouts ..."

"Tell him about the time we gave you a birthday cake," Frank interrupts. "You were all choked up, and shit."

"Time out," Bob says. "I wanna tell him about training camp in Lauderdale. So, I'm down there with Kevin and George, couple the Regulars—"

"Tell him about the cake, you fuckin' dick," says Frank.

"Time out, Frankie. We're driving from the hotel to the ball park, half an hour, 45 minutes maybe, looking at all these maps. After four days, we realize we're half a mile from the stadium."

Bob sees Frank standing up with a look of terminal displeasure, and decides to tell me about the cake: "So I'm out here one night and they're singing 'Happy Birthday.' They got a cake, so I sing with 'em. But when they get to the 'Happy Birthday, dear ...' part, they're like, singing my name."

Bob pauses, to let the mystery sink in. "It's my thirty-second birthday. The cake's got my name on it too. It's probably like the biggest thrill of my life."

The Angels take the field for the bottom of the seventh, and Frank and Bob ask me if I've heard their "Mickey Mouse" cover:

> Hey, Chili ...
> M, I, C.
> See you real soo-oo-n.
> K, E, Y. Why-y-y?
> 'Cause we don't give a fuck about you.

"I love that one," says Frankie. "And, first time I heard the 'Gang Bang,' I was on the floor." He stands up, glares at the air an inch above his head and five feet in front and screams, "The Yankees suck what?" then begins punching the air. Bob shakes his head and finishes telling me about Lauderdale.

"So we get some pictures, the three of us with Dave, meet some other New Yorkers in the hotel—they weren't there for the training, they were on some other business. The biggest thrill was with Dave. What else is new?"

"Do you guys know him?"

"Yeah, we know him. Not personally, on a social level, but he sees us on the street, he knows, 'Yeah, the Bleachers.' We give him a plaque last year, congratulating him for his sixth consecutive year hitting 100 RBIs. He didn't do it, he ended up with 97, but we give him the plaque anyway."

"I met Dave once," says Frankie.

"Time out, Frankie. So we're down there, waiting by the gate for Dave to come out. There's a couple guys there, had their kids or something, and we ask, 'Dave come out yet?' And they're like, 'Don't waste your breath, Dave don't stop for nobody.' So he comes out, and the three of us are like, 'Dave, Dave, Dave.' Big smile. He's like, 'What the fuck are you guys doing down here?' signing autographs. He remembers the plaque. Suddenly"—Bob pauses to savor the irony—"the guys with the kids are like, 'Hey, we're with these guys.' That was like the biggest thrill of my life."

Frankie looks hurt. "I thought it was the cake."

"Nah, that was the biggest thrill of my life out here," Bob corrects him, standing up and brushing off his pants as he heads down to Row A. "Talk to the man, Frankie. He'll make you famous."

•

Against the back-drop of the "Get the Fuck Out Song" and the "Gang Bang Song" (a series of knock-knock jokes ranging from "Eisenhower"/"Eisenhower Who?"/"Eisenhower late for the Gang Bang" to "Gladiator"/"… before the Gang Bang"), I listen to half an hour of Frankie's fantasy life. It's a familiar fantasy to anyone growing up in New York: being outnumbered and having the numbers to escalate.

"I would never suggest," he begins, "for anyone to come out to the bleachers and to hit one of the Regulars. I would not suggest that. And I would never suggest what happened here, one time, when Yankee Joints got his bag taken by some guy. He asked for it back, and five guys stood up in his face, at him. So I walked over there and like, 50 guys jumped up behind me, it was like a wave. I tried to explain to these guys, I got like, 50 guys behind me, and every last one of them's willing to hit you. They don't need no reason."

I ask if there are a lot of fights out here. "This dude says, 'Whenever there's a fight, I never see you anywhere. Why?' Why-y? You ain't looking in the right place," Frank answers. He seems convinced that it was me who asked the question. "If you ever see a fight," he says, poking my chest hard, "look under the pile.

Under the pile. That's where you'll find me. Under the fucking pile. But like, if, like, this guy"—Frankie points to a fan two rows back—"like, if this guy were to hit Bob or Ike or Cousin Brewski, it would be suicide. And if I stood up in … his face"—Frank points to the same fan—"and said, 'You gonna hit me, you gonna *fucking* hit me?' I swear, 20 people will come behind me."

Frank looks at the guy suspiciously, then tells me how five enormous security guards came to the bleachers for him one day last summer. "Now, that is the most idiotic thing in the world I have ever heard. If you got 2000 fans and 3000 guards then maybe, maybe you could talk. But if you got five guards, I don't care what size they are, I'll throw 20 midgets on you to kick your ass. But they don't think that way over there in Security."

I ask Frank how he came to be an umpire.

"I was playing football and I got hurt bad. I could still move around and holler but I couldn't ever play again. I was going home and the bus driver asked me did I want to umpire little league ball with him. And I enjoyed it, a lot. See what happened was, my first game, I threw the manager out. And I said, 'Damn, I'm 13 and I just threw this 40-year-old man out.' So, I grew up and went to umpiring school in San Bernardino. I do college now, and the Dominican Leagues in the winter. With a little luck, I'll make it to the majors."

Frank looks down at the field, where the Yankees have just gone down three straight, then over at the Regulars, who are singing "Syphilis." "One day," he nods his head, "I'll be umping at the Stadium and I would have to make a close call against this team."

Frank continues nodding his head. "See, I know that would happen," he adds with conviction, "And the Regulars would nail me. I know that. Fuck them. I call them like I see them. And I will be a Yankee fan till the day I die. I know that."

A 4 train rumbles overhead and Frankie starts thinking about something, shaking his head and moving his lips with a repeated, unspoken sentence. "Everywhere I go," he finally says it. "Everywhere I go till the day I die."

He stands up and looks down at the first rows. "Like, I was on the subway," he says, "wearing my cap. And this guy's wearing a Mets cap: 'You should get a better cap.' Get a better cap?! What?" Frankie takes his black Yankee cap off his head and pounds it into shape. "When you win as many World Championships as the Yankees," he tells me. "When you win as many pennants. When you win as many division championships, as many World Series as this franchise, in its history, then you come back and see me." Frank screws his cap back on his head, shoots me a hate-look, then heads down the steps to join the Regulars. "And I'll meet you on this train," he yells up at me, "three thousand years from now."

Little Big Mouth

The Unfunny Comedy of Andrew Dice Clay

A hundred or so surprisingly subdued leather boys and their women are guzzling Budweiser and Bud Lights on a bottlenecked New Jersey Transit bus to the sold-out, 21,000-seat Brendan Byrne Arena in the Meadowlands, headed to the sixth show of Andrew Dice Clay's Fall 1989 Tour. Twenty-six rows deep, everyone is coupled up. A rough census of diamonds, ring fingers, and averted glances shows the majority are wed or engaged, with no one mani festly overjoyed to be so. From the occasional sibilant snippet around me, in fact, I get the feeling this entire busload is "completely fucking disgusted"—from working all week, with their lovers, or both. I look at my calendar watch—there are only twelve days left of the 1980's—and think about how old I'm getting: Ten years ago, these people would have been loud, stoned, 'Luded, or tripping, headed out to see Queen or a Zappa Halloween Show, and traveling in the prurient "co-institutional" packs of a Catholic high school game bus—guys on one side, girls on the other.

Through the bus' green plastic window, I look down at the same scene inside the four-mile line of cars stalled under the bright lights of Route 6: A stony-faced man stiff-armed at the wheel, as though he's going 80 mph, a woman with Big Hair facing forward in the passenger seat. It's a bizarre sight, and one I imagine will recur in the 13 states visited by the Dice show: An hour-long vituperation on women, dwarves, dogs, Latins, Pakistanis, Arabs, beggars, paraplegics, Oriental business acumen, and deejay Howard Stern, with whom Dice had some words over complimentary tickets. Born Andrew Clay Silverstein, Dice doesn't tell Jewish jokes.

In fact, Dice doesn't really tell jokes at all. He lacks the media range of a Morton Downey or the metalhead mass appeal of Axl Rose, but he has exactly their audience, plus the tailwind of the late-1980s fervor for "comedy" behind him and the demagogue's genius for the lowest common denominator. In the last year, his shows have moved from the club circuit to hockey arenas, stadiums, and concert halls of 12,000 to 21,000 seats. Last month, in less than two hours, he sold out the bulk of just under 200,000 seats across the East Coast and Midwest. This is a feat no "comedian," Eddie Murphy and Richard Pryor included, could ever approach—for reasons that become apparent as the night drags on. I haven't seen a black or Latin face since the bus left. But for a 60-year-old Marielito manning the elevator to the Byrne Arena's VIP lounge and a heavily booed lead-off act, Ed Griffin (introduced as "the talented young black comedian Dice personally discovered at the Comedy Store"), I won't see another till I get back to Port Authority. I can't escape the feeling I've landed in the middle of some Erskine Caldwell story about a leisurely Saturday afternoon lynching.

In this year's push to have not just "a cult following ... I'm going to have everybody" (i.e., a big Hollywood/TV career), Dice Clay has stripped his Bensonhurst-style racist-homophobic-classist act down to 90 percent sexual/misogynist remarks, which has simply proved his safest material: "I give 'em what they want. Pull their hair, rap 'em in the head a few times, say all the little things they want to hear, like 'Fuck, pig, howl, skank.'" Other than a rehash of a few Richard Pryor jokes about black men's penises and testicles (which wave fearfully out of Dice Clay's mouth, like a white flag) and a diatribe on the boredom of Geraldo Rivera's show (beginning with a fierce scream of "Spic! You keep me up to 3 a.m. to watch this shit!?"), Dice's remnant slurs are aimed largely at what Pryor once called "the new niggers"—Asians, Arabs, and Indians. Delivered with his pseudo-Guido malaprops and monotone, they bring an atypical vitriol to his voice and body language: "What are these people anyway? They're kind of like urine-colored." His rage over the limited English of recent immigrants has given rise to what has become his theme joke, repeated, in fake Italian-American accent, by his entire audience: "If you don't know the language, leave the fuckin' country!"

"Dice's got the Brooklyn attitude to a T," a sweet-faced kid from Park Slope named Paul explains to me, opening his third 16-ounce Budweiser since Port Authority. "He's a real Flatbush tough ... even if he's really Jewish, out of Sheepshead Bay. Doesn't matter. It's a sort of persona he picked up along the way. He hit some kind of nerve with it. Dice shows are an event, a spectacle, kind of a religion. Everybody knows his material pretty much verbatim by now. They go to chant the jokes, those poems."

I ask Paul if he finds the man funny. Watching the video, "The Diceman Cometh," and listening to the 450,000-selling LP, "Dice," it never occurred to me to laugh when someone calls a black woman with braces a "Black and Decker pecker wrecker" or recites:

> Georgie Porgie pudding and pie,
> Jerked off in his girlfriend's eye.
> When her eye was dry and shut,
> Georgie fucked that one-eyed slut.

"It's not really humor we're going for," Paul admits, including his girlfriend Christine as he swallows a quarter of the can. "We're going to get shocked. With Dice, just when you're going, 'I've heard this shit before,' he'll hit you with something like, 'Don't move your ass so much, I'm trying to watch the ballgame,' or, 'You know the slob you're eating is a pig when you can't hear the stereo.' You just can't believe what you're hearing. A lot of it," he concludes, grinning about fat asses and stereos so widely he can't polish off his beer, "is about women ... sex and stuff."

I ask Christine if she finds Dice offensive. She says "Nah" and Paul puts his hand around her shoulder. "She's really liberal about stuff like that." I ask Paul what he does for a living, and he suddenly looks dumbstruck. "I deliver furniture for a rich woman in the Slope," he begins, the rest of his answer trailing off as he stands to admire a convoy of stretch limousines just inside the gates of the arena. The crowd outside the bus is packed so tight they seem joined at the shoulder. "Look at that," he says to Christine. "Last time we saw Dice was in Town Hall, a year and a half ago," he says, not really looking at me. "They were selling T-shirts with those dinky stick-on letters. See what they got now. Maybe this guy's only a fad," he tells me, "but he's huge."

•

Information on Dice Clay is kept scarce. Ascertaining his age from his L.A. publicity firm takes over an hour (he's 32), and an embargo on interviews, press tickets, and cameras and tape recorders has been placed on this tour. The moves are ostensibly a reaction to his bad press, ("I wipe my fuckin' ass with my fuckin' reviews," he now tells his audiences) but one can't help but feel he's terrified of having the veil lifted from the *Face in the Crowd* character he's created.

"Andy's been around a long time," says Richie Tinken of New York's Comic Strip. Dice Clay, he says, "underneath it all is a nice, hardworking Brooklyn Jewish boy who's found a niche. He was doing all this material in a shirt and tie for years before he hit his gimmick. I seriously doubt he's going to monkey with it now."

I ask Tinken why Dice Clay's hit so much bigger than a comic like Sam Kinnison, who's far more vicious—and funny. "Simple," he says. "With Sam, you could tell he was genuinely enraged at something, blacks, Hispanics, women, whatever. He started out a preacher, or at least comes from a family of them. You know there's something behind everything he says. But with Andy, you get the feeling, alright, he'll put on his leather jacket, say a few nasty things about women, then go home and put on his normal clothes."

Originally a drummer at bar mitzvahs, Clay entered show biz at the end of the *Saturday Night Fever/Rocky* craze, doing Travolta imitations at Brooklyn discos. He spent 10 years building a standup career and a following at increasingly big clubs, eventually falling under the wing of Mitzi Shore at the Comedy Store in L.A. Parts in four low-budget films culminated last year in an HBO comedy special that aired on New Year's Eve, the starring role in a Bruce Willis - intended vehicle, *Ford Fairlane* (the trailer is shown at deafening volume before tonight's show), and a spot on the MTV Awards, in which his obscene language earned him a lifetime ban from MTV, a lengthy disclaimer from the network, and 12 notches up the Billboard charts for his album. Pat Hoed, publicity director of the LP's label, Def American, says Dice Clay spent most of his career "working one-liners and his dumb impressions [still part of the act]. He just flowered into this character about three or four years ago. Because he is doing a character."

•

Eight permutations of the Dice "character" are selling (at $18 apiece) like six-packs at stands in the Byrne Arena tonight—black T-shirts showing Clay in a black T-shirt, jeans, shades, an array of ugly black leather jackets and holding, reaching for, or having just taken a drag of a Marlboro 100. Intended to portray him as a drug-free, slightly thinner Vegas Elvis (his hero), c. 1971, they seem more like the ultimate fantasy of a Rupert Pupkin— Scorsese/DeNiro's caricature of a desperately hungry comic in *The King of Comedy*—somehow become flesh.

For each of these permutations, a thousand in-the-flesh variations are standing straight up, like a field of denim and leather asparagus stalks, against the walls or in the aisles of the arena, chain-smoking while their women wait on endless lines for the concession stands and bathrooms. A rather dapper specimen catches my eye: an immaculately coiffed blond man in his late twenties, wearing Guess ? jeans, paisley snakeskin boots, and a low-cut Danskin-looking T-shirt under a red, white, and blue leather jacket. A friend, Mussolini-sharp in a black turtleneck and a black acetate suit, gingerly pats the fine line of white-walled hair around his ears as he glares at me. On the back of his jacket is a cluster of gold studs spelling SUPPORT YOUR COUNTRY. I realize that I'm being rude, and tell them I'm just a reporter, taking notes. They both look like they're dying to kick the shit out of me. I ask the blond man, whose name is Vince, what he thinks of Dice Clay.

"Why you ask so many questions?" his friend demands.

"Let him do his fuckin' job," says Vince. "He's a cub reporter. He's going to make me famous."

"Looks like a fuckin' Jew to me," his friend shoots out. I immediately calculate odds on getting in a sucker punch and getting out alive. Knowing I wouldn't get five feet, I think to ask if he knows Dice Clay's real name, then get a nasty inspiration. "What," I ask, "do you do for a living?" It's good for about two seconds.

"I work an appliances/electronics store. Assistant manager," he adds, puffing himself back up. I ask Vince the same question, and he lights a cigarette. "I'm the other assistant manager," he tells me, then urgently taps his friend's shoulder, to check it out. A pretty woman, a bright red ribbon woven through a huge permanent, whizzes by with a Harry M. Stevens tray holding two franks and six beers. She begins to spill beer.

"Repulsive fuckin' assholes!" she screams, not even bothering to turn around.

"Whew, she got some mouth," Vince says admiringly.

•

A pair of wailing guitars, the intro to "Whipping Post," calls everyone back to their seats, and a traffic jam forms at the gates to the seats. On the empty, black stage, I can make out a set-up for a 12-piece blues band, with two drum kits. The music, however, is coming from 10 overhead speakers—*The Allman Brothers' Live at Fillmore East*—including a large amount of crowd noise from 20 years ago. The girl with the red ribbon is glaring, sandwiched between two guys with huge pecs under red T-shirts just in front of me. I tell her I'm just a reporter. She really does have some mouth.

"You guys write shit about Dice," she lets me and several hundred people know. "You don't know Thing One about it, and you nevuh, evuh, fuckin' will. The man is rock and roll. The man has got a brilliant voice. The man has got the goods."

I ask if the goods she's referring to aren't the same she just heard from Vince and his friend. The question seems to inspire her.

"Dice is a comic," she says, turning off at her aisle. "Those guys are just a bunch of fuckin' comedians."

As Clay enters from the rear of the stage, backlit so he looks like

Terminator on elephantine legs, the entire crowd's on their feet, and deafening. Gregg Allman starts singing

> *I've been run down*
> *I've been lied to*
> *And I don't know why*
> *I let that woman make me a fool ...*

Appropriately enough, Dice Clay raises his hand and snaps off the music at the lyric, "Sometimes I feel." As he stands in the narrowest possible spotlight for a two-minute ovation, two enormous screens off the side of the stage show him in close-up, his face exultant and contemptuous: the only feelings, other than infantile oral aggression, that I'm going to see for the next hour.

"So I'm doin' this huh-mah-nicka solo on this litt-tle pig's-s fudge flaps-s," he breathes the first of his thick, emphatic consonants into the mike. He waits out another ovation before continuing with the little pig's response, an insecure, whining, grating warble that is going to be tonight's blanket "impersonation" of everything from women, to homeless men begging for a quarter, Geraldo Rivera, and Moonies. Ten minutes into the show, he delivers the punchline of his first actual joke, everything till now being either the assertion, "I'm the greatest comic ever walked fuckin' earth," or citations of people and situations he hates, followed by "Fuck you" or "Suck my dick." Halfway through, I pick up what seems to be an echo in the speakers, then look around to see the entire arena chanting "trim that pussy, it's so hairy," a follow-the-bouncing-ball routine that continues for the ensuing half-hour of nursery rhymes modified to feature genitalia and anal sex, followed by some fantasies culled from masturbatory responses to his childhood TV shows ("OK, Jeannie, you wanna please your master? Make your tongue six feet long and lick my balls from across the fuckin' room").

Though Dice Clay never slips out of character, it becomes obvious that one is watching a "performance"—not of some stereotype Brooklyn tough, but of the interior life of a man who's in serious regression. After a strange, est-like sermon about Following Your Dreams ("Just like I did"), delivered half in "Dice" grunt, half in a recognizably different, pudgy-kid-in-the-back-of-the-class voice, the blues band is called onstage, and the real psychodrama begins. One last doff of the cap to the "Dice" character—a five-minute ditty with one lyric: "Suck my dick/and swallow the goo"—is all he needs to settle into the entertainment portion of the show, a painful rendition of "Love Won't Let Me Wait," which is followed by a blast of Led Zeppelin from the P.A. system.

For a full three minutes of "Rock and Roll," the band members chant "D-I-C-E," while Dice Clay does the rim of the stage, playing air-guitar and thrusting a fist into the air (the other holds an imaginary microphone), clearly lost in some fantasy of being both Robert Plant and Jimmy Page as he pumps the audience. While the music lowers, he runs triumphantly to the second drum kit for his show-stopping finale, a tap-for-tap cover of the entirety of the dueling drum solos on Santana's "Soul Sacrifice" off the *Woodstock* album. Both video screens above the stage show Clay's face for the whole number—living out his Sheepshead Bay basement fantasy, looking as blissful as Little Oscar drumming unseen beneath the bleachers during the Danzig rally.

Dice Clay runs to the front of the stage when the number ends, yells, "I'll see you at the Garden in February," and then charges offstage. The lights go up and the suddenly silent crowd files out to Blood Sweat & Tears singing "God bless the child that's got his own" (the music programmed by Dice Clay). Stunned, I look around for someone to explain what I've just seen; I wind up looking at my watch, just for some bearings. The show's lasted exactly 50 minutes. I count out the remaining days, hours, and minutes of this "low, dishonest decade," and finally just get angry: Tomorrow afternoon, I realize, I'll be paying my analyst half a day's wages for the privilege of putting on the kind of performance this idiot's making millions for.

Superhuman, All Too Superhuman
The Short, Happy Second Career of Mark Gastineau

"Yeah, I played football," a wiry, blond-haired young man named Fred is telling Mark Gastineau on the casino floor of the Clarion Hotel. "I played defense. Just like you, Mark," he confides over the din of hundreds of slot machines, a nearby craps dealer, and a band covering early Heart and Fleetwood Mac singles. "I wasn't big or anything, but I could hit. I was a cocky kid."

It's a little before midnight on a slow Sunday evening at the Clarion, the newest casino in Reno and the last place to gamble on the road through the Sierra-Nevadas to Carson City. There aren't many rollers here, just package tourists, losing rolls of quarters among the pastel South Sea motifs, and a lot of locals like Fred, who come for the loose slots, $2 beers, and friendly help: A nearby craps dealer, for example, is patiently explaining to his only customer the "vigorish"—the two- to 10-percent odds the house has at each table; and the Sports Book, a nice guy in short sleeves sitting in a small booth near the Purple Parrot Restaurant, didn't mince words when I asked why he'd posted odds for Haugen-Mancini, the Main Event of Friday's "Tough Guys Don't Dance" fight card, but not for Gastineau-Liebergen, the card's "Special Feature Attraction": "Don't all his guys just fall down or something?"

Fred, who wears a red CATERPILLAR cap and a dirty blue nylon windbreaker with his name stitched on the chest, is drunk, and seems to have taken the marquee outside:

MARK GASTINEAU
TRAINING CAMP
FREE ADMISSION & MEET
MARK GASTINEAU

at face value: "I really wanted to box, too, you know, but I didn't have the hands," he's telling Gastineau, his eyes going white as he drains the last inch of his Corona Light. "I had a lot of heart, though. You have to have a lot of heart for the fight game, don't you, Mark?"

Gastineau, playing a bank of $5 slots cordoned off by a white silk rope, nods earnestly for half a second, then pivots on his heel to play a second bank of machines behind him, a calf muscle the size and shape of a Blimpie Regular forming and unforming as he does. Over six-six and 265 pounds, he's so perfectly proportioned his immensity hardly registers at first; down to seven percent body fat, his face is unnaturally gaunt, and every thought and impulse seems to appear there instantly, making him look haunted and simple at the same time. When he moves, it happens in fluid, super-concentrated pulses: Feed three coins, Pull the lever, Scan the floor, Stretch the neck and shoulder muscles, Consider Fred's confession of his lost potential, Give a $5 coin to the waitress who brings the extra-large cranberry juice garnished with fruit and small plastic animals, Feed three coins. The frosted glass seems no bigger than a Dixie cup as Gastineau folds it in the crease between his thumb and index finger, and the coin, which looked like a nickel in his hand, becomes huge in the waitress's.

His stablemate and sparring partner, Joey Winters, a cruiser-weight from Smithtown, L.I., steps over the rope and begins collecting Gastineau's winnings in a plastic bucket. He wants Gastineau to cash in now, so they can get upstairs by midnight and keep training for their six a.m. roadwork. Gastineau doesn't want to hear it: "Feed those in for me," he says. "Will you, Joey?" After half an hour of playing these machines he's up a good $900-$1000.

"Jesus, Mark," says Fred, "you're huge. I mean, you used to be ripped, but now you're like, big all over. It's really different."

Gastineau puts coins in three or four different machines fast as he tells Fred about the differences between the old regimen of Unified Training, which bulked and slowed him, and Accumulative, which "trains a muscle to think independently, unconsciously," so he can throw a punch with each part working. "With Unified, it was just upper body, lower body. Now ... Keep feeding 'em, Joey ... it's legs, chest, my back, my arm, his face." His voice has a taunting, Southwestern twang, and he sounds impossibly naive. When Joey, who seems dizzied by the act of throwing away $15 every five seconds, pleads with him again to cash in, Gastineau just needles him: "Feed 'em in, O.K., Joey? Be a pal? To me? For once?" Within five minutes, he's down to less than $200.

I introduce myself when he cashes in a few minutes later—for $15, which he takes in coins for the dollar slots. "I don't have much to tell you," he says automatically, feeding three coins in one smooth motion. "I train, eat, sleep, train, and fight. The high point of my day back home is riding the Long Island Railroad from Atlantic Beach into the city to train. I'm not a controversial person any more."

The machine hits three somethings and 20 coins clang into the tray. Joey looks disgusted. Gastineau, fishing out almost all 20 coins in one handful, looks possessed. "And I've blocked out the entire state of New York from 1980 to 1990," he says, "so you can write whatever you want about my past. Football just seems like a 10-year vacation to me now, you know, compared to boxing. And that other stuff—headlines and stuff?" he asks ingenuously, his face going blank and happy. "It's like something that happened to someone else with my name. In a gossip column somewhere."

•

Gastineau's name—once worth half a million a year in endorsements and synonymous with the "Sack Dance" he performed after tackling quarterbacks—survives largely as a measure of greed (a "Gastineau contract" is for a previously unheard-of amount), vanity (after a 1982 add for Norelco shavers, he was less famous for football than for shaving his chest so his pecs and long hair could be better appreciated), a five-yard penalty (the "Gastineau Rule" is for excessive celebration of one's own heroics), and as a boilerplate metaphor for grandiose celebrity and sudden obscurity. Since retiring from the New York Jets seven weeks into the 1988 season, when his fiancée Brigitte Nielsen was mistakenly diagnosed for ovarian cancer, he has attracted increasingly smaller, sparser, and more sarcastic squibs: Reports of a $480,000 palimony suit by a Phoenix waitress named Jodee Dominici; gossip column items about his possessiveness, smothering love, and various split-ups with Nielsen; a *Wall Street Journal* story about a precedent-setting child support/alimony judgment awarded his outspoken former wife Lisa (inspiration for such tabloid headlines as "He's Pathetic," "I Call Him Joe Isuzu," and "Wife Says Gastineau Sacked Closet"); and wire-service fills about imminent signings with various football teams, which always seemed to break down with Gastineau demanding his former salary, his old number 99 on his jersey, and the right to wear his hair long.

Gastineau's decision to begin training as a professional boxer met with a similar indifference when he and Nielsen—wearing rings with "9"s fashioned out of diamonds (so that they formed the number 99 when they held hands)—made the announcement to a Vancouver press gathering in 1989. "I know my potential, my capability, my aggression. My aggression has to be controlled." The 6'1" Nielsen, who had briefly left Gastineau six months earlier, citing physical abuse ("We're not dealing with four-eleven," she told a *USA Today* reporter, "we're dealing with six-six and 300 pounds"), supported the decision wholeheartedly: "I've always felt that Mark is too unique, too special, too strong to be a member of a team. I also think he is the only white man on this planet who really has a chance to let Mike Tyson know what strength is all about. I definitely would not like to see Mark in the ring with Tyson if I did not believe in him," she added. "Because I love him." Asked about his chances in the ring, Gastineau said he planned to give the sport its due respect, and that he had grown the hair back on his chest. "Brigitte," he told the newspapermen, "likes hair."

The training began in earnest, however, only when the couple parted for the last time, in April 1990. Nielsen, who'd announced a 1988 break-up to a Milan press conference by reading haiku from a book of her poems ("We sacrificed our/Love to mean people. Oh God/Darling, it's so sad"), kept it simple this time: "I'm through with men." (She was married six months later in the Silver Bell Wedding Chapel in Las Vegas.) Gastineau, looking "to do something positive with my life," put up a $6,000 regulation ring and a shed for the heavy bag in the backyard of his home in a high-end Scottsdale, Arizona, development. The ring was a foot too high and the shed the wrong color for the development's codes, however, and he was over $9,000 in arrears for summonses, missed court dates, and legal fees when an Associated Press stringer visited him two months later. Gastineau said he wanted back into football at any cost: "I'd cut my hair. I wouldn't care if they gave me number double X. I'd go out there without a number."

He did return to pro football later that year, but it amounted to little more than a four-game, helmet-swinging brawl midfield up in Canada for the BC Lions. "I was in great shape, down to boxing weight," Gastineau tells me. "I was running with every team, kicking ass and taking names. But the coach had a big attitude problem with me, and the offensive linemen I was up against were all Canadians who just wanted to punch my face in." His final retirement—he was placed on injured reserve, then waivers, and finally let go—received far less attention than a third-degree assault indictment the following May for fracturing a man's nose and right eye socket with one punch in a Long Island bar late one night. Turning himself in to Nassau County police the next morning, he listed his profession on the arrest report as "Unemployed— Football Player." The following Saturday he was a guest on "The Joe Franklin Show," part of a short-lived bid to become a television sports announcer.

His professional boxing debut a month later was seen by only 700 fans in the 5,000-seat-capacity Civic Center in Salem, Virginia. It made the national papers, however, when his opponent, Derrick Dukes (listed by Gastineau's promoter, Rick Parker, as a 2-1 heavyweight), collapsed after an innocuous left hook, 12 seconds into the first round. Dukes (whom a later computer check showed was a professional wrestler with no boxing record) went into spasm on the mat (tripping Gastineau as he headed for a neutral corner), then left the arena apparently unharmed a few minutes after the fight. (Rick Parker announced he'd been taken to a hospital, but this seems to have been a falsehood.) The Virginia boxing commissioner vowed to investigate. "To me," he said, "the fall didn't look right"—a perception shared by Dukes' colleagues at the Fridley 49er Days Pro Wrestling Spectacular in a Minneapolis suburb, who recognized it as a standard wrestling move called the "bump." En route to his next night of work—at the Blaine Blazin' Brawl in Blaine, Minnesota—Dukes was quoted as intimating he could have beaten Gastineau, but, "You've got to do what you're paid for."

It's difficult to learn the details of Gastineau's seven other fights—one- and two-round TKOs in Oklahoma, Indiana, Missouri, and California that everyone involved refers to collectively as "tuneups." "They were just, you know, fights," says Rick Parker. "Maybe a little more violent than your usual fight." The second, which took place either in Akron, Ohio, or Hammond, Indiana, was stopped by a ring doctor after blood started trickling out of Gastineau's opponent's ear. In the converted conference room of a Howard Johnson Motor Lodge in Oklahoma City, he hit a first-time professional named Irish Tim Murphy with a punch several people say made Murphy spin 360 degrees and land in a full split, though no one—including his cruiserweight brother, Irish Dan Murphy—can remember what kind of punch it was. And Gastineau lost three teeth in a fight, though it's not clear which: He remembers it as his sixth; a "Rick Parker Presents" press release says it was the fifth victim—a 16-17-1, 213-pound hairdresser/bouncer named Jimmy Baker, who lasted until 1:09 in the second round in the ballroom of an Indianapolis airport hotel.

Though his appearance on the "Tough Guys Don't Dance" card—a heavily promoted pay-per-view event—marked his national-TV debut, Gastineau seemed blasé at the New York prefight press conference, held at Mickey Mantle's restaurant this past

February. Asked about his opponent, Frank "Gator" Lux (described by promoter Al Goossen as a "veteran of 40 fights with a .500 record ... who'll fight and not just fall down"), Gastineau spoke only of his happiness with his boxing "family": His manager, Jimmy Glenn, a former cornerman for Floyd Patterson and owner of the Times Square Gym, and Willie Dunne, a moody man in his mid-50s who moonlights as a trainer between shifts delivering the *Daily News*. "I have ... people around me who want to see me do good now," Gastineau said. "In football, there were people around me who wanted to throw water on me whenever something positive happened." There were some dreamy comments made about the next "Great White Hope" and a showdown with a Top-10 fighter within the next year, but Gastineau clearly harbored no further illusions about himself: "My name is something that's maybe a draw," he said. "Probably the draw comes from wanting to see me get knocked out. But whatever it is, it's a plus for revenues."

•

Red, white, and blue balloons are blowing in the wind outside the Purple Parrot's windows, escaped from the grand opening of a new R.V. park down the street. The shadow of a huge cloud is moving fast across the Sierra-Nevadas, just beyond the last shopping mall in town. A father and his pre-teen son, whom Gastineau assures me are Oklahomans, stand at the cash register after paying for lunch, wearing jeans, cowboy shirts, and matching wide-mouthed boots and white hats, picking their teeth in unison.

"Where those people live, those boots are called cutaways," he tells me, making his way through a modest plate of salad bar and his fifth glass of iced tea while Jimmie, Willie, Joey, and I eat burgers and fries. He looks super-gaunt after his five-mile run up in the Sierras this morning. "They come off your feet automatically when you get thrown, so you don't get dragged by the stirrups. Hey," he hollers across the room. "Like your cutaways."

"You're Mark Gastineau, aren't you?" the father says. "Christ, I remember you as a lot bigger."

Gastineau beams out a ten-second smile, then tells me how he lost his mount during a "Lifestyles of the Rich and Famous" segment about his life with Nielsen. "I mowed a 50-foot swath across the arena," he says pedantically. "I wasn't wearing my cutaways."

Nielsen is the Banquo's ghost of this fight camp—a taboo name around Gastineau, until he drops it. "I've made mistakes in my life," he tells me. "But I've also learned one thing about life: When you have God up here"—he holds his right hand above his head and builds a staircase of descending values with his left—"and everything else below, things will just work out. And it doesn't matter what's Number Two and what's Four. They'll just take their place. But only if you have God at Number One," he concludes. "God the Father."

"Speaking of which," says Jimmy. "When's your Dad coming?"

"Jimmy's my Dad, really," Gastineau assures me.

"Big Ern was a fighter too," Jimmy says.

"Yeah," says Gastineau. "And he became a professional football player the same day I did."

I ask Gastineau what he means, and he says, "You'll see. Ern's got a way of taking over your personality."

Jimmie and Willie chuckle, and Gastineau lets out a deep sigh and looks happy. "Even with great people like this behind you," he says, "when you step up into the ring everyone just disappears down below. There's nowhere to run, no time out, and no team-mates to hide behind," he says, exiling something white and fattening-looking to the far side of his plate. "It's just you and your little friend."

•

Three days before the fight, Ernie comes to the Mark Gastineau Training Camp in the Oasis Room, a carpeted reception room on the mezzanine level that's been outfitted with a ring, punching bags, 25 folding chairs for the audience, and a big stereo system cranking dance music. He gets a row of double-takes from the crowd as he enters, asking, "Where the hell is Mark at?" He does look remarkably like his son, 20 years down the road and with a third of the air taken out: His hair is cut in the trademark shoulder-length feathercut bouffant, his legs and upper body are pumped and deeply bronzed, and there's only a hint of fat and vein and wrinkle showing at the vents of his purple running shorts, matching purple tank-top, and purple hightop Ponies. He has a silver and gold Rolex Oyster on his wrist and is missing the little finger of one hand—lost, he later tells me, while roughnecking in the Oklahoma oil fields.

"You know where the hell he is?" he asks Joey, Jimmy, Willie, another "Rick Parker Presents" fighter, and a cruiserweight who's been brought here from Oklahoma to spar with Gastineau. "Of all the ... He's got a couple dozen people waiting half an hour to see him train. This is no way to behave." I mention that he looks like his son, but Ernie doesn't buy it for a second. "Mark looks like me a little," he says, his vowels broader and longer than any I've ever heard. "May-ay-be."

At 5:15, a tuxedo-dressed emcee with a microphone comes in to distract the restless audience with trivia questions: "How many times has Mark Gastineau been married? No, seriously. What college did Mark Gastineau go ... East Central Oklahoma?! How did you know that?" He hands out some two-for-one dinner coupons at the Purple Parrot, then puts a blues and R&B tape on the deck, shrugs his shoulders, and leaves. The fighters are working rhythmically to Hammer's "2 Legit 2 Quit" when Gastineau rushes in at 5:30, looking hounded by the Fates, already exuding his sweet, androgynous musk: of sweat that runs free and odorless and Abolene beauty cream, which he wears a thick coat of during training, to promote sweating. He hands Jimmy his huge leather pack, Rolex, and room-key and says, "Hi Dad, when'd you get here?" then starts jumping rope at double-time to the beat.

"What do you call that, Mark. The soft-shoe?" says Ernie. "You look kind of feminine."

"If you ever were a fighter, Ern," says Gastineau, "you'd know about jumping rope." He's raining sweat when he puts the rope down a few minutes later and laces up, working with Willie to get a few yards of tape on, then standing by himself in front of the mirror with the gloves on.

"Vanity," says Ernie, "thy name is wahh-min."

Gastineau starts shadow-boxing, then working with the overhead bag, keeping good time. "And this is the heavy bag, Ern," he says, hitting it so hard it swings like a hanged man. "Just in case you were wondering."

"You want a towel, Mark?" Ernie asks. "You're sweating pretty hard."

Gastineau starts hitting a combination of jab, hook, and right hand—his big punch. The right comes so hard Willie and Jimmy have to hold both the bag and the eight-foot overhanging rig to keep it in control, and Gastineau starts nailing them in compulsively, his eyes fixed on one spot in the center of the bag, a yell coming out when he exhales with each right hand, sounding like a Doppler effect: "RaaahhhHHHhhh!!!"

"Drink a little, Mark," Ernie says, coming over with a bottle of some hideously red stuff called Carbo-Lyte, which he holds above Gastineau's mouth. "Sip it, son, or you'll cramp up," he says as Gastineau tilts the 16-ounce bottle with the back of his glove and takes in half in one swallow. "And wipe off the sweat, Mark."

"Big Ern's right," Gastineau says, wincing as a quarter-inch stream of sweat washes through his right eye. "The older you get the longer it takes to warm up. Get that cassette out of my pack and put it on, Joey?" he says, summoning Willie up into the ring for a round of hitting the trainer's gloves—heavily padded, oversized mitts that Willie wears as targets on both hands. "Crank it up, Joey. Let's make a little noise here. Right, Dad?"

Mr. Big comes on, singing: "She led me down the road to ruin," and Gastineau starts exhaling his RaaahhhHHHhhhs as he pounds the trainer's gloves with right hands across the body, knocking Willie off balance and back a step with every punch. Willie keeps talking about balance, patience, and concentration, but Gastineau obviously just wants to hit someone or something for a little while.

"Your strength isn't in your hand, Mark! It's in your balance. Your big right hand gets a quick left hook's going to knock you on your ass one day," he says, hooking Gastineau in the shoulder with the mitt whenever he loses concentration and throws the punch in a way that leaves his right side open. "Give the other man a chance to make a mistake, Goddammit. Why the hell do you always have to be the one that makes them all?"

After two minutes of right hands, Gastineau finally starts moving in the ring, faking every third punch, responding to Willie's hooks. "Patience! Finally," Willie yells. "Now you're a fighter, Mark. Now you're living in patient time."

"Now I'm warm," Gastineau says, walking to the center of the ring to gaze into the full-length mirrors on both sides. He seems to like what he sees, as well he should: He looks superhuman—not only huge but thoroughly agile, quick, and intelligent.

"Blue, 32," he yells to the crowd on the far side of the ring. "Blue, 32," he repeats, climbing through the ropes and leaping high over his father's head. I ask what "Blue, 32" means.

"Nothing," he says, draining the other half of the Carbo-Lyte. "It was just a cadence number at the Jets' training camp. It doesn't mean a thing."

•

"You wanna know something about me?" Ernie asks me, sitting across the dinner table in the Purple Parrot. "I have interviewed more people in my life than any reporter who's ever lived. And I am the only person who knows everything there is to know about Mark, from Day One. See, I've been thinking about writing a book, or a movie. Mark and I have always been best buddies as much as father and son—water-skiing, roping steer, out on the boat at the lake. Mark is a champion speedboat racer. I don't know if you knew that, for example. At seven or eight he could swim 80 feet underwater. Mark is one of the greatest success stories in the history of America. And the thing about me is, you really couldn't write a book about him, or a screenplay about his life, without me. Over the years, I have collected everything that has ever been written, photographed, recorded, entered in the record books, or timed on a stopwatch about Mark Gastineau. And when the United Scouting Combines held their camp in Arizona in 1978, where they clocked Mark for a 4.59 in the 40-yard dash, I ran it in five-flat myself. In my street shoes."

"You better believe it," says Gastineau. The word "believe" is all Ernie needs by way of a segue.

"I'm probably the only man in the world who has believed in Mark 100 percent since he played fullback in his freshman year in high school, and even before that. See, Mark had a terrible accident to his leg when he was nine years old. He was climbing the swimming pool fence to get a volleyball his sister had thrown over, and he got his little leg trapped in the gate-hinge. He almost couldn't walk because of it. But I'd love him even if he couldn't play any sport. I love Mark's younger brother, for example. He's a 17-year-old who's six-two, 217 pounds ..."

"Now there's a carbon copy of my Dad," Gastineau says. "I look exactly like my Mom—we're like two peas in a pod."

"I have an unconditional love for people," Ernie says testily. "It's a love that makes me as happy as the ones who I love. And I haven't had a single unhappy day in my life since divorcing Mark's mother after 37 utterly miserable years of marriage. See, the power of unconditional love is very great. Why should I waste your time and my time figuring out what I don't like about you, when I could be agreeing with you and doing some business together. And let me tell you one thing about myself: Sitting right across from you, if only a few things had gone different, I would have been one of the greatest athletes that has ever walked the planet."

Rick Parker comes over, the light of a cellular phone glowing in the pocket of his flowing gray-green suitjacket. An overweight man with shoulder-length blond hair, scraggly red mutton chops, a small fortune (acquired from a door-to-door business selling "True Blue," a cleaning concentrate for oily driveways), and the recently acquired nickname "Elvis," he wears orange-tinted aviator glasses dangling from a beaded chain on his neck, loafers with tassels, and a tiny 14-karat-gold boxing-glove charm on his necklace. I ask about Lon Liebergen, who became Gastineau's opponent after the *Daily News'* Michael Katz revealed that Frank "Gator" Lux was not a ".500 heavyweight," but a 190-pound cruiserweight with a 15-18 record.

"Man, we got barbecued by the media about that Lux's record," says Parker. "Liebergen is, I believe, a 10-4 fighter, about six-two, fights out of Davenport, Iowa, with, uh, Michael Nunn."

"He's from the same stable as Nunn?"

"Not really the same stable. The same"—Parker forms his hands into a globe and shakes them for emphasis as he sits down next to Gastineau—"town."

"I know I'm going to heaven," Ernie tells me, leaning over and touching my wrist assuringly. "See, I might not be the most honest man in the world, but I know for a fact there's no one more honest than me. This is what I instilled in Mark: That you don't have to be literally the best in the world, just that no one has the right to be better than you. That's what this country's all about. I was up in the plane the other day, talking to the fellow next to me, a venture capitalist, about my outlook on life, how I am the ..."

Gastineau, deep in conference with Parker, is talking about a venture capitalist he knows up in Canada: "You can talk to him one day and get the whole world promised on a platter. Next day, it's like he's never heard of you. He's like a manic-depressive or something." He's also listening to every word of Ernie's:

"... So I get up at the end of the flight and a woman in back of me says, 'Excuse me sir, I don't want you to think I was eavesdropping on you, but I've got to say that your motivational speech throughout this plane ride has changed my life. I had just about given up until I heard you,'"

Gastineau's head swivels in astonishment. "What'd you say you were talking about on that plane, Ern?"

"I was talking about life, son."

Gastineau turns to me. "See, this is what I cannot believe. I cannot ever ..." He locks his father's head in a huge bear-vise. "My whole life, I've listened to you talk, Ern, and it sounds"—Gastineau shakes his head three, four, five times before continuing—"completely off the wall. But there's always some woman there saying, 'Sir, I cannot tell you how much you've helped me.'"

"It's just a power I have," Ernie explains, working his chin free of his son's forearm. "A power that comes from making someone happy." He grabs Gastineau's hand and smacks it affectionately. "It's the power," he says, giving me a wink, "of unconditional love."

•

Pre- and post-fight ceremonies at the Reno-Sparks Convention Center are held in a large, airless room cluttered with schedules for livestock auctions. At the weigh-in/medical exam for the "Tough Guys Don't Dance" program, where a few dozen media people and boxing personalities are trading cards and cigars and gossip, there's a turndown mood of Opening Day at some low-rent trade convention. The card has been beefed up with a few well-attended "prospects"—the 1988 silver medalist Roy Jones, Jr., who weighs in flanked by men in silver lame karate outfits, and former San Francisco mayoral candidate Irish Pat Lawlor, who steps on the scale in emerald-green shorts and a T-shirt that reads IT'S GREAT TO BE STRAIGHT—but there's not much glamor here, just the smell of filthy lucre in short supply. All but the main-event fighters are seeing their opponents for the first time, and seem bewildered. The prospects just look like professionals, come to add a workmanlike notch; their opponents—the "tomato cans with the day-jobs," grateful to be fighting for more than a few hundred dollars—try to seem mean as they stand on the scale, and look remarkably like lambs at the slaughter.

Gastineau goes through his weigh-in wearing glowing multicolored warmup clothes, strapped to a yellow Walkman with a tape blaring George Michael's "Father Figure," oblivious of everyone in the room—including a woman from the promoter's office who hands him an IRS garnishment on his purse, rumored variously at $40,000-$75,000. Though he talks about his love for his new sport, he seems anomalous in this world of shysters, freaks, and hard-luck people. His name comes up only in some occasional, envious quip about his purse—20 or 30 times what most of these boxers are fighting for—though no one here has any illusions about the logic of boxing money. Jimmy Ellis, the former Oakland Raiders' defensive end who recently made $475,000 for losing to George Foreman in one round, stands in a corner like the Ancient Mariner, telling anyone who asks how he made $1,700 three weeks later, losing to some journeyman heavyweight in five rounds in Reseda, California.

Lon Liebergen stands in the same corner with his brother and wife, a nondescript, average-sized man with blond hair, a healthy complexion, biceps that are slightly larger than normal, and a gut you can see through his red windbreaker—the result, he tells me, of the 10 pounds he's put on in the last few weeks to move up from cruiserweight to heavyweight. A steel worker at the mini-mill in Bennett, Iowa, he played defensive end in high school—well enough to get tryouts in the USFL and CFL—and started boxing after winning a 1986 Tough-Man Contest in a Masonic temple in Davenport. He won his first pro fight, 30 days later, and after working his way into a swingshift position at the mill that gave him more flexible hours, spent four years scratching together a 7-4 record. He's had trouble getting a fight since he was knocked out by Frank "Gator" Lux in the seventh round of their Iowa Cruiserweight Championship fight last year. "I guess I got this fight because of that one, though the logic," he says, "escapes me."

His eyes widen as Gastineau walks out of the medical examiner's suite with a huge smile and a swagger. "He's not that big," Liebergen says. "I thought he'd be a lot bigger somehow."

Gastineau waves at me to come over; he wants me to "go ask the doctor about that exam I just took. I'll kiss your ass," he says, "if he's ever seen a 35-year-old man like me." When I mention whom I was talking to, he looks deeply betrayed for half a second, then gets the smile back on. "Just ask the doctor what condition I'm in," he points to his chest. "The old man's never been in better shape."

•

Liebergen dances in the red corner with a fearless look before the fight next evening, keeping his eyes off Gastineau, who wears a thick coat of Abolene and a coat of grease put on his face from Jimmy Glenn. They both seem awed by the all but sold-out crowd of over 5,000, a sizable fraction of which, now four fights into the night, is drunk. People are yelling the kind of obscenities normally reserved for a wrestling event, and a carnival/hanging-day atmosphere is settling over the arena. From 10 rows away, the fighters don't seem that different in size, but from the floorboard perspective at ringside Liebergen disappears entirely behind Gastineau's shoulders when they touch gloves in the center of the ring.

He comes out jabbing and throwing body shots, ducking a wild combination from Gastineau, then a pair of jabs that miss. A minute into the round, Gastineau is dancing away after every Liebergen punch or feint—a tense, sideways motion that throws him out of step and makes his hands droop and lag, as if he were reeling in a marlin. He lingers, gaping, at Liebergen's jabs and rights—a fraction of a second longer with each—as though he's estimating the damage they could do. When he throws his punches, they come off-balance or off the wrong foot entirely: a straight-arm jab he seems to transport more than throw, a right hand Liebergen ducks under easily, hooking Gastineau on the shoulder with a left that gets him circling the ring for another 10 seconds. Gastineau lunges forward with an overhand right that misses narrowly, and they clinch for the first time.

As the referee steps in to separate them, Liebergen holds on to the clinch for an extra second. With his head wrenched slightly to the side by Gastineau's forearm, his nose buried in the Abolene-scented hair around his breastbone, he looks like he's registering Gastineau's size for the first time, and seems traumatized. He spends the remaining :53 trying to stay out of the corners and the center of the ring, Gastineau stalking him, breathing hard, his face rapt with concentration, his movements coming easily and naturally now. They finally square off in the center and Liebergen throws a pair of jabs, connecting with both, then flees back into the ropes when Gastineau's suddenly starts charging. A huge "RaaahhhHHHhhh!!!" escapes Gastineau's mouth as he raises his right arm and moves across six or seven feet of the ring in a kind of stutter-step, then drives a haymaker down the left side of Liebergen's face. It snaps his head back two inches, makes his teeth vibrate loud enough to be heard from ringside, and spins him 180 degrees into the ropes, where he stands and sways with his eyes wide open, reaching blindly for some rope to hold onto while flashes from a dozen cameras go off.

The fight is still on, and Gastineau, who's clearly never been trained for such a situation, looks bewildered, angry, and strangely helpless: He stares at the referee, who for some reason isn't calling off a count or a standing-eight; at the back of Liebergen's head; at Jimmy and Willie in his corner; then with mounting anger back at the referee. "Do something, schmuck," someone screams from ringside, and Gastineau raises his right hand for another overhead and takes a hurtling half-step forward. Liebergen, beginning to turn around and instinctually raising his gloves, is in no shape to be punched again, and Gastineau holds the right in, throwing a left hook that whisks above the top of Liebergen's head, making him cower pathetically until the referee finally steps in to stop the fight.

Gastineau hears the roar of the crowd and raises his chin, looking, for the first time since I've met him, like the photos of the old 99: thick-skinned and tight-jawed, arrogant as hell. He raises his right fist, pulls it down, then his left, not in victory but by way of cranking up the machinery for a five-second sack dance, which from ringside looks like a manic squat-thrust drill. He's soon joined in the center of the ring by Rick Parker, who, apparently overcome with emotion, jumps up and down, his glasses, stomach, and tiny gold boxing glove flopping wildly as he tries to latch on to Gastineau's neck and shoulders.

•

Liebergen seems only half-conscious when he knocks on the door of the men's room serving as Gastineau's dressing room at the back of the arena half an hour after the bout. He has something on his mind, but after apologizing several times for not putting up a better fight, leaves with a confused look. After midnight, he tries to call Gastineau from the hospital—where he's being diagnosed for compound fractures to his cheekbone—but Gastineau has gone downtown to celebrate. Diagnosed next month for a fractured skull as well he announces that his wife has convinced him to give up boxing.

By then Gastineau is living with his 21-year-old girlfriend, Missy Berkowitz, and her parents in Woodmere, Long Island, having lost the lease to his apartment in Atlantic Beach. His black 4 x 4 is parked haphazardly on the street, his two huge dogs, Ruby and Ronnie, are dozing in a fenced-in dog house, and his heavy bag is hanging from a hook on a huge maple on the front lawn. Missy's swing, which had hung on that hook for 15 years, lies in a heap at the foot of the tree.

From downstairs I can hear him training in his room at the top of the stairs, an extra bedroom-cum-gym equipped with six Exercycles, treadmills, and Stairmasters. It's almost 80 degrees outside, but Gastineau has the windows closed and is running a space heater at full blast. Bottles of amino acids, vitamins, and lipotropics are scattered all over, and his third half-gallon wide-mouthed jug of water of the day is balanced on the control panel of his treadmill, a dozen lemon halves bobbing inside. Over his unmade bed is a vibrantly colored oil painting of a nude, ripped, heavily mustachioed Gastineau—painted, *a scuolo di* Leroy Neiman, by his former hairstylist Danny Tarantello.

"He didn't do that from life," Gastineau tells me. "He copied it from a spread *Playgirl* ran on me."

Though he's been living here for less than a week, the room has his unmistakable odor of beauty cream, and Gastineau, on his fifth mile of the morning, is glowing with health and aggression. I can practically smell his testosterone level—he's gone celibate until after his next fight, scheduled in Nebraska in two weeks—and his usual friendly, cornball manner has given way to imperiousness. He has me on one of the bikes in no time, then yells downstairs to Roberta, Missy's mother, to get upstairs and ride the other.

"Your midsection is where you live," he says, getting off the tread-mill to apply a fresh coat of Abolene to his stomach. "If you have a strong center of gravity you can take a lot of stress ... ROBERTA," he screams, getting back on. "YOU'VE GOT TEN MINUTES."

"NO WAY, MAW-WW-WWK," she yells from downstairs.

"TEN MINUTES," he yells.

"WHATEVER YOU SAY, MARK. IT'S YOUR AMERICA."

"TEN MINUTES. THEN I DESTROY THE HOUSE."

Gastineau finishes the fifth mile, bolts off the machine, and scam-pers downstairs. He comes up a minute later, hauling Roberta by the collar of her shirt. She's screaming and her face is livid as he drags her into the room, lifts her in the air with one hand, places her on the bike, and goes off to shower. "My God," she says to herself as she starts pedaling. "It's like having ten people in the house."

Gastineau appears at the door half a minute later, buck-naked, hiding his groin behind the door jamb, holding the black sneakers he was running in. The dye is running off onto his hands—he's simply sweated it out—and his feet are tinged with black. "I want you to take these back to Foot Locker," he tells Roberta.

"For Chrissakes, Mark, put a towel on. I'm not your mother."

"I want you to take these back for me!" he hollers. "If they can't hold up to their specs I want my money back. And tell them I had to do my roadwork in boxing boots."

•

Gastineau's still pissed about his sneakers as we head down a bumpy road that runs parallel to the LIRR tracks between Woodmere and Cedarhurst. I ride his mountain bike and he jogs beside me in a pink, green, and royal-blue Givenchy warm-up suit and calf-length boxing boots, his huge leather pack on his back and my briefcase slung over one shoulder for extra weight. It's one of those rare Long Island roads still lined with pleasant, unostentatious houses and old, overhanging trees, and one of those perfect early-summer days full of limitless possibility. We've been out over an hour, going at a snail's pace in the shade, and Gastineau is far more relaxed and expansive than he was on the treadmill, talking about Ernie. When the subject drifts to the childhood injury Ernie mentioned to me over dinner in Reno, Gastineau stops running and says, "Let me show you something about that."

He unties one boot and pulls the sock down to show me a scar: an inch-long, oyster-shaped hole gouged out of the side of his ankle near the Achilles tendon. Using both hands, he carefully folds the skin of his ankle around the scar. "Now, you tell me," he says emphatically. "What's that look like?"

"It looks like a vagina, Mark." The way he's manipulating the contours, the top ridge is even protruding like an erect clitoris.

"Not a vagina," he says, looking disgusted. "A big, huge gaping one."

I ask if he's ever heard of *vagina dentata*, and he gives me a strange look.

"Ernie said you almost couldn't walk because of the accident."

"Yuppp, but I sure didn't want to hear it," he says. "The leg was facing 90 degrees out by the time Mom came and got me free of the gate-hinge it was caught in. I'd broken bone and ligaments and tendons, but no skin, and I kept saying it was O.K." He takes a step with the leg bent at a right angle—to show me how distended it was. "I kept saying: 'I'm O.K., Mom. I'm O.K. Just let me walk it off.' It was crazy."

"The first cast they put on came loose, and the second was on so tight I began getting a strange itch underneath. They took that cast off a week later, and it had eaten straight through the ankle." Gastineau picks up a slow jog again as he tells me about the two skin grafts needed to cover the wound. "You could see daylight at the end ... Remember what I was saying about keeping God at Number One and everything else below? That's when I learned that."

"How's that?"

"Well, I came to in the recovery room after the operation. Mom and the doctor were standing near me, whispering, but I could hear what they were saying. I pretended I was still out. The doctor was saying I'd probably never walk again, and that if I did it would be all deformed."

Gastineau stops to show the club-footed walk the doctor predicted for him, then begins jogging again. "I closed my eyes, and started praying." He stops again to look me dead in the eye. "I prayed 24 hours a day. Day in and day out: 'Please God. Let me be able to walk. Let me able to run. Let me be able to play.' And I wound up not only being able to run, I ran the fastest 40 yards in history for my size. That's how I know about keeping God at Number One."

"But you haven't always kept Him there?"

"No, but I did for the longest time. See, college for everyone else was discos, music, you know? Sex? Yeah, well, when everyone else was at the party I was under the stadium, lifting, or out on the track sweating out 40-yard dashes until after midnight."

I've been backpedaling to keep balanced every time Gastineau stops jogging, and the pedal suddenly comes off. Gastineau gets a tiny wrench out of a kit-bag under the seat and gets to work trying to pry off a gasket cover whose gears are stripped—a hapless task made ugly by the sweat that starts pouring off his forehead. He hears the whistle of the 3:47 into the city, a few miles away, and empties his pack, looking for a wrench-set. "Damn," he says, "I've gotta get in to spar with Joey." Among the cassettes and T-shirts and bottles of pills is a sandwich, wrapped in plastic with a love-note in block capitals from Missy: MARK: I MADE THIS SAND-WICH FOR YOU BECAUSE I LOVE YOU AND I WOULD NEVER DO ANYTHING TO HURT YOU. Gastineau hears the whistle of the train as it pulls into Cedarhurst and starts working feverishly at the gasket cover.

"I really liked the first school I went to," he says. "Eastern Arizona. I was a Freshman Year All-American there."

"Why did you transfer?"

"My Dad told me to go to Arizona State. To get more publicity. Ern's got his faults, I know, but he really did believe in me from the start. I hated the coach at Arizona State, but when Dad says Go ..." The train sounds its whistle again and Gastineau switches to a smaller wrench. "The next year, Dad sold the ranch and 80 acres where we lived in Arizona and moved to Oklahoma. I went to see him and visited East Central Oklahoma. I really liked the guys on the team there. Good guys, born-again Christians, not the kind who hit you over the head with it, but you know ..." Gastineau stops working the wrench for a second to look me in the eye. "I really believe in God, you know."

His eyes bug as the train comes into sight around the bend. Cramming everything into his pack, he gets it and my briefcase on his shoulder, and starts running along with the train, at a steady jog, then a full-out heat as it starts passing him. I struggle for a minute to get the one-pedaled bike going, then look up. He's already hundreds of yards down the tree-lined street, waving at the conductors, then at the breakman at the rear of the train. Suddenly he's running back, telling me to get off the bike, which he hoists up on his left shoulder. "Don't forget the pedal," he says.

When I get to the station in Woodmere, the conductors are gathered around Gastineau and the waiter from the train station coffee shop is proudly holding his bike. Owners and customers of the adjacent shops stand outside to see what's keeping the train in town, the gate is down, and the main road is backed up for half a mile with cars honking loudly.

"What's that guy's name in the back who held the train for me?" he asks the conductor when we pull out past the station.

"His name's Bob."

"I'll be right back," Gastineau tells me. "I gotta go thank Bob. Things like that really mean a heckuva lot to me."

•

An hour later, we step out of the GNC on 37th Street and Seventh Avenue with over $100 worth of concentrated bark extracts, liquid johimbo, amino acids, lipotropic creams, tiny vials with eyedroppers, and half-gallon bottles of Hydra-Fuel and Amino-Fuel. I ask Gastineau about the love-note on his sandwich, and he says, "Let me ask you something. How you can tell if your woman's cheating on you? Can you ever know for sure?" he asks.

"You can't, you know," he answers with resolution. "And if you could, you wouldn't be interested in the first place. There's got to be that little area of mystery, even if it's just a five or six percent chance, just a little area. Even if it's just a one or two percent chance," he says, showing a tiny space between his two-inch-wide thumb and index finger. "It's like those 98-percent slots back in Reno. If they returned 10-percent of your money, you know, you probably wouldn't even play them."

A well-dressed man with an autograph book stops Gastineau, and flicks through his book for a blank page. "I'm a collector," the man says, "not a dealer. This is for me, it's not for sale."

"I don't care," Gastineau says. "Sell it if you want to."

Every other man or woman we pass is either gaping at him, saying his name familiarly, or asking for an autograph. The men's attention flatters him, and he'll spend a minute with any who stops him, patiently repeating the same answers to the same questions. The women who look at him make him enraged.

"Why do they bother you so much?"

"They don't bother me," he says. "I don't care what they do."

"Why do you want them to stop looking at you?"

"You don't get it. I want them to look at me. I want them to want me. I just want them to be better," he says with utter conviction. "That's all. I want them to behave. You know that 60, 70 percent of them have husbands or boyfriends. They've got no business looking at me."

Crossing the corner of 42nd & Seventh, Gastineau asks if he's looking good in the ring. I tell him I'm a little concerned by the ways he hesitates when he's about to get punched. His brow darkens with incomprehension, but he knows what I'm talking about. "You think I have a death wish or something? I don't see anything in that ring that looks like death to me."

Gastineau gives me his "I really do believe in God" look for a good ten seconds. Then he grabs my forearm and gives it a squeeze, steps into Seventh Avenue and starts crossing against the light as a bus approaches. He squares his shoulders and deliberately slows his pace, and the bus pulls up with a groan of hydraulic brakes. By the time it passes he's across the street, grinning manically.

"You ever try that?" he asks when I cross.

"No."

"I've been doing it for years," he says. "It's one of my favorite things about this city. Scares the crap out of the drivers. You want to try it? Look."

An M104 is coming down 42nd Street, an 18-foot White Rose delivery truck barreling headlong in the next lane, a car's-length behind. Gastineau steps out against the light and slows the M104 to a standstill, then disappears as he steps an inch past its fender. When it passes, I see he's flattened himself, chin against his neck, shoulders hunched, his hands held rigidly at his side. He has a huge smile on his face as he leans away from the White Rose truck, the lower panel shaving his back as it passes him.

•

I lose touch with Gastineau a week later. There's no one home when I go out to join him for his last week of roadwork, and from brief phone calls with his new "family" in Woodmere and his boxing "family" in the city, I can tell things aren't going well.

The fight in Nebraska doesn't come off. A month later, Gastineau is substituted into USA Network's "Fight of the Week" at San Francisco's Civic Auditorium, fighting a 17-15-1 journeyman heavyweight/cruiserweight named Tim Anderson, a pudgy, 213-pound former stunt-actor who has the nickname "Doc" because of a small pharmaceutical distribution company he runs in Miami. Gastineau is so stripped he can't fit his boxing trunks, and after getting a coat of grease on his face from Jimmy before the bell, comes in wearing cut-off black sweatpants with frayed ends that reach halfway down his thigh.

He gets a big round of applause, but by the end of the first round the crowd is booing his usual opening-round timidity and USA Network announcer Al Albert is opining from ringside, "His toughest fights thus far have probably been with Brigitte Nielsen." He's thrown two punches in the round, and seems mystified by Anderson, who's neither putting on a show of bravado nor cowering from Gastineau, just dancing and waiting to see what his opponent, with his extra six inches and 50 pounds and a 10-inch reach advantage, has to offer.

In the blue corner, Jimmy tells Gastineau to start throwing punches. "Take his head off, Mark," Ernie screams repeatedly from below the ring. Gastineau tries to take him literally, flying out of his corner with a flurry that immediately has Anderson up on the ropes, shielding his head. They're strange punches: not combinations so much as a series of three- and five-punch tantrums that gradually subside with exhaustion; when Anderson leaves the ropes, unfazed after a little less than a minute of this, Gastineau's gritting his teeth for breath, and has clearly shot his wad for this fight. By the end of the round he's lost the stamina needed to concentrate until the bell, and in the last ten seconds loses sight of Anderson long enough to get clocked with a left hand that snaps his head back. It enrages him, and he comes out charging sluggishly in the third with a right hand that looks like some open-field maneuver and push-tackles Anderson into the ropes. Two minutes into the round, he gets hit with the same kind of punch that knocked out Liebergen, and it gets a similar reaction: a spin into the ropes, where he looks dazed while he's counted to six by the referee. "All right" he yells, for no discernible reason. "You know? All right."

By the fourth round, the fight has become a freak-show. Al Albert is talking about Gastineau's problems at the Jets: "Right now is when he might need some help from those teammates of his. This is fourth and one and he needs the sack." Gastineau's hands are rarely above his waist and he looks like he's underwater and staring at a strange new world, stumbling derelict from corner to corner and playing games with his mouthpiece, occasionally getting inspiration for some strange hop and skip of a jab, taking endless shots to the head and body with no more capacity for defense than turning away, stiffening his shoulders, and raising his hands over his head. When the two fighters clinch halfway through the round, it's clear that Anderson's exhaustion is the only reason he hasn't yet knocked Gastineau down.

With 20 seconds to go, however, he summons enough wind for a round-ending salvo: Chasing Gastineau to the ropes near his corner, he pounds his body, then fires a low shot to the groin that doubles Gastineau over and makes him howl. They go into something vaguely resembling a clinch—Anderson has Gastineau's head locked in his forearm, and he seems to be trying to knee him in the face as Gastineau screams at the referee. When they break, Gastineau, who looks like he's choking, takes a step toward the blue corner, registers the cast of characters there, then looks angrily at the referee as he takes a giant step into the center of the ring to complain about the low blow. He's utterly oblivious of a roundhouse left that jolts his head back, makes his eyes go white, and gets him all but horizontal in the air as he falls flat on his back.

He gets up halfway through the count, somehow, and takes a wobbly step forward as the bell rings, staring glaze-eyed across the ring at a neutral corner. The referee turns him back to his own corner, four feet behind him, where Ernie and Rick Parker are screaming at him and the referee, their hands pounding on the mat. Jimmy wipes Gastineau down and rubs his shoulders while Willie yells: "Wake up, Mark, damnit. It's time to go to work, Wake up, Goddamnit." Jimmy asks, "What round are you in? Mark! Tell me what round you're in?" Gastineau knows he's going into the fifth and Jimmy puts one last coat of grease on his face and sends him into it. Willie's still screaming "Wake up" and Gastineau tells him to shut the fuck up as he gets off the stool. Rick Parker is up and screaming something about bashing this guy's head in, and Willie tells him, "Shut up, man. Just shut the fuck up." Gastineau takes a step into the ring, oblivious to Ernie asking him, "Are you sure you're OK, Mark?"

He lasts another standing eight after a big right hand, and a minute of taunting and body shots from Anderson, then gives it one more shot: a strange combination of a left hook, a jab that looks like a tennis backhand, a forearm swipe he lifts upward like some vestigial memory of an off-the-snap drive, and a lunge that drives Anderson hard into the ropes, smiling and grimacing. When Anderson comes off, he walks from corner to corner for the last 45 seconds while Gastineau tries to stalk him, losing sight of him almost every time he turns a corner. In the final seconds Anderson rounds a neutral corner a little quicker than he has been going and blindsides Gastineau with another left hook that all but knocks him out. Once again, the referee has to walk him back after the final bell.

Gastineau seems strangely at peace and cogent for the post-fight interview. He insists he hadn't forgotten his boxing trunks—"They were just too big for me," he tells Al Albert. "Me and you both could've fit in"—and that this defeat just makes it "more of a challenge to get that Top-10 fighter." Every question suggesting he'd moved up to national exposure too quickly gets the same response: "I'm probably going to have to get a new girlfriend ..." As he drains a quart of Evian and talks about "having a more stable home life," "getting my rest at night 'stead of arguing," and "You can't have family problems, you know, you can't and do ..." he looks utterly dazed and clearly doesn't know who he's talking to.

What Becomes a Legend Most?

Sitting on the Rim With Earl Manigault

Stretched out on his bed in Room 517A in St. Luke's Hospital, Earl "the Goat" Manigault is clutching the pole of the IV unit he's hooked into as he gazes out the window at Morningside Park. Beside a half-eaten piece of carrot cake on his night table is a Federal Express Overnight mailer with the sum of his personal effects: clippings, a few photos of himself as a young man, a dog-eared 49-cent notebook he keeps phone numbers in, under $20 in bills and coins, and a Xerox of a six-figure option from a Hollywood production company for the rights to his life story—sent by his agent, Sterling Lord.

It's a sports-filled Sunday afternoon, and Earl and a catatonic-looking man strapped to his bed across the room seem to be the only ones in the wing not watching. His 16-year-old, Earl Jr., wearing unlaced L.A. Gear hightops and a brightly colored parka with the hood up, chews absentmindedly at his gold neck-chain as he glares at a Knicks-Bulls game from the foot of the bed. Darren, 24, watches a golf tournament from his perch on the windowsill. "Reporter's here, Daddy," he says, raising an eyebrow in acknowledgment before turning his attention back to the T.V. He doesn't seem like the kind of kid who'd say Daddy.

The man Kareem Abdul-Jabbar once called "the best ballplayer his size in the history of New York" is still, at 45, a six-foot column of those flat, articulated muscles and rounded angles one seldom sees outside a Marvel comic. Wearing a canary yellow print hospital robe that fits him like a mini-dress, at first glance he looks as perfect as the 20-year-old ballplayer in the photographs in his clip file: self-possessed and utterly natural, his smallest movements full of quiet, languid grace. Then notice the uneven maze of brown, black, and thick white keloid on his forearms, the legacy of a 14-year heroin addiction that reduced him, two decades ago, to living-legend status, petty thief, and two-time penitentiary inmate. His face, hands, and neck are also dotted with blackened patches, scars, and tiny gouges, his chest is bifurcated and sunken at the sternum after a pair of double-bypass operations, and two wide triangles of discolored skin lead from his breast to his collarbone, remnants of a fire he set while nodding in bed one afternoon in the late '60s. A pair of missing incisors make his otherwise haunted face seem boyish every time he speaks, which he does only when he has to—his sentences filled with a strange, apologetic morbidity, almost inaudible, and free of adjectives, adverbs, and most articles. Whenever possible, he answers questions with a shrug, smile, or two-sentence set-speech. Ask about heroin and his lost career, and he'll say the same thing every time: "For every Michael Jordan, there's an Earl Manigault. I didn't hurt anyone but myself."

As he sits up to greet me, I see that his "springs"—the "million-dollar legs" that vaulted him to a 28-point scoring average in high school, and the one area of his body he refused to put the needle in—are bloated from ongoing treatment for walking pneumonia. A recurrence sent him into St. Luke's a week ago, days after relocating himself and his two sons from Charleston, South Carolina, where he retired a decade ago to go cold turkey for the last time. Other than a few sentimental journeys back, Earl hasn't been in New York since 1981, when he was released from a two-year stretch in Sing Sing on robbery and weapons charges. Though he's hoping for a new start on the strength of his movie deal, the project is still at the treatment stage half a year into the option, and the $2,500 he received on signing is long gone. His return, already chronicled in *The New York Times* and the *Daily News*, has a doomed feeling: Four months from now, he and Earl, Jr., will go back to Charleston on a borrowed $100 bill, leaving behind Darren, who'll become a crack addict and thief a month after their arrival.

Copying phone numbers from his book, Earl tells me he doesn't feel much like talking today. It's an unusual melange of contacts: disc jockeys, journalists, a foundation trustee, directors of rehab programs, a Princeton Sovietologist. He also lists two out-of-print books devoted wholly or in part to his mythos, *The City Game* and *Double Dunk*. The spelling of the most rudimentary names and words, I can't help but notice, is way off. "Fact," he says, leaning back on an elbow for his carrot cake, "I really don't enjoy talking about myself at all."

Earl takes a slow bite and chews it with that quiet revulsion ex-junkies never seem to lose for their food. "That's what reporters are for." He reaches forward with a roundhouse flourish and swats Earl, Jr., on the back of the head. "Laugh when your father makes a joke," he says. "And take the hood down." He directs my eye to his son's unlaced sneakers, smiles, and then polishes off his cake. "How you ever going to be a legend like your father?"

•

Earl Manigault's legend has grown large over the years: On a few dozen basketball courts in New York and North Carolina he accomplished all that he ever would by his ruination at 22. Those gyms and playgrounds and that fall have become the stuff that Nike ads, off-season sports columns, and park-bench cautionary tales are made of, but there wasn't a word of contemporary coverage on him, and it's been said, probably accurately, that there isn't a box score in existence with Earl's name on it, though he dominated a team of future NBA All-Stars for almost a decade.

At 13, recruited by every community center team in Harlem, he was already able to dunk two volleyballs at once, and he owned the city's junior-high-school scoring record, a 52-point performance in a game his team lost. By his 15th birthday, his reputation was established: an inner-city Billy the Kid who roamed the boroughs, 12 to 15 hours a day, in search of the local aristocracy: Bedford-Stuyvesant, the Bronx's Patterson Projects, the Rucker Tournament playground on 129th Street and Seventh Avenue. "At sixteen," his former running mate Bobby Hunter remembers, "Earl was already neither man nor boy but a cult, a neighborhood of one, a whole other trip than your average walkaday legends of the community. Earl was the hero of a golden era that made nothing but heroes, greater and lesser. The only villains were villains unto themselves, because they could not dunk the basketball."

As he grew to six feet, an increasing number of Earl's points came from further and further above the rim. Among the youngest of that generation of 100 or so ballplayers who went on to elevate the NBA to its current altitude, he became known as the "master of tricking"—dunking on the big man, tipping it in over the big man, snatching the big man's jumpshots out of the air, pinning layups to the backboard. During one unofficial citywide all-star game, held at Riis Beach on the Fourth of July Weekend, 1962, he stunned a crowd of hundreds by hovering above the rim for what seemed like minutes before dunking it on Lew Alcindor and Connie Hawkins.

By Earl's senior year at Benjamin Franklin, a now-defunct high school in East Harlem, he was packing every house he played, from the Renaissance Ballroom on 138th Street and 7th Avenue (which became a regulation-size full court in off-hours) to the old Madison Square Garden during the City Championships. The Championship finals were covered by local writers and national college scouts, but the opportunity for discovery was lost every year by a point or two:

"My junior year," he remembers, "we're down by a point against Clinton, semi-finals. I get the rebound off Lucky Peterson's jumper and break out of the pack real fast, ten seconds left. Our big man's alone under the basket, Aubrey, and I get it to him. He just stays in the three-seconds, waiting for someone to come down so he can dunk on them. After five seconds, the ref finally calls him on it. End of game."

A month after Earl's eligibility to play high school ball ran out, he was expelled for smoking dope in the locker room, a false charge, he insists, brought by a track coach he'd refused to high jump for. After four years of grades arranged by Bill Spiegel, his "win-at-all-costs" coach (and the school's dean of discipline), Earl was functionally illiterate and, at 18, suddenly unknown: He and his contemporaries had been recognized by the big schools and the national scouting combines, but scholarships went only to the stars of a few brand-name schools that delivered passably educated students: Power Memorial (Lew Alcindor), DeWitt Clinton (Nate Archibald), and Boys High (Connie Hawkins). Earl won't criticize his years at Franklin, but there are many who will; you can hear the tales of a dozen or so every June, when the Franklin alumni come down to Morningside Park for the Rucker Stars of Yesteryear Games. Now a hardcore, mean-looking group of men in their mid-40s, they first regrouped for pick-up games in 1967, calling themselves the Franklin 11. By 1968, the number had dwindled to five. "Junkies," Earl says with a sad smile, "every one of us."

With a similar smile, he remembers accompanying his friend Alcindor out to UCLA that August, "hoping for miracles." He managed to catch Coach John Wooden's eye during a three-on-three—grabbing a jumper of one of his starting forwards out of the air—but when the term began there was nothing left for Earl but to go home. Recruited by St. John's and Iona, despite his lack of diploma, Earl decided against it. "I really wasn't ready for college," he says. "I still had high school to get through."

But for the intervention of tournament director Holcomb Rucker, the Goat legend would probably end at this point. Rucker showcased Earl that summer in his Senior League Tournament, on a team that included Alcindor and Charlie Scott and lost every game. In September, he put him and a friend on a Greyhound to Fayetteville, North Carolina, armed with letters for Frank McDuffie, coach and principal of Laurinburg Institute, a highly regimented black prep school that specialized in reforming dropouts and kickouts like Dizzy Gillespie and future All-Pros Sam Jones and Jimmie Walker.

Enrolling as a 19-year-old senior, Earl spent the best two and a half years of his life there; while learning to read and write, he led a team hailing from two square miles of Harlem that sported an all-slam-dunk layup line and defeated every college within a hundred-mile radius. (Charlie Scott, two years shy of setting ACC scoring records that would stand until Michael Jordan, couldn't make the starting five until Earl graduated.) McDuffie remembers taking a special interest in this "gloomy, quiet kid who defied the laws of gravity." He kept the gym open at night, because Earl couldn't sleep if a new shot occurred to him; he scheduled a board of teachers to hear Earl's term-recitation from the American Standard Lesson Plan, because he was scared to deliver it to the morning audience; when Earl grew homesick for New York and complained of hunger, McDuffie seated him at his table. He also assigned two coaches to wake Earl at six each morning, take him to the football field, strap 20-pound weights to his hips, grab him by the ankles, and make him drag them the length of the field. "It was like being in prison," Earl remembers. "I loved it. We wore our blue blazers with the gold crest everywhere we went, so they'd know we were McDuffie boys, and string up someone else. We were the only ones who could sit at the lunch counter in town."

Word on Earl had spread by the spring of 1965, and letters of interest came in from 73 schools, including West Point, UCLA, and Michigan State. "I didn't want to embarrass myself, though," Earl says. "I was still pretty book-weak for those schools. I just wasn't ready"—a recurring motif with Earl when discussing his past. He took a scholarship at Johnson C. Smith, the all-black school nearest Laurinberg, and became increasingly enraged while he sat on the bench and played garbage time for five months: His coach, Bill McCullough, didn't take to his showtiming, though Earl's only start produced 27 points and Smith's first win of the season. In New York for the Christmas break, Earl decided he couldn't face returning to Smith's bench.

But for a year of 60-point performances at Green Haven State Prison in 1969-70, and an unsuccessful training camp in 1971 with the ABA-champion Utah Stars (club-owner Bill Daniels invited him after reading Pete Axthelm's *The City Game*), Earl's playing career ends at this point, January of 1966. Nine months of haunting the parks and gyms he'd dominated as a kid proved too much for him as an adult. He became a junkie a week after his twenty-second birthday. Though he never courted the press, his community's idolatry, or the book, film, and job offers he received, a second career as living legend began with publication of *The City Game*: Half a year out of prison, he found himself spending weekdays with sportswriters, p.r. people, and what he calls "ball-freaks"—white men with an insatiate yearning for their unfulfilled potential on the basketball court. Every Friday he'd drive out with WABC deejay Murray the K to coke-filled weekends among an adulating crowd in Montauk. "Filmmakers, writers, this private eye, lots of cover girls," he remembers. "Skinny-dipping. Riding horses on the beach. It was a little unreal. They were talking about the Olympics, making an art movie. Movie never happened, or the Olympics. Utah didn't happen either. After three weeks of training camp, they went back with the same team as the year before."

Back at home, Goat tales were growing tall: Playground historians told of a junior-high-school kid who could throw it in, backwards, from a flat-footed position anywhere inside the paint; of a 15-year-old who took quarters off the tops of backboards and "made change on the way down"; of a six-foot junkie NBA centers begged, in the half-court circle before Rucker Senior League games, not to slam on them while their wives were looking. One dunk, executed on a Friday evening in 1963 in the packed gym of P.S. 113 on 113th Street, has become truly mythic. Various incantations have Earl beginning his leap against six-five Vaughn Harper and six-nine Val Reed anywhere from the foul line to the top of the key, and executing one or two 360-degree rotations in midair before slamming it in—backwards, forwards, one- or two-handed, Around the World, depends who you ask.

"It's true, Earl dunked a basketball on me and Val at Thirteen that night," says Harper. "And it's true that we were humiliated." A two-time Syracuse All-American, Detroit Piston "for about a minute," WBLS deejay since 1976, and a man who's "been telling Earl's untold story to reporters for two decades," Harper hastens to add: "But that was one play, in one game, in one summer of tournaments with literally thousands of plays like that. Nothing but that one dunk lives from all of that."

"Thirteen rocked for a solid ten minutes," insists Bobby Hunter, a former Harlem Globetrotter, sometime savior of Earl, an assistant coach at Long Island University, and a true bard of the old school. Over a long liquid lunch in a booth in Goody's, on 135th Street and Malcolm X Boulevard, Hunter drinks vodka gimlets—"with very little gimlet"—and lays out a Goat chronology for me that's equal parts detail, alliteration, and elegiac hexameter. Six-four, with a huge, vicious smile and fingers that seem a foot long when he waves them past my face to conjure the years going by, Hunter stresses the "need for interpretation" when chronicling Earl. Sitting next to him, swaddled in a grey trenchcoat, green scarf, and a black beret, Earl quietly nurses his health and a Grand Marnier on the rocks, his eyes bulging incredulously from time to time.

"They had regulation officials there," says Hunter, "who could not believe what they'd seen. The scaffold above the gym was waving perilously through the air, with dozens of people screaming on it. Chairs were thrown on the court, chairs that people had had to fight for, because there were nine bodies to every space in that gym. Those who had not gotten in sensed the enormity of what had happened, and they began to riot on the streets. All West Harlem vibrated for a week.

"But there's many, many stories to that slam. A thousand people were in that gym, and every one of them saw it their own way." I point out to Hunter that there's room for no more than 300 people in the gym and he gives me a "Now you're catching on" alligator grin. "And I've spoken to 5000 who swear it happened their way. I, personally, have never seen its equal," he avows, raising his glass to order another round, "and I was in Detroit at the time."

Hunter saunters over to a party of four women eating smothered pork chops at a side table and comes back 15 minutes later. He's even more eloquent when conveying Earl's affect off the court. "A legend," he says, "can only be a legend where he's from.

"I recall that one day Earl put on a cheap silver bracelet; I believe it was the proceed of some less than moral transaction. By sundown, all Harlem wore cheap silver bracelets, except for Earl, who'd taken his off, the more precisely to shoot his trademark J—a linedrive that left his hands heading downwards, characterizing an era of power and rage, of speed and spin, and of the cheap tin backboard. Same with his Afro, which he was the first to be seen sporting, and his Afro pick. And his copy of *Sketches of Spain*, because Earl caught on to Miles when everyone was still dancing to Tito Fuentes. And the leaflets he started handing out, to Make the March. And we must never forget the era of the tan duffel. If you did not own a tan duffel coat you stayed at home and you could not go to the park."

Earl's was a "world of parks," Hunter says, parks that from the age of 12 he didn't play in so much as haunt. "Parks with that sweet smell of success: girls, fresh air, ball. *Reputation*, which is the only reliable currency up here."

"A common delinquent without a ball in his hands and a park to play in," as Raymond Diaz, a later, less eloquent associate puts it, Earl was rarely seen anywhere else. "And he was always alone," says Hunter. "Earl brought thousands of people together, but he was alone. He came alone, he saw alone, he threw it in your face alone. He shot up his arms alone, he went to prison alone, kicked the drugs alone. He was never more alone than in the park, because Earl was not a team player. He was a team. He was an alone team that snatched everyone's jumpers out of the air. Except for mine.

"But it wasn't merely his renowned jumping ability, because a man named Jackie Jackson had already invented the art of the leap, up on 143rd Street. Earl imitated it, and added the *rocketalization* of the Goat."

"Connie had real rockets," Earl enthuses quietly.

"The Hawk educated the world at large, true," says Hunter. "And the Doctor perfected it. What I'm saying is that all those men flying across the TV now are mere after-images of this distant concept that you, as the Goat, brought into existence."

While Earl tries to tell me about how fast Connie Hawkins went up, Hunter executes a flowing glissando with his fingertips to show just how distant the concept is, then covers the entirety of Earl's face with his left hand and points his right index finger at himself.

"But I am talking about Earl. I am talking about his quiet, alone behavior that made him a cult. Because Earl was always the quiet man, with a soft voice and a gift for explosive movements that can only come from the heart, and from the slow, steady, solitary sipping of blue Concord wine. Even in '67, when no one was seeing Earl, who was otherwise engaged on a rooftop or in some toilet somewhere, on every other park bench it was still, 'Remember when Goat … ?' 'How 'bout the time Goat … ?'

"Like, one thing we did in 1969. Earl came down to Morningside Park, and so did everyone else when they heard the Goat was back. We dug a hole, stuck a pole in, and we had a tournament. It was a crisp afternoon. We had a heavenly hash made of horseshit and wine, and it was a good year. We had legends, we had junkies, we had powder-blue uniforms. Millbank [Earl's community center team] came down, a team that made cults; Forty-Three [the 143rd Street playground players] came, and Thirteen came too, because Earl had many cults. He was a weakened man, a step and a half gone, with tracks on his arms you could see from downcourt, but nothing had changed. Earl got the ball on the tip, went up, and that first dunk brought back all of Thirteen—*in a whisper*."

•

A decaying 20-by-30-foot billboard reading, WHAT BECOMES A LEGEND MOST? shows Lena Horne in a three-quarter sable down the side of an abandoned tenement on the corner of 113th Street and Martin Luther King, Jr. Boulevard. A dozen young men are milling on the stairs outside; occasionally, one hurries inside through an open space where a front door once was, looking like he's arrived at a party. Halfway up the block, next to a Jehovah's Witnesses storefront with a Gothic-lettered marquee advising passersby to WAKE UP AND BE SAVED! another doorway has drawn a similar congregation, bright and early this Saturday morning. By afternoon both of these crowds will have dispersed. A beautiful, abandoned brownstone with bricked-up windows on the corner of Adam Clayton Powell, Jr. Boulevard becomes the hub once night falls.

"Motherfuckin' crackheads," Earl explains as we head toward P.S. 113. It's the first time I've heard Earl curse. His sons look over their shoulders, impressed—particularly Darren, who hasn't been up north for years. The last time I'll see him, he looks like Earl today: same peach-fuzz pencil mustache, slow gait, and long-suffering innocence about him. Sired during Earl's first year at Laurinberg, he has an eight-year-old of his own, whom he shows me a picture of. I mention that the kid looks no more than five years old, and Darren admits he hasn't seen him for years, then shows me a passport-sized photo of his estranged wife. The promise "I will love you forever" is written inside a heart on the back, with the words GOAT CHILL chicken-scratched below.

"Used to be a nice block," Earl says apologetically. "Great basement club, two streets down. Sneak in at 2 a.m., when everyone was wasted, see Miles, Monk, Mingus. Malcolm X spoke on that corner over there, the time I was handing out the leaflets for Bayard Rustin. At least people did their nodding on the corner then."

Avenue blocks in West Harlem are long, two to three times the length of most Manhattan blocks, and constitute virtually separate neighborhoods, each with its own identity, income strata, regional hatreds, passions, and legends. Thirteen doesn't have the cachet of Fourteen, the maple-lined block of Stephen Foster Homes that Bobby Kennedy made a showcase (and an anomaly) of in the mid-'60s, or the notoriety of Sixteen, where Robert Kennedy, Jr., was mugged while buying heroin in the mid-'70s, but it's a very proud street, despite its abandoned buildings and its three shooting galleries.

"You could make a professional all-star team from the boys who happened to be on Thirteen any given day or night of the week," Jim Edwards explains in his ill-equipped office in P.S. 113, where he's been running a community center since 1954. "At least in Earl's day you could. The days before decentralization"—a word he pronounces rather than says—"all the budget crunches." A barrel-chested man in gray sweats, a whistle dangling from a cord on his neck, and the words "legend of the community" never far from his lips, Edwards gives me a partial list of the ones he knew as preteens. While he does, my eye wanders to two board games, Stratego and Chutes & Ladders, sitting on top of an empty "Recreation Cabinet" in the corner—games I haven't seen since childhood, and that haven't been replaced, I realize, since the era he's describing:

"Lew Alcindor, Charlie Scott, Connie Hawkins, Satch Sanders, Cal Ramsay, Vaughn Harper, Helicopter Knowings, Zeke Clements, Willie Hall, Roger Brown, Ray Felix, Joe Hammond, Pee Wee Kirkland, Jackie Jackson—my God, but he could leap. For overall ability, Earl had more potential than any of them. All you had to do was look at him and you'd see he was going to be worth millions, soon. The only way he could go was climb. That's why they called him the Goat."

Edwards pauses to break a $10 bill for the lunch matron and to say hello to Harold, a painfully shy-looking man who lives across the street, wearing thick double-knit trousers and a red-and-blue flannel jacket as a shirt. Harold apologizes for interrupting the interview, then stands in the doorway, constantly changing his eye glasses for reading glasses and then back again. When the subject strays from basketball, Harold, "a good point guard" in his day, and a man who's seen every game of importance at Thirteen, brings it back quickly. Until last year he owned the only surviving footage of Earl in action, a Super-8 film of a "double dunk" that was lost in a fire.

"I've always taken Earl's fall," Edwards says, "back to one day in his senior year. He was standing alone in the Indoor Gym downstairs"—he points down the hall to where Earl and Earl, Jr., are sitting, a 40-foot court broken at 10-foot intervals by supporting pillars. A dozen kids under 16 are trying or pretending to try to dunk volleyballs and punchballs while another dozen or so run a heated full-court. Darren, who was a high school star in his day, spins a ball between his legs before throwing it over his shoulder from 20 feet out. It almost goes in.

"Earl was holding a basketball, like always," Edwards settles into his story, "but he looked terrible. 'Why?' I asked him. Suspended? A month before he was All-City, All-State? Non-attendance in class? But that was no secret, till he wasn't eligible anymore. You don't just chuck a boy out. Where's he going to go?"

"The double dunk," Harold nods his head, "was the ultimate humiliation." He takes a step into the office to pantomime the shot: "Earl throws it in your face, once"—he lifts a tight right elbow, slams it down—"twice"—he does the same with his left arm, then repeats the whole chicken dance again: "Threw it in on the way up. Caught it in his gut out the net, and one more time coming down."

"And I have always seen Earl's fall," Edwards nods, as though he's picking up where Harold left off, "as the fall of this community. Just look down Seventh Avenue: patches of concrete and emptiness, empty housing complexes. Those houses were thriving in Earl's day."

Harold steps out of the office, nodding: "It'd take weeks to recover."

"Thirteen has always been a neighborhood of fence straddlers," Edwards says. "Boys who're perched high, and who're going to fall, either into this house or into that house outside."

Harold steps in again, folding both hands inward. "Earl had to cup it," he explains. "He never had the hands to take it off the dribble, like Connie or Joe Hammond or Pee Wee."

The mention of Hammond's name galvanizes Edwards. "Now Joe was a magician." Standing at his desk to show Hammond's great shot—going around the basket in midair and dunking it backward—Edwards looks up at the ceiling, joins his meaty hands over his head, like a ballerina in third position, and then slams them down behind his head.

"Never forget the time Earl did that to Joe," Harold admonishes, demonstrating Earl's one-handed method of the reverse dunk. He slams into the door of the Recreation Cabinet as he throws his hand backwards, and Edwards suddenly remembers himself. "But what am I saying?" he says, sitting back down. "You can't describe this kind of artistry. It's like a Charlie Parker solo from 1954. Lost. It was a situation that arose in a game played 30 years ago in the Upstairs Gym that brought Earl's sense of movement out. It's lost forever now."

•

Three flights up, Earl's face crinkles into something resembling a smile as we head up a short stairway to the Upstairs Gym. Only the bottoms of six pairs of sneakers in midair can be seen. "Nothing but treads," he says, pretty much to himself. "Spalding and Converse only. All-star games every Friday. Us and the Bronx versus Brooklyn and Queens. College stars coming back for some real ball."

"Did they talk about being away?"

"No. They just came to bust our young asses."

He points to the low ceiling. Music is echoing from an enormous radio that a pair of 200-pound girls in red, black and green sweaters and L.A. Raiders caps are walking down the far side of the court, taunting everyone who misses a shot. There are over 100 kids in the gym, and half as many adults on the sidelines, wearing sweats and sneakers. "That ceiling's why my game was so inside," Earl says, "'cause you couldn't shoot so easily. It was even worse when the scaffold was up for repairs, and that stayed up the whole time I was here. By that far wall, I played Climb the Wall, when I was in the Midgets: Three steps, push off, and I could dunk it, once I learned to cup. It was beautiful, you know, watching Connie pick it up off the floor, pass it, lay it up, whatever he wanted. He was the best of us. When you cupped it you had to invent."

I ask if he remembers any particular shot, and Earl flashes me an amazingly arrogant look. "I remember lots of particular shots." He juts his chin and hunches his shoulders, swaggering in place. "One time, this is the Rucker, I took it in the cup just inside the paint. Lost my man"—he raises an elbow and feints to one side, looking like a 1950s Ivy League fullback posing for the yearbook shot. "At the hoop, still two big men guarding it. Give them a fake, head, shoulders, hips, till I could feel them going with it. When I came out of it, everyone's over ... that way, and I just floated in."

"So there were times you dunked it from the foul line?"

"I suppose so."

"Did you ever surprise yourself?"

"All the time. According on the situation you're in. Everybody's out there to get a name, stop you. It's more like playing by myself sometimes. Best of times. I never believed one man can stop another man. After I was cut from Utah, they offered me a job, assistant manager, advise how to stop a man like the Doctor. All I could tell them is just pray he's off, stop himself. You can't guard a man like that, 'cause you can't understand him. He doesn't know what he's going to do, how're you going to know?"

"Still, it sounds like a good job they were offering you."

"Yeah, talking job, though. I never did much conversating with the group. Never hung with nobody. They used to say, in therapy in prison, whatever, I needed to talk more. I saved up my anger, held it in till it came out on the court. Or went up my arm, after ball was over. I couldn't say about that."

"You don't think heroin had anything to do with anger?"

"Maybe so. Thing was, you know, I didn't really know what heroin was till I was strung on it. Too late then."

"How could you not have known?"

Earl shrugs his shoulders. "I was misled," he says, looking around the gym with a self-conscious smile. I get the feeling he doesn't want to talk about heroin here, and ask about his dunk on Vaughn and Val Reed. "Nah, that was just a regular dunk, nothing new," he says. "Big moment for the crowd, though. Two big men get embarrassed by a future junkie. I bet half the crowd was strung that night."

I ask about Joe Hammond and Earl gets excited, telling me how Joe "busted Jerry West's ass for an entire Lakers' training camp," was offered $50,000, and asked to wait a year until West retired. Hammond, who Earl says is "always on the move—can't ever catch up with Joe," left word behind that he could make more on the street. "He's kind of a traveling salesman," Earl says with a wink. (Hammond's currently serving a multi-year sentence for selling crack.) "Just wasn't pro material," Earl says. "Whatever that is."

Vaughn Harper had told me that many of the "legends" of his generation, particularly Earl, were not "pro material." "Earl had the ability," he says. "He was a pure natural athlete, and one of the great leapers, but he was all street. There was no way he could have shifted gears to the NBA's team play, or even a good Division A college." Though I find no one who shares the opinion, and dozens who strongly disagree, Harper's words have a ring of truth. Earl's greatest admirers talk about his lone-wolf presence on the court: Some say he was more dangerous to play with than against, because you never knew when a pass would come at you, hard and at face level; others talk about his game as though he played a vaguely different sport than everyone else on the court.

When I ask Earl about the pros, he talks about his tryout for the Utah Stars, which he feels was mostly a good-natured publicity gimmick. "I don't think about my 'lost pro career,'" he says, "because I never came close. Most of us didn't. I mean, a guy like Jackie Jackson. There was no way he could've gone pro."

"So he didn't leap as high as everyone says?"

Earl gives me a quizzical look. "Jackie was a God," he says. "I saw him in the Rucker one summer, and I couldn't believe it. Nobody could. Six-five, and he just hung up there. He pinned Wilt Chamberlain's hookshot to the boards, maybe 15 inches above the rim."

"Did you ever play against Jackson?"

"Nah. I walked up to his park once, though, the summer before Laurinburg. I really wasn't looking forward to leaving."

I ask why he didn't play against him, and Earl shakes his head and gives me that look again. "Because he was working there."

"Working?"

"Yeah, working. Green uniform, black patent leathers. Standing in the little red house. I went over, though"—Earl nods imperceptibly, showing his greeting to Jackson, then shakes his head with even less animation to show Jackson's denial. "I was just a kid, he was a man. He was the Park Man."

"What did you do?"

"I played some and went home. There was no competition, 'cause everybody had already left for college. I walked past him, though, to the water fountain." Earl nods his head once and raises an eyebrow, showing Jackson's approval, ending the story.

"You didn't try to see him again?"

"No need," he says. "I was ready to go."

•

It's only after months of taking the measure of Earl's solitude that I can understand how he could have remained oblivious of heroin until the mid-'60s. "I saw it, you know, from '59 onwards," he says, "heading to the Rucker court on Twenty-Nine. People nodding, two-, three-deep on Seventh Avenue. I knew something was wrong, but I never questioned it. All I ever thought about was ball, you know. I stayed pretty much to myself."

That stretch of Seventh Avenue has been deserted for years now, and the Rucker Tournament was moved 20 blocks uptown a decade ago. All that's left, when we walk these streets together late at night, is a sense of isolation, and of an almost unearthly disen-franchisement, feelings that never go away in Earl's presence. Taking a gypsy cab from one abandoned building he lived or nodded in to another, walking along a teeming Lenox Avenue and 125th Street at 2 a.m., so he can show me a block-long gauntlet of 11-foot-high street signs he used to smack, the loneliness begins to gnaw, though he's known by every third person we pass. Earl has a welcome gift for sidestepping sentimentality, but the abandoned, overpopulated Harlem he shows me begins to feel so disaffected and immaterial I find myself longing for something—however maudlin it might be—to connect what I'm seeing to his past. An endless series of gyms, shops, clubs, playgrounds, boarded windows, vacant lots, street corners, schools, community centers, and buildings, half of which no longer exist, it emerges from his shy half-sentences with an increasingly fleeting reality: the memory of one childhood-long rush to the basketball court that still leaves everything else a blur. I stop asking, "Who were you with when …" knowing the response: "I think I was by myself then, heading to the park."

The ninth child of a family in Charleston, Earl was conceived, he tells me, when "Moms stepped out one night"; his father refused to keep him, and he was given to a retiring, childless country woman named Mary Manigault. He spent his first six years like a 20th-century Kaspar Hauser, essentially without connection or language:

Mary's house was a one-room tar-papered house with no electricity, heat, running water—or Mary, whose double shifts as a cleaning woman kept her in Charleston most of the day and night. "We were just out in the woods," he says, "surrounded by tall blue grasses, high as the house. No other places in sight, big brown snakes crawling in through the windows."

Earl didn't go to school until Mary, through relatives, found a job in a laundromat on Manhattan's Upper West Side in the early '50s. Six or seven years old, he was placed in second or third grade (he can't remember), and transferred schools regularly while Mary tried to find a permanent apartment. He made no friends and remained silent and mystified until discovering basketball in the fourth grade. By then he lived alone in his room at the Hotel Pennington on 95th Street and Riverside Drive, an S.R.O. Mary managed for the next 35 years. From the few conversations I have with people who knew Earl before his high school days, I gather that Harlem recognized him for what he was—country—and left him pretty much alone. A phrase that comes up several times is "mother-wit."

"By sixth grade," Earl says, "I'd learned I had the springs in my legs. I'd go everywhere I could to find the big man. Watch all day. Dream about what he did at night, figure out how I could do it, then add one more thing to it, to make it mine." Earl says he sometimes considers his life a failure because he was never able to sit on the rim after dunking it, a shot conceived while looking down through the rim during a double-dunk and seeing his gut level with the bottom of the backboard. "I could have pulled myself up, sat up there my whole life," he says. "Never known a thing about it."

Returning to New York in 1966, Earl still didn't know; when he found a plastic bag full under a bench in St. Nicholas Park one October afternoon, a former Millbank teammate had to explain. They snorted it up and vomited it out at a dance at St. Aloysius Church that night, then the high came. "Some people look on the street and find a $100 bill," Earl says remorselessly. "I looked down and my life was over."

After eight months in New York getting "more and more

frozen" from having warmed Johnson C. Smith's bench for a term, Earl couldn't resist the instant oblivion. "The white lady," he calls it sometimes. "It's like snow falling, Christmas every day. Big, heavy dreams. I never sat on the bench my whole life." He still bristles when I ask about Smith's coach. "You know how it is. He plays his seniors till there's six minutes left," he tells me in Goodbye Columbus, a bar on 95th Street and Amsterdam he favors for the jazz the day bartender plays. "Looks at the board, 22 points down. Looks down the bench: 'Son, I want you to go in there and do this job for me.' He wants a miracle. I can't deliver that."

Earl points to a squat, nasty-looking man standing outside a bodega across the street. "That's Felix, the Coke Man," he says. "Delivers every day. Used to be the Junk Man. Motherfucker."

Earl is furious today. The owners of both apartments the Manigaults have been sleeping on the living room floors of for 14 weeks have sworn out complaints for Darren's arrest for burglary. "Earl [Jr.] saw him in Columbus Circle last week," Earl reports with a strange objectivity. "Said he weighed about 85 pounds. Either the drug'll kill him, or someone on the streets will. A year or two in jail's the only thing that can help him now. Penitentiary's really what saved me."

He peers out the window toward the Happy Warrior Playground, four blocks up. Site of the "Goat Tournament" that Earl ran from 1972-81, it's the locus of the only period of steady employment of his life; almost every day finds him back there for eight hours, sitting on the bench with a Colt .45 while the locals gather round him and tell Goat tales. The summer tournament, funded in its early years by drug-dealers like Felix, helped Earl and many of the ballplayers to "Just say no to drugs"—he says this with a wicked smile—"at least once every summer." From time to time, it provided him an opportunity to help a few young ballplayers: Ronnie Ryer and Ray Shirley, both now playing pro ball in Europe, are two names he mentions often. "I think all Earl really lived for, those 10 years of his tournament," says Raymond Diaz, whom Earl made his 11-year-old "commissioner" in 1974, "was to find another Earl Manigault on the streets, and save him." By 1979, Earl was directing it from the Bronx House of Detention, where a *Sport* reporter "discovered" him, carrying around his thumb-worn chapter from *The City Game*.

Earl's first dozen or so brushes with the law—for possession, weapons, finally for stealing mink coats off the racks in the garment district—brought him an unusual clemency. "Nine times out of ten," he says, "the cops, D.A.s, even the judges let me off. Ballfreaks." One summer evening in 1967, a man approached Earl and two friends on a court on 143rd Street. "This millionaire from Clifton, New Jersey," he remembers. "He wanted to do some good, and we listened to him. Pretty sad guy." They went with the man to Atlantic City, in a vain effort to dry out. "Problem was," Earl says, "somebody brought a cigar box full of drugs. We walked the board-walk for two weeks and went home when all the drugs were gone."

I ask where "home" was at this time. "Any place I woke up," he says. "I never let the people see me high. And if anyone tells you, 'I used to see Earl ...' you know he's lying. I always did my nodding where I couldn't be found. Hallways, basements, up on the roof." He points to the 24th Precinct house, three blocks up. "I used to nod out in their bathroom. Had a lot of fans there." Earl juts his chin angrily toward Felix. "I really don't like that dude. It bothers me, man. People saying shit about Darren: 'like father, like son' stuff. Soon enough, word gets around: 'The old man's back on.'" I'm a little surprised Earl's strongest reaction to Darren's troubles is for his own reputation, then remember Bobby Hunter's "only reliable currency" comment. Earl's been living on his reputation for close to 20 years.

The bartender puts on a Freddie Hubbard tape, and Earl mellows out. He lapses into a long silence when I ask why he stayed on heroin so long. "It really wasn't how long," he says finally, "but how much. It's a little like this trumpet player. He's looking for his note, and he won't stop till he hits it. I had it every day of my life till ball ended, kept looking for it afterward, with dope. I'd be up in a hotel room with some females and four, five thousand dollars worth. More money than I'd seen in my whole life. Two days later, it's back on the streets for more."

"Didn't you think about the pros?"

"Yeah, but as I got deeper involved all that just faded away. There was no hardship then, leaving school early, till Connie did it in '69. I was the second, coming out of jail and going to Utah. But I didn't make it."

"How about schools that had recruited you from Franklin, like Iona or St. John's?"

"Iona was a hundred million miles away, man. I was really lost. Just stopped thinking about it."

"What did you think about?"

"I thought about money. And I thought about how to get money."

Earl's three-year crime spree ended early one afternoon in the spring of 1969. Running down 37th Street toward 8th Avenue with seven boxes of dresses under his arm, he looked up when he heard the word "Halt," and saw a policeman pointing a gun at his head from six feet away. "I was really scared," he says, then starts cackling. "I still can't believe how ridiculous this is. I got a man pointing a gun at my head, and all I'm thinking is, I haven't had my quota for the day. I didn't care about getting busted, or pistol-whipped. I was busted dozens of times. Had my ass kicked, hard, more times than that. All I knew was the craving. I took the boxes, threw them in his face, got away."

Earl was arrested in Penn Station ten minutes later, taken to the Midtown South Precinct's basement and chained to a radiator. The cop he'd assaulted came down a half-hour later and put a hole in his head with a lead pipe. "Would've been okay if he'd left it at that," Earl says, "but he wanted my ass."

Twenty-four hours later, Earl found himself in the Tombs, facing the longest 19 days of his life. "Everyone in there was kicking. If they could. My third day in, the guys in both cells next to me hung themselves at the same time. I could hear them fighting for their last breath. You call out for help, but it doesn't come. Two aspirin by the seventh day, maybe. Look at the pillow and see the worms crawling. The rats come out at night and get up on the bed with you, and you're so doubled over with the cramps you can't get them off. Once you pay that piper you never go back."

"But you did. Several times in the '70s."

"Yeah. I just wasn't ready to quit then. Wasn't till I went back to prison."

"So you have a 10th anniversary coming."

"Man, every day's my 10th anniversary."

In September 1969, the month Lew Alcindor joined the Milwaukee Bucks for $1.4 million and Connie Hawkins arrived in Phoenix after winning his hardship suit in court, Earl got his first basketball contract. After his "Orientation Period" at Green Haven, three weeks alone in a cell, the assistant warden who ran the basketball league came in with a paper for him to sign. "If you want to play ball and get along up here," he told Earl, "there's only one team to play for."

"Hell's Kitchen," Earl remembers. "Guys who scrubbed the pots and pans. Easy job. Terrible team. I'd just kicked, still sick, I really didn't feel like playing. A few weeks passed and I figured, what the hell. So I got on the court next day, and a bunch of guys started talking shit. They were right. I could barely hold the ball. I slept on it, or tried to, but this guy named Stretch, big man, started yelling across the cell-block, 'The Goat ain't shit. I swear to God, the Goat ain't shit.' Next day, it was movie day, Tuesday, the yard was empty. At halftime, I had 54 points. People ran to the theater and told what was going on. That kept up the whole year I was in. Game time was four o'clock, when the guards changed shift. They didn't even leave. And nobody went to the movies," Earl says with hopeless pride. "It sounds ridiculous, I know, but this was kinda the high point of my career."

With none of the self-abnegation, Bobby Hunter had made a similar point during our lunch.

"When Earl returned—forget about the Utah Stars, because that was not The Return. Basketball is a game of the streets. It is not a Mormon sport. The Return was that a man who had been almost parallel to those streets had stood up again. And this is the Return, because this is the greatest human ability. To come back, to never go back."

Earl had looked mystified. "Come back from where?"

"From death's door. And to leave from the other side."

"Where does this ability come from?" I'd asked.

"It went right back up my arm," Earl had said, though Hunter wouldn't hear it. "Nothing's as good as being as good as you are. I learned that from Holcomb Rucker, who saved my bacon, Earl's bacon, probably half the butts in this bar. He said, 'Some will never be players, because they never played. Others will always be, because they did.'"

•

I meet Earl for the last time a week later, on the benches outside the Happy Warrior Playground. He's brought a rose wrapped in plastic for the woman he and Earl, Jr., have been crashing on the past week. "A rose," he says, "is a rose, was a place to sleep."

Three men his age, wearing leather sneakers and sweats, are passing a quart of beer and discussing Michael Jordan's 43 points against the Pistons last night. A 62-year-old mailman pulls his cart over, says, "Neither rain nor sleet" as he pulls a half-pint of Bacardi from his breast pocket, and begins a last round of Goat tales: How Earl dunked two balls, backwards, 36 times in a row one night to win a $60 bet, how he went over Big Al Williams, Ray Felix, and the Helicopter during one 47-point game in the Police Athletic League Championships ...

Some kids finish a three-on-three on the court in front of us, and I walk over with Earl to shoot baskets. His jump shot, flatfooted now, is a tight, self-taught, awkward-looking one-hander that brings powerful memories of Dick Barnett and Oscar Robertson, Earl's two heroes as a kid. He takes a while warming up, but after ten minutes he's got his shot back, and there isn't a doubt in my mind this man was "pro material." When he drives the lane, looking exhausted after a half-hour of popping nine, ten straight, some imp of the perverse overcomes me, and I jump in front to block his shot. The ball, cupped between his right hand and forearm, vanishes behind his back when my hand is an inch away, reappearing a half-second later on the side of the backboard with an impossible-looking spin that sends it through. "Let that be a lesson to you," he says, crashing to his seat against the playground fence. Though he's smiling, he looks like he's a million miles away. "I'm trying to figure it all out," he says, still catching his breath a minute later.

Earl leans his whole body into me and looks me straight in the eye, as he's wont to do in his rare moments of confidence. "All the time I was growing up, I didn't think about nothing but making something new happen on the court. I slept, thought, talked, shit, fucked, drank, and ate, and it was ball. I never made it to the pros. College was a wash. Things just didn't turn out like I was hoping, but ..."

His voice trails off with a sense of insoluble paradox. During the minutes of silence that we sit there, I try to piece it together myself, for I've felt this subjunctive agony almost every time I've been with Earl: One coach who could've helped him rather than used him, one game he would've won and not lost by one point, one corner he should've turned instead of the one he did. I grew up a mile south of Earl, on many of the same courts, idolizing the local approximations of his talent and grace, that natural ability to make something beautiful out of the ugliness of city life. It just doesn't seem possible that nothing could have come of all that but a life spent miles below the poverty line.

"But, you know, I gave the people what they wanted," he says finally. "And I can't walk more than a block in this city without someone stopping me, spend some time with me, buy me a beer, pack of cigarettes. I'm recognized for what I did and what I gave, and I don't think they'll ever forget."

It still—even after months of watching Earl's reputation in action—doesn't begin to answer the feeling of loss. "But that isn't enough, is it?" I ask.

"No, it isn't enough," he says with a gap-toothed smile. He seems happy I've finally asked him that one question. "It really isn't."

In the Land of the Fischer King
The Strange Defense of Bobby Fischer

The foothills of the Montengrin Alps above the Bay of Kotor are a mottled green-brown, and the rock-strewn mountains rising thousands of feet above sea-level are parched and ugly. In addition to the sounds of shelling from Dubrovnik, 50 kilometers up the Adriatic coast, and the arrival of the U.S. Sixth Fleet, enforcing the worldwide embargo against Serbia and Montenegro, the summer has brought a terrible drought. The olives, wine-grapes, and tomatoes the region is famous for are tiny and shriveling on the vine. The bay, briny from lack of rain, heaves up a thick salt musk that makes the beaches smell like mussels. The rich Italians, fleeing Feragosto, who have saturated this vacation paradise with money, color, and motorcycles for 30 years, failed to show up this season, and everyone from the royal family and mountain warlords to the local Mafia chieftains are cash-poor and nervous.

On the tiny fifteenth-century island of Sveti Stefan, however, 200 feet offshore, imported champagne, Krstac, and the domestic grappa called *loza* are flowing, and a ballet troupe, jugglers, a seven-foot contortionist, belly dancers, and a 32-piece folk orchestra dressed as chess pieces stroll across the flagstone causeway that connects the island to the mainland beaches. In the twilight, the island itself, a former fisherman's and pirate's village, looks like a confabulated chess piece: a maze of ramparts, villas, cathedrals, dark piazzas, tiny, covered passages, and stone stairways spiraling off at extreme angles.

On the westernmost castellation, a Carrera marble terrazo cum three-star hotel restaurant, Bobby Fischer sits like an idiot king with his back to the setting sun. Boris Spassky, who sits alone in his tennis whites two tables over, savors the last of his mineral water as he takes in the pinks and oranges over the Adriatic, impassive but for an occasional suave pass of a hand through his thick silver hair. Fischer, in a newly handmade aquamarine suit, beige shirt, and a pair of strangely designed, Herman Munster-like black shoes, has every eye in the restaurant but Spassky's on him. Flanked by three bodyguards and a pair of waiters, an elbow on the table and his cheek propped on his fist, he shovels in a second bowl of melon and ice cream, washing it down with full glasses of Krstac. He's gained a good 60 pounds since his last public appearance, and his formerly gaunt and beautiful face, now covered with a scraggly red-brown beard, has filled out so much it's almost unrecognizable. Only the eyes are the same: hazel, wide open, relentlessly shifting, loaded with feeling, confusion, and suspicion.

Throughout his four-course dinner, he's been talking in animated flurries to Eugenio Torre, the serene Philippino grandmaster serving as a second (all-night study partner and researcher) for his World Championship Match against Spassky, the strange comeback that Fischer has decreed to commence 20 years to the day after the conclusion of his famous Reykjavik victory in 1972, 17 years after he forfeited the title. A hot wind blowing off the hills across the bay is taking most of Fischer's words, and I can hear only fragments, but the accent is unmistakably Brooklyn, the Brooklyn of Ebbets Field, Barbra Streisand, and transistor radios: "… There's a lot of people without homes now. It's, uh, y'know, like illegal. Like squat-tuhs. They should be arrested or somethin' …" "… In America, prisons cost money. In China, they make 'em work. And if they don't work, they beat 'em. Hah. Hah-hah-hah.…"

With a thick stench of Havana cigar, a rustle of silk, and the click of alligator leather over marble, Jezdimir Vasiljevic makes his way across the terrazo, trailed by four bodyguards. "Svakako! Svakako!" he's telling one of them: "No shit! No shit!" A small

man with a farmer's physique, mutton-chop sideburns, and a wooly
haircut that looks like the "After" photo in a Moscow barbershop,
c. 1962, he wears a brown, double-breasted gangster suit that's an
inch long at the shoulder, wrist, and heel, and carries a rectangular
case of expensive brown leather, a mystery accessory that never
leaves his side. Referred to as the "paradigm of the new busi-
nessman in Serbia-Montenegro" in the Serbian tabloid *Borba*, and
as a black-marketeering, arms-dealing Mafioso in the Croatian
tabloid *Novi Viesnik* in a "country" like this there's not much
difference. On Sveti Stefan—which he calls "my town"—they
simply call him "Mr. BIG," after his bank/holding company,
Yugoskandic B.I.G.: Biznis-Informacije-Glamur. Any *informacije*
about this man's *biznis* would have to be massively double-
checked, but this is impossible. "I am mysterious man," he loves to
tell you. "I cannot talk now." Like Fischer, he has a 20-year hole in
his c.v. (when he was "abroad") giving rise to various *mon oncle
d'Amerique* rumors: that he smuggled Albanian mercury, or fenced
South African diamonds in Sweden. Most often cited is that he
dealt arms to Israel, and made his fortune during the 1982 invasion
of Lebanon.

As for *glamur*, he has pulled off the Serbian publicist's equiva-
lent of raising Lazarus in bringing Fischer here to play this $5
million "Revenge Match of the Century," but he doesn't seem very
happy just now. He had planned to found a corporate mini-state in
Sveti Stefan—a two-percent tax zone a la Monte Carlo, that would
lure foreign business to his bank—but this has been crushed by
U.N. sanctions, and he's in serious arrears on the five-year, $570-
million lease for this island, three nearby hotels, and 150 acres of
adjoining property. Telexes from the U.S. departments of State and
the Treasury—threatening huge fines and prison sentences if
Fischer breaks the embargo by playing the match, are reportedly
coming daily, putting Fischer on edge: Half a mile up the mainland, a pair of high-backed swivel chairs and a huge oak chesstable
emblazoned with the match logo sit like corpses at the entrance to
the playing site in the Hotel Maestral, the first casualties of
Fischer's demands for perfection. (By the start of the match, he will

have vetoed 11 more tables and two other pairs of chairs.) Hammering and high-pitched drilling are heard throughout the night from the 75-yard-long playing hall, as workmen construct the floor-to-ceiling concrete barricade that will separate Fischer and Spassky from the audience, leaving a 10-foot aperture in the center through which the players can be seen.

Fischer is standing with his palms open in great drama as Vasiljevic approaches his table, and they leave the restaurant immediately in a phalanx of bodyguards, Vasiljevic swinging his briefcase, Fischer toting a leather pocket chess set and two books. "I got so much to do tonight," he says as he heads up the stairs toward his villa on the other side of the island. His walk is unnatural—left arm and left leg together—and driven-looking. Vosco, the cashier at Under the Olives, an open-air restaurant across the causeway, has been filling me with Nosferatu-ish stories of Fischer's dead-of-night ramblings through the mainland forests, every other night in the month since he's arrived. The other nights, a small motorcade rushes him and Spassky across the causeway to play tennis on an old, dimly lit clay court surrounded by blue spruce and cypress. They say he's phenomenally competitive, and that his agonized screams are heard echoing down the hillside when he loses difficult points.

Spassky gets up to leave a few minutes later and I try to make conversation. "Of course you want to talk to Bobby," he says. "But this is impossible. He does not like the media." Spassky's voice is a comical Bela Lugosi baritone that swells and falls with dry humor and a strangely unctuous self-doubt. Though he's a natural performer, he shares Fischer's contempt for journalists, and tries at all costs to avoid interviews.

I mention the war, and he asks for the latest news about sanctions. A naturalized French citizen for over a decade and a virulent anti-Communist, he seems genuinely mortified to learn of the extent of European condemnation of the match. (The Madrid daily *El Pais*, for example, is running the headline "Chessboard of Blood.") "But you cannot blame only one people," he protests. "In Bosnia and Serbia, both are the same people in power. Bolsheviks.

In Bosnia, they get weapons through a special route. And in Serbia"—he raises a pale, beefy index finger professorially—"in Serbia, they have also a lot of weapons. They are bandits. Worse than military. Both sides. It would be nice," he says, filling his lungs with salt air, "if they could make a corridor, like with fire, so that we could get here safely and be here safely."

I ask Spassky if it's true Vasiljevic offered him life insurance as part of his contract. (It's also rumored that a clause in Fischer's 17-page contract stipulates that no noise from the war shall interfere with his concentration during a game.) "Yes, this is a very special question. My safety. We have to look into this. Come," he says, leading me a few steps to the turreted wall facing the mainland. To the left and right, a series of pristine beaches and U-shaped, emerald-green harbors sit perfectly at peace in the gloaming. Two blue cigarette boats with MILICIYA (Police) signs and Browning 50-caliber machine guns on the prow patrol the waters around the island. It's hard to know who they're protecting: Seventy-two of the 100 or so yachts anchored within eyeshot, CNN reported recently, were stolen this summer from the harbors in Dubrovnik.

"Look at this," says Spassky. "A piece of paradise. You know, I used to drive on the coast from Trieste to Bugogno. A beautiful city, but it probably doesn't exist anymore. Do you realize there used to be 700 kilometers of coastline? Now, less than 100."

"Why do you think Bobby has decided to play this match here then?" I ask. "And why now, in the middle of a war, after 20 years of refusing?"

"These of course are the crucial questions," Spassky says portentously. "I can say only, Bobby wants to create the very special atmosphere of Reykjavik. He was the great hero of the West then."

•

These "crucial questions" feel increasingly moot with each war-weary photographer, wire stringer, and television crew that checks into the various Sveti Stefan hotels the day before the match's opening ceremonies. When they gather at night, trading war-stories over *loza*s at Dusko's, a dark, Western-style bar with cheap plastic tables along the sea-wall and Dean Martin and Ricky Nelson trading the harmonies on "My Pony, My Rifle, and Me" on the boom-box, it becomes clear that this war—its headlines of 1,000-year racial enmity and "ethnic cleansing" notwithstanding—has, at trench level, become the anarchy of freak individualism run amok, and the total collapse of the marketplace. You get the feeling there's no place in the world that Fischer, who singlehandedly inflated the value of chess and then turned his back on countless millions, belongs more.

"It's like Kipling's 'The Light That Failed' here," says James Mason, a photographer for Black Star who's been covering the war for over a year. "A lot of people who just want to kill people. Americans especially, extremely lost survivalist types going around with headbands, sawed-off shirt-sleeves, and Rambo knives, fighting for either side. They're going crazy in Dubrovnik, firing machine guns and listening to the voices in their heads. They come because there's no daily accounting necessary here."

Ben Hawke, a sometime producer for Australian "60 Minutes," says he's run into "characters straight out of *Road Warrior*, literally having gun battles off the sides of petrol trucks. There are parts of this country where 10 American dollars won't buy you a litre on the black market, which is where Mr. B, I, G, comes in. Almost every flight in the country's been cancelled because of no fuel, and he has his own filling station across from his little island for the BMWs. He *is* the black market, only he does it legally, through his bank. He's giving 30 to 65 percent interest, monthly, depending on the foreign currency you give him."

Dejan Anastasijevic, a UPI stringer from Belgrade, tells me about the two dozen American mercenaries he met during the leveling of the Croatian city of Vukovar: the Fred Perry Brigade, who "liberated" a lifetime's supply of tennis shoes, T-shirts, camouflage pants, and floppy hats with Fred Perry logos before flattening the boutique with bazooka charges. In Sarajevo, he met a farmer in one of the Serbian strongholds who sold his combine and bought a Russian T-55 tank from the Federal Yugoslav Army, which he drives into the hills after work each evening, so that he can fire on Muslims. "The day I met him it was a ceasefire, but it didn't matter. 'This tank is my private property,' he said. 'No one can tell me how to use it. Communism is over. I'm living in the West now.' While he was talking, I finally understood that Hannah Arendt phrase, *the narcissism of small differences*. That's exactly what this war is."

For 20 years of intractable petty demands, Fischer personified this narcissism exactly. A strange boy with an I.Q. of 181, he grew up in small rooms studying chess with the radio on, refusing to wear anything but corduroy pants and striped sportshirts, developing strange ideas about people—particularly those he loved to call "Commies" and "World Jewry." He shares a "small difference," half-Jewishness, with two "Commie" world champions, Spassky and the current champion, Garry Kasparov (born Garik Weinstein), whom Fischer has accused of "pre-arranging" the games of his matches with Anatoly Karpov. Fischer's father, a German-born physicist who may or may not have worked for the Wehrmacht in the early stages of the war, and his phenomenally strong-willed, Swiss-born Jewish mother, Regina, separated bitterly after news of the Holocaust in 1945, when Bobby was two. The father is said to have moved to South America.

Regina, Bobby, and his older sister Joan lived in various parts of the Southwest before settling in a fourth-floor walk-up in Brooklyn, when he was six. The following year, Joan bought him a cheap chess set at the candy store on the first floor of their apartment building. Though he had a phenomenal knack for puzzles and games, he didn't take to chess immediately; the fascination dates from a year later, when he came upon a dusty old book in the library of a house in Patchogue, Long Island, that the family was visiting. Its pages were filled with pictures and exploits of the 19th- and early-20th-century masters, and their elegant clothes and austere faces filled Bobby with wonder. He became freakishly singleminded. "All I want to do is play chess," he announced. "Ever."

"Bobby was simply a boy with no relations outside chess," says Viktor Korchnoi, the former challenger for the world championship that Fischer vacated in 1975 to Anatoly Karpov. He met Fischer for the first time in 1960, in Buenos Aires. "Bobby is not crazy, like they say. And believe me I know crazy. He simply failed to keep up normal relations," adds Korchnoi, who recently finished his game (via a psychic) with the 1920s Hungarian grandmaster Geza Maroczy. "This is a great danger at that age, because chess can take over the mind. Even if you don't want to, you must keep up normal relations, which for a boy that age, of course, is school."

School for Bobby was a blur. A science teacher at Erasmus Hall High School wrote "NOT SATISFACTORY" on a test he got a 65 on. "TOUGH," wrote Bobby, who felt his teachers were "all mental cases." At 14, already U.S. Champion and a year shy of becoming the youngest grandmaster in history, his notebooks were filled with drawings of grotesque heads and radio-babble: "Hey everybody, gather round, cmon, let's dig these Rockin' Sounds, we got the rugs on the floor ... Come on now I wanna swim with you." He dropped out at 16. "The stuff they teach you in school," he said, "I can't use." The radio was his source of truth: "I was with Bobby in Yugoslavia in 1968," says the prolific British chess writer and international master Bob Wade, one of the few people Fischer has ever trusted (he once hired Wade to research an opponent's games— something he normally did on his own). "His only real interest was listening to the news on the radio." In Sveti Stefan, Fischer carries a yellow Sports Radio wherever he goes.

He developed a passion for Yugoslavia in 1958, when he came to play his first international tournament, an elimination qualifier to determine the next challenger for the world championship. The Yugoslavs, who are chess-crazy, unconditionally took in the "Corduroy Killer," as he was known in New York, and Bobby played brilliantly, earning a return to Yugoslavia the following year for the final qualifying tournament. Mikhail Tal, the "Magician from Riga" who won the tournament and became the next world champion, defeated Fischer decisively, however, enraging him. Tal, a relentless joker, walked past Fischer on the bridge outside the playing hall, flapping his hands and saying the word "Cuckoo" in a high-pitched voice. "Bobby," a journalist here named Miluivka Lazarevic tells me, "ran back to his room in tears, developed a cold, and went to bed. Bent Larsen [the Danish grandmaster who served as his second in the tournament] had to read him Tarzan and Mickey Mouse stories until he got better."

When Fischer returned here in 1961, he got even in a beautiful game in which he sacrificed his queen, not just beating but hoisting Tal, who is often cited as the greatest attacking player of the modern era. The personal element was hardly unintentional. Now 18 years old, Fischer had an understanding of the depths of competition, and could no longer be "psyched out," as he later put it. "It is difficult," said Tal, "to play against Einstein's theory." (Einstein, who submitted to an I.Q. test, scored dozens of points lower than Fischer.) After a long barnstorming in Argentina, Brazil, and Chile (during which Fischer is said to have seen his father for the only time) he also had a new look. In one of two adjustments he would ever make to reality principle, he had given up his corduroys for suits. Seventeen, all handmade in Argentina, England, Trinidad, California, New York, and East and West Germany. "If you get 17 suits," he believed, "you can rotate them. They wear a long time. That's where the poor man gets it coming and going. His suits wear out fast."

Fischer's second adjustment is said to have come a year later, over the radio, when he joined the Worldwide Church of God, after hearing a sermon by Garner Ted Armstrong. It advocated a mixture of Jewish Sabbath and dietary ritual and apocalyptic Christianity: the Second Coming, the end of the world, regenerative baptism, (which Fischer apparently abstained from) and, of course, tithing. He did this in a big way—$93,315.35, according to an interview he may or may not have given in 1976. He followed the Church in the late '60s to its headquarters in Pasadena, and has remained there, despite his eventual break. That came, depending on who you ask, after the failure of the world to end in 1972, of Jesus to appear in 1976, or, more credibly, over his disillusionment with the alleged fiduciary and moral profligacy of Church leaders: In 1972, Garner Ted was accused by various members of adultery, and by 1976, the Church's yearly take of $75 million had outstripped Billy Graham's and Oral Roberts' combined.

The break was bitter: There was a flurry of leafleting by Fischer outside the Church's Ambassador College in 1976, a late-night incident of assault on an ex-Church woman he felt had violated his confidence (he later settled out of court with her), and a $3.2 million lawsuit. It left him essentially homeless (he had lived, after his victorious return from Reykjavik, in the basements of the luxury homes of various ministers) and penniless. After 1975, when he resigned his title (because only 43 of his 44 demands for a title-defense match had been met), the rare accounts of his situation all mention cheap rooms in Pasadena and L.A., months of his crashing on former friends, and days spent riding the orange citybus between L.A. and Pasadena, analyzing chess games on his pocket set. At the end of Fischer's one public statement since Reykjavik, a 14-page, Gogolesque pamphlet titled, "I Was Tortured in the Pasadena Jailhouse!" (he had it printed in 1981 after a case of mistaken identity led to his two-day incarceration), he wrote: "When I left home that Tuesday I had nine dollars in cash and well over another dollar in change ... either a five dollar bill and four ones plus well over a dollar in change or nine ones plus well over a dollar in change (I'm 99% sure it was the former)."

Other than royalty checks for his 1969 collection, *My 60 Memorable Games* (probably the most cogent chess book ever written), he seems to have depended on the curiosity of strangers. Through back channels, one could place a telephone call to Fischer, for $2,500; $5,000 was the fee for a meeting. One also had to pay him $1,000 to open the letter requesting the meeting, and that letter had to be addressed: Mr. Robert James Fischer, World Chess Champion. Yasser Seirawan, the highest-ranked American grandmaster since Fischer's abdication, knows of at least 20 cases where the money was plunked down, including rabid chess player and fellow religious recluse Bob Dylan, whose tour manager is said to have bought him the meeting as a birthday present.

Most of the other known meetings involved multimillion-dollar offers from various fascists and despots, to play chess in their countries. "Dictatorships," the English grandmaster Raymond Keene tells me, "have an enormous weakness for chess, particularly for Bobby." Ferdinand Marcos' Philippines offered $3 million, the

Shah of Iran and Qatar $2 million each, and South Africa, Chile, and Argentina are said to have put up similar amounts. Last year, a Francista millionaire from the south of Spain sent a Basque chess-playing journalist named Leontxo Garcia with a $4 million offer. Garcia spent a few nights walking around Pasadena with Fischer before he was told, "Nah. The figure's too low." "Fischer," Garcia says, "has some very strange ideas, but he is the most brilliant man I ever met. I believe he is more intelligent than Einstein. He didn't seem to care about the money, either."

"Fischer," agrees Bob Wade, "never cared about money. His only desire was to prove that his choices were correct: He wanted chess to be important, because he was a chess player, and he wanted to be important. Bobby knew money was important, but he didn't have a clue why, outside of clothes and status. The only way he could accomplish what he wanted was to fight for a lot of money. Once he got it, he gave it away. He did not know how to spend it. And once he'd become champion, after, essentially, sacrificing his life for it, he didn't know how to spend his time."

Time does seem to be the key to Fischer's return. In 1990, he registered a patent in New York for the Bobby Fischer Anti-Time-Pressure Chess Clock. Unlike standard chess clocks, which tick away remorselessly while a player thinks, this one awards what Fischer calls "bonus minutes" every time a move is made. "It is a gross overstatement," says Korchnoi, "but in chess, it can be said I play against my opponent over the board, and against myself on the clock." With the Fischer Clock, the faster you move, the more time you gain. Only a man who lost 20 years of his life could have conceived it.

Since registering his patent, Fischer has spent much of his time abroad, staying with families outside Brussels, Manila, and, for over a year, in the Bavarian countryside outside Bamberg. Each of the three families had a young child Fischer developed a great affection for. It's said he spent hours teaching each one to play chess.

Janos Kubat, Press Director of the Match, speaks of a "fairy tale motive" behind this match: a series of "It's never too late" letters sent to Fischer, who's about to turn 50, by a Hungarian chess master, Zita Rajcsanyi, occasionally referred to as his fiancée. I spend an afternoon playing chess with Zita—an incredibly patient, mothering 19-year-old with thick glasses, a pony-tail, long, wrinkled skirts, T-shirts, and high-top Converse that she laces all the way up her calf—and find it easy to believe Kubat's "fairy tale." Fischer, in her telling, is an open and very simple book. "He is completely natural. He plays no roles," she says. "He is like a child. Very, very simple."

•

"We've waited 20 years," says Nebosa Dukelic, the moderator of the match's opening press conference. "It's good we wait some more."

Flanked by Fischer, Spassky, Vasiljevic and a Serbian engineer who has perfected the model of the Fischer Clock that will be used in the match, Dukelic has a huge, helpless smile as Fischer, in a gray business suit, off-yellow shirt, and floral-print tie, keeps some 175 members of the media sweating for 15 minutes under the arc lights while he leafs through the questions he has insisted be put to him in writing. A miniature version of the Serbian-Bosnian war is breaking out in the first few rows between the battle-hardened print and electronic journalists, fighting for space. Swiveling in his chair before them, raking a finger through his beard with bizarre lese-majeste, Fischer smiles, grimaces, and raises an eyebrow: "Hah-hah. That's a good question"; or "Who typed these up anyway? There's a real lot of typos in these questions." Every few minutes he swivels 180 degrees to read the 15-foot sign behind him: THE WORLD CHESS CHAMPIONSHIP. He never looks at the journalists, even when a shoving match breaks out between an AP stringer and an Irish cameraman who's just arrived from Sarajevo.

"Perhaps there is a question for Mr. Spassky?" says Dukelic.

"Nah, I'm first," says Bobby.

"Yes, it's right, the World Champion goes first," Dukelic immediately apologizes. "Perhaps I can help you eliminate some repetitive questions?"

"I wanna choose 'em. That's my agreement," Fischer says, looking over at Vasiljevic. "Alright. We'll start with some typically impudent questions from *The New York Times*." He says *New* so that it sounds like *Jew*. Lest anyone miss the point, he identifies the man as "a Mr. Roger CoHEN." Sitting next to me, Josef Lapid, an elderly Yugoslav who emigrated to Israel in 1948 (he's the editorial writer for the Tel Aviv daily *Ma'areev*), starts murmuring: "He can't get away with this. He must answer for this." On Cohen's fourth question: "If you beat Spassky, will you go on to challenge Kasparov for the World Championship?" Bobby brings the house down by swiveling 180 degrees and pointing at the sign. "Can he read what it says behind here?" Roger Cohen is doubled over with laughter. So is Josef Lapid.

The laughter turns to dumbstruck applause when Fischer, looking remarkably like Lenny Bruce reading transcripts of his obscenity trials, answers a question about defying sanctions: "Just one second," he says, rifling through his briefcase until he finds the Treasury Department's August 21, 1992 "Order to Provide Information and Cease and Desist Activities." "So!" he bellows. "This is my reply to their Order not to defend my title here." He hurls a gob of spit on the Order, thick enough to leave a smudge when it's Xeroxed and circulated to the media.

And on he goes: 20 years of private vituperation squeezed into 90 minutes of this and one other press conference a week later. He accuses Kasparov, Korchnoi, and Karpov—"really the lowest dogs around"—of pre-arranging the seven world championship matches they have contested since 1977; World Jewry of blacklisting him for 20 years; the Moscow publisher, Physical Culture and Sport (which published a Russian edition of *My 60 Memorable Games*), of owing him royalties of "let's say $100,000, just to open discussions"; and the U.S. government and Time, Inc. of conspiring to defraud him of "tens, maybe hundreds of millions," this dating to his mid-1970s $3.2 million breach-of-contract lawsuit over an exclusive Fischer sold Time, Inc. for Reykjavik. (The suit was thrown out of court when Fischer, representing himself after firing his lawyers, refused to answer questions such as his name and age, on grounds that it was private information.) To understand "why I was singled out for such treatment," he says, "well, you have to understand a lot about the world scene and who controls

America ... what kind of religion they have."

When he begins to analyze communism as "basically a mask for Bolshevism, which is basically a mask for Judaism," Josef Lapid is up on his feet and hollering: "No, we can't leave this anti-Semitic outburst unanswered ..." Lapid's ejaculation seems to remind the Irish cameraman and AP stringer that they have unfinished business. As another shoving match starts in the first row, Fischer looks up at the audience for the first time and begins to swivel in his chair, a small but extremely satisfied smile playing itself out on his face.

•

Seven hours later, 45 minutes before the $1 million Opening Spectacle on Sveti Stefan, he still has that smile as he marches ceremoniously across the causeway to the music of a Montenegrin 25-piece brass band, shoulder to shoulder with Vasiljevic, Zita, and Spassky and his wife Marina. I've come early, to talk to Vosco at Under the Olives, and seize the opportunity to try to meet Fischer. Falling in line with the procession, five feet behind him, I pick up his marching beat, a self-conscious lope that from moment to moment looks like a stutter-step at a New Orleans funeral, or a goose-step. Lapid, the Israeli journalist, steps into the procession 20 paces later with a fragile, 82-year-old man, Sadik Danon, the Chief Rabbi of Yugoslavia. "Bobby was the greatest." Danon is soon whispering to me, unconsciously picking up the goose step as he looks at the back of Fischer's head. He pronounces the name so that it sounds a bit like *Boobala*.

"Are you going to file a protest against his remarks?" I ask.

"No," he says. "I don't want to hurt Bobby. He's just crazy."

Vasiljevic leads the procession to a cafe 200 yards from the causeway. With a flourish of both hands he invites Fischer, Spassky, Zita, and Marina to sit down, and as two dozen bodyguards form a half circle around the table, he instructs a waiter to bring big bottles of mineral water. It's an incredibly hot, still evening.

"I wanted the, uh, you know, individual bottles," Fischer says when the waiter comes out with a tray. "The small kind."

The waiter brings out five small bottles a minute later. Fischer's talking about bug repellent. "It's natural, your stuff?" he asks

Marina. "Is it natural?" He has a large mosquito bite on his forehead and a crazed look. "I bet it's chemicals, right? I've got a machine that kills them with a beep. You know? They fly in. Bzzzz. Then, beep, pow! Bye-bye bug. Hah-hah. Bzzzz, beep, pow!"

"Mine you put on your skin," Marina tells him.

"Right, the roll-on," Fischer says with great distaste. "See, that's chemical." Sweat is beading up on his forehead, and Spassky offers him a tissue from a packet, which he accepts with great suspicion, then a feeble chess joke as he wipes his whole face: "Usually, I avoid exchanges in the opening. Hah-hah." Spassky offers another two tissues, then the whole packet. Fischer repeats his joke about chess openings as he examines the packet thoroughly. "Ah. Yeah," he finally says approvingly. "German."

Vasiljevic comes to the table with two tall, dark and heavily-bearded men, Milo Djukanovic and Momir Bulatovic, the Prime Minister and President of Montenegro. Fischer looks distrustful as they are introduced—they look like the Smith Brothers, and he clearly doesn't believe Montenegro has a president—and offers the tips of his fingers by way of a handshake. The crown prince fares no better a minute later. Fischer only wants to talk about "those fixed games of those criminals."

"I'm not a specialist on this pre-arranged business," Spassky says with enormous reason. "But I do believe Kasparov and Karpov agreed beforehand to a draw, the 19th game in Lyon, in 1990. This time, I agree, was a fix."

"What you're saying now, Boris," says Fischer, "is just a pinprick. I'm going to demonstrate it all in a book. Proof positive." He has to stop to explain to Spassky what *pinprick* means. "See, the 19th game in Lyon is where it gets really ingenious. They made that one look obvious, so you'd say, 'If'"—he raises an index finger, and a terrible, manic glint comes into his eye—"'If. Maybe. Just that one.' And you'd forget about all that other injustice."

"It's like the Mafia," says Spassky.

"Nah, Boris, the Mafia's got honor."

"Yes, because they must deal with other Mafia."

"These guys are much worse than the Mafia. So much worse."

Vasiljevic comes over to explain the procession back to the Opening Spectacle. Spassky, who seems for the moment overwhelmed with the absurdity of it all, says something that makes Vasiljevic respond, clearly with some offense taken, "I have no monkeys on my island." Fischer gets confused each time Vasiljevic pronounces the word *spectacle,* a la Française. "We will march back to the bridge, where we drink the Schnapps with the dignitaries. Then, through my town, past the dancers and the circus people, to the Spectock-ck!"

"Through your town?" Fischer asks.

"Yes," says Vasiljevic. "The town on my island."

"Your island." Fischer looks hypnotized. I think about an interview Fischer gave thirty years ago, at the age of 19: "I've got strong ideas about my house," he told the man. "I'm going to hire the best architect and have him build it in the shape of a rook ... Class. Spiral staircases, parapets, everything. I want to live the rest of my life in a house built exactly like a rook."

"Yes, Bobby," Vasiljevic says, taking a cigar from his pocket and firing it up. "My island."

•

Fischer stays for only half the Opening Spectacle, which, with its two orchestras, innumerable dance troupes, six-year-old violin prodigy, two sopranos, three folk-singers, six banquet tables, and full fireworks to the tune of the "Hallelujah Chorus," seems to leave him unsated. I follow him to a small, dark piazza in the center of the island, where he watches the contortionist and some rather erotic folk-dancing for half an hour, Zita and Vasiljevic at his side. One of the dancers begins to gyrate a foot in front of him, the guest of honor, and he blushes, vividly, and starts perspiring. "Gotta go," he says, getting up quickly and rushing out of the piazza trailed by a half-dozen bodyguards. At the back of the pack, Zita is looking over her shoulder at the dancers with an enchanted smile.

The match itself is an anti-climax. The question of Fischer's greatness is left unanswered: His play, which through a 16-year career had its own steadily developing logic ("It began to feel," says the international master Walter Shipman, "as though you were playing against chess itself"), now has no signature of its own. The first game is brilliant: "Every move perfect," says Yasser Seirawan. "Terrifying." More to the point, however, is that its perfection and terror are pure Kasparov and Karpov. It has Kasparov's trademark pyrotechnical attack on both sides of the board at once (on bookend pawn pushes—his 19th and 40th moves—you can practically feel Kasparov's hand moving the pieces), and Karpov's patented suffocation technique, in the grip of which the opponent can only watch his pieces slowly rendered useless. In chess terms, it reads like a successful, but extremely didactic attempt to show that the game hasn't passed him by.

His subsequent failures in the next four games, particularly pusillanimous losses in Games Four and Five, have very much the same feeling. It's not that Fischer has lost it, or as Kasparov rather hopefully opines on Finnish television halfway through the match, "The legend of the best chessplayer has been destroyed." He's simply playing like one of those well-read but insufferably solipsistic lunch-counter philosophers he sounds like in some of his rants.

His form is outstanding by the time they leave Sveti Stefan at the end of the match's first half, but it just doesn't seem to matter. There's no tension, except for a few comical demands he's laid down: To have the first three rows of seats removed, and to have a sign placed behind the board, reading WORLD CHESS CHAMPI-ONSHIP, three times, so that no photograph can be taken without that vital information. He has a blue curtain placed over the ten-foot aperture, then has it sealed off with glass. The curtain rises with him and Spassky already seated. They're chatting away happily, as though at the beginning of some domestic comedy, and you quickly get the feeling this is no match at all. When Fischer amiably shrugs his shoulders after his first defeat, saying, "That's what chess is all about. One day you give your opponent a lesson, the next day he gives you one," you get the feeling this simply isn't Fischer either: The old Bobby would have been foaming.

•

At the airport, heading back to Belgrade, I notice Vasiljevic and four bodyguards entering the police captain's office, and through a crack in the door watch them check in their 9mm pistols. As Vasiljevic reluctantly snaps open his rectangular case and surrenders the Heckler & Koch machine gun inside, he sees me and waves his hand imperiously. "Go way," he says disgustedly.

At the gate, however, he comes over and sits beside me. "Now you know my business secret," he says. "I am no longer mysterious? The *Jerusalem Post* says I am 'of mysterious origins.'"

"Did you sell weapons to Israel?"

"No," he says with a big smile. "Stupid, stupid. I sold medicine to Israel. Printing paper. I saw you at the cafe, before the Spectockck. If Bobby knows you are press, he runs 25 meters. And, believe me, if he knows you are Jewish, he runs 50 meters."

"They say that you are a creation of this war. That your money comes entirely from the black market and from all this killing."

Vasiljevic gives me a big grin and tells me that I don't know what war is. "I have seen more wars than this. I grew up with war. Believe me, you don't know war."

"Tell me about yourself."

"No, nothing. I am mysterious. I have two sons, named David and Levy. I invited Sadik Danon to the Spectock-ck. Why don't you ask how I know you are Jewish?"

"Was your sons' mother Jewish?"

"Don't ask. I tell Bobby, 'My two sons are ... have the Jewish names. You tell me about your chess table. You tell me about your pieces. You can tell me about the light in your chess hall. But my guests, you stay away. He respects. How can he no. It's my town."

"Do you think he's crazy?"

"No, he's like Hegel."

"Hegel?"

"Yes, everything fascist, and Marx and Hitler follow him. It's like Bobby, a little. You know, Hegel stayed in only one town his whole life. Bobby never goes out either. He hates change."

"Do you mean Kant?"

"No, Hegel. I know philosophy. You don't know."

"Did you get Bobby by promising him his own island."

"No," he says with an impish smile, "by being mysterious. He is not so difficult. Only for you, you know."

"So you don't agree that Bobby is crazy?"

"No. Not crazy. Irrational judgment. Trauma of the childhood."

"His mother?"

"No, the father. If you mention the father, he will not speak the whole night. Mother, he calls every day. And the sister, crazy sister. I like you," he suddenly says. "I could give you exclusive with Bobby. But it doesn't matter. I talk with him 12 hours, all night, no stopping. It's one word, maybe two. Trauma of the childhood. Bad instruction."

Vasiljevic shrugs his shoulders as he gets up to board the plane, where he has the entire first class section booked for himself and his entourage. "Poor Bobby."

Sympathy For the Devil
The Greening of Charles Manson

"The world of sanity," Blue tells me, "is a little box. The world of insanity is endless, perfect. Charles Manson *is* the Universal Mind. He can think through the mind of a shellfish."

Blue's voice on the other end of the line, calling collect from a small town in the vast doldrums of the San Joaquin Valley, is precise, girlish, and full of strange, dogmatic music. Forty-six, she sounds almost identical to the 24-year-old ex-graduate student and daughter of a San Diego stockbroker named Sandra Good one can see at the tail ends of '60s documentaries, the parts about where the decade went wrong: an X carved into her forehead, her head shaved, a beatific smile on her face as she tells a crowd of media people outside the L.A. County courthouse, "You are all next!" The only difference is an inflection of self-doubt that creeps in at the end of her speeches, making them sound a bit like questions: "He's powerful, I swear. And he's still out there in the desert watching ... as a raven!? Then, boom, he's out in the bush, with the bushman, or in the mind of a ... Norwegian biologist!?"

It's not easy to get to Blue. She is one of less than half a dozen members of the "Manson Family" (a term she hates) still loyal to Charlie. The others have scattered widely, most returning to the small towns in California, Nevada, Wisconsin, and New Hampshire they had fled before joining up with Manson in 1967-69. Some married neo-Nazis, or became single mothers, musicians, carpenters, or homeless. Two went on a crime spree in Canada. One opened a dog-grooming salon, another became a disciple of J.Z. Knight, the woman who channels Ramtha, the Enlightened One (a male presence first incarnated 35,000 years ago), for a following that includes Linda Evans and Shirley Maclaine. One died of thyroid cancer; another in a car wreck. One is the vice-president of a southern California bank; another is in Chapter 11.

Half of Blue's last two decades have been spent in state and federal penitentiaries: six months in 1971 for aiding the prison escape of an Aryan Brotherhood member, then 10 years for conspiring to threaten business and government leaders she felt were destroying the environment. She's spent the other years in a self-imposed underground of collect calls, P.O. boxes, borderline poverty in temporary rural addresses, and fleeting alliances with like-minded people, many of whom seem to be in or fresh out of prison. She became "Blue" in 1974, when Manson, transferred to the California Medical Facility at Vacaville for 15 months of thorazine and solitary confinement, initiated the Order of Rainbow, a color-coded restructuring of his world. A new clock was ordered: "Morning is red, noon is gold, afternoon is green, evening is blue, and night is sleep time." All governments were to become one, with headquarters in China, and all monetary systems reduced to one, placed on computers, so that the screens would read out Manson's name: 666. The women, now considered nuns, received colors.

Blue and Lynette "Squeaky" Fromme (who'd become Red) were living then in Sacramento, to be near Manson when he was in Folsom Prison. They began dressing in body-length red robes with peaked elf-caps, visiting graveyards and industrial plants, and recruiting members for the International People's Court of Retribution (the IPCR): "a wave of assassins," Blue claimed in a bizarre press release she hand-delivered to the Associated Press, "... several thousand people [who] have been silently watching executives and chairmen of the boards—and their wives—of companies and industries that in any way harm the air, water, Earth and wildlife."

The IPCR's work seems to have been largely epistolary and

anonymous—hate-mail to Dow Chemical, Standard Oil, and lumber companies, leaflets promising death and the return of Manson, assassination instructions to the occasional acolyte, etc.—until Red made the front pages on September 5, 1975 by pulling a loaded .45 from her robe and pointing it at President Ford. Blue, tried for conspiracy six months later, burned a $100 bill before her jury, announcing, "This is your truth, trust, and faith ... I want life in prison too, I want to be with my family." She was given 15 years. "Manson," she said, "is the head of the IPCR, and only his hands, only his move can call them home."

After a five-year parole in Vermont, Blue came "home" in 1991, to Corcoran, "Farming Capital of the USA" an inhospitable town in the center of the San Joaquin Valley that houses the maximum-security prison in which Manson will probably spend the rest of his life. Barred from visiting him (because of a prior conviction for aiding an escape attempt), she relocated to a town 25 miles away, where she grows her own food, travels locally by bicycle and tries to avoid the media, agreeing to talk because I've expressed an interest in ATWA, the acronym (Air, Trees, Water, Animals) for environmental awareness Manson coined in 1982. Our first conversation, a surprisingly pleasant one, ends with an invitation to meet a week later, provided I first make a pilgrimage to Sequoia National Park (to witness its natural majesty and the ravages of acid rain) and call a man in Chilicothe, Ohio—a white supremacist who sounds as though I've awakened him at 4 p.m., and who vets me for half an hour with questions like: "You realize Manson's only in prison because he's a white male?"

I broach the subject of white males with Blue when she calls again and all pleasantries vanish, as does the chance to meet her:

"We were left to die in prison because we were white man. And where were your liberal humanitarians when we were facing the gas chamber for trying to save Earth from people ... getting drunk on the blood of children!? Even child-murderers get to point the finger at Charlie, accuse us of killing unborn children. Peck, peck, peck, peck down the order. Sharon Tate's baby dying? A baby that would grow up to be a fat fucking hamburger-eating, earth-destroying ... soul-destroying piece of shit!? What we did was necessary to start a revolution against pollution. We made a statement and we wrote it in blood in the Tate house and in the LaBianca house: 'This death you look at? This is your children. Tate-LaBianca is the house of the future.' We were the little kids, trying to save the sheep from the wolves—and I don't mean, you know, to put down wolves!? And where are Abbie Hoffman and Bernardine Dohrn and all you liberal humanitarians now? Crying about Nelson Mandela? Like, Spear of the Nation isn't a violent organization? About jobs for the homeless? Jobs that destroy Air, Trees, Water, Animals? About some guy in a wildlife-destroying fur coat who left home without his rubbers, got fucked up the ass, and got AIDS!? Excuse me, but that is just White Liberal Guilt Fear, the same that can't forget nine little murders, and yet will ask me to lay down for a black man ... and commit genocide!?"

"Genocide?"

"Genocide. That's essentially what you do when you go to bed with someone who's not of your own race. You breed your own genes out of existence, you breed theirs out too, and any goddamn fool can see that. The blacks don't even know how to dance anymore. Yet in one swoop of guilt-fear, they'll ask me to destroy thousands of years of Anglo-Saxon, Teutonic, Celtic genes and lay down ... for some African!? Excuse me, but what are his genes? Hottentot?"

Blue stops, apologizes for ranting, then talks at length and with eloquent fury about the rape of the environment: the arsenic tailings left by silver mining, rain-forest beef, water tables, dioxins, paraquat, and the U.S. Bureau of Land Management's abandonment of wild horses in Nevada. The subject of nature, however, leads inexorably to eugenics, then white men in prison, then to one particular white man in prison:

"Childhood is a part of perfection, at least if they're genetically-O.K. kids. You can't understand us, or ATWA, or anything we were living through, until you understand perfection. A naturalist can. Einstein knew it. The perfection of a spider, a leaf ... coral!? It's the differences in life that make nature so beautiful. *A red bull in a green field.* You get a genetically-O.K. kid, and you can just love 'em. And if people can't understand that, fuck 'em. I can't wake the dead. I'm still a kid. I won't ... grow up!?

"I remember all these people who came up to us after the murders—reporters, book writers, film and TV people—asking us questions, acting like they understood. I remember sitting on the corner outside the courthouse and looking up at them, so handsome and smart and pretty. Now they come and they're younger than me, still so handsome and smart and ... and I look at them, and all I see is Mom and Dad. All they want to talk about is murder, and they still don't understand the first thing about Charlie. No, I don't want to talk with you.

"I just got a postcard from him," she says in conclusion, her voice cracking with what sounds remarkably like maternal pride. "I can't believe this guy. Living in a cell with a stub of a pencil, four sheets of paper a week, and he's telling me about Having a Good Day. He is a man at total peace. As long as he is held down, until he is given his will to set policy for survival on an international, environmental global order, there is no hope, no order, no love. Just the ghoul your guilt-fear made him into."

•

"I am totely & compleetly alone & when you are compleet alone & compleet you are what my words call me. PUT IN YOUR WORDS that HERESAY dont HAVE the LAST WORD."

Manson's letter arrives half a year after I'd written him: two pages of legal paper covered from top to bottom with punctuation-free, unsyntactical sentences, with afterthoughts like "50 years ahead is 50 years behind because forever goes ahead & behind—up down round & round til you center the vortex" thrown in lengthwise down the margins and across the back of the envelope.

"Its like as if Everyone had the person I was gona bee befor they seen me—so as to fallow there own fears Death wichs & money ... Faces off—In 21 yeers I never met no one in the press who wants to know the truth behond words. Our vocabalary starts in prison. New words begin in the Under World—your world out there is dying & its smaller than my world in here and what people say about Manson

is there own dreams. They see[m] to come through a Heavens body
to form real from the demon's soul ... [their] own reflections to say
what is real or is not real."

•

Twenty-two years after he made news, people still come to
Manson—"through a Heavens body" or otherwise—at a phenomenal rate. He receives more mail than any prisoner in U.S. history, a
weekly average of 10 pounds: letters from young men, wanting his
approval to kill, single mothers in Anchorage, proposing marriage,
divinity students in Gdansk, wanting to discuss The Book of
Revelation and gnosticism. The bulk come from girls aged 14-19:
"Everyone's playing something different with the thought,"
Manson said in 1986. "They're playing boats and planes and trains
and rabbits and ducks and swings and hearts."

He leaves the bulk of his mail unanswered, though in February
1987 he responded to a request for auctionable items from a
Colony Theatre of Wasilla, Alaska, 300 miles south of the Arctic
Circle, sending an autographed Monopoly dollar, half a used
prison canteen coupon, four letters from Red, a Salvation Army
address book he autographed and catalogued as "one address
book from the army of some faraway place," and a doll woven
from the unraveled yarn of his socks. One of many he's sent out "to
do little jobs" in the past 15 years, the dolls, which include voodoo
figures, insects, and scorpions, are said to be his response to
"Charlie's Angels," which he felt was lifted from the mythos of his
control of women. "I call them my Mansonettes," he's said. "If
they don't have any hair I call them my Mansonites. I got 'em in all
colors." (The Colony Theater failed to elicit a response from Red:
"I'm trying to save some whales in Massachusetts," she told a
friend by telephone from the Federal Prison in Alderson, West
Virginia. "A theater would be way, way down my list of priorities.")

There are weeks in which Manson receives 75 requests for televised interviews. His rare appearances, invariably accompanied by
a network apology, are known to triple a show's ratings. "I always
know when it's Sweeps month," says Adam Parfrey, publisher of
The Manson File. "My phone doesn't stop ringing. The TV tabs,

calling about Manson. They ask about him in prison a little, and about the murders a little. Mostly, they want to talk about sex."

Parfrey—who is also the publisher of an authorized biography of the satanist Anton LaVey, a novel by Goebbels, *Tortures and Torments of the Christian Martyrs, Rants and Incendiary Tracts*, and the childhood memoirs of an Aryan Brotherhood man—prides himself on being the only editor on the mailing list of "Singin' Dose Anti-Psychotic Blues," a newsletter for mass-murderers issued by a 24-year-old Brooklyn man named Frank. Under deadline on a feature about a San Diego paraplegic sex-cult when I visit his East Hollywood home/publishing house, he can't drive me to the nearby LaBianca house (site of the second night of "Family" killings and a de rigeur pilgrimage for any Manson scholar) but takes the time to show me his art collection: a haunting oil painting of a 10-year-old cowboy, being hanged by two rustlers at sunset; a functioning miniature plywood gallows, built by a Folsom prisoner; his "white elephant," a swastika-red, hyper-realist poster drawing of a nude, prepubescent Shirley Temple, balancing a riding crop between her labia; and his prize, a signed original canvas by John Wayne Gacy, the Chicago mass-murderer of 33 young men, which depicts the seven dwarves emerging from an anus-like cave.

Though he has had trouble placing ads for and distributing his lists, Parfrey has all but sold out a first printing of 10,000 copies of *The Manson File*, a collection of the letters, stories, poems, and artwork Manson has sent from prison. It's a bizarre, disordered œuvre, and (once one learns to accommodate the omnipresent swastikas and invocations of death, evil, Satan, etc.) an immensely compelling one: A simple line-drawing, a street scene featuring a menagerie of animals, spirits, vehicles, and swastikas, is enough to keep the eye moving for hours, until the cosmology of Manson's world leaps out at you.

"Charlie's got a fevered brain," says Parfrey, "and he's just gotta scratch it. You never know why these things come. He just zings them out there. He's totally non-linear, and, I think, far more fascinating in what he's not than what he is. He's an 'insane mass-

murderer' who's neither insane nor a murderer. And though he is a
true heretic, he's far more interesting in his digressions than his
philosophy, which I think is intentional, if you could ever use that
word with him. Charlie's archetype is the Trickster."

•

*"ALOT of people, have me as they think & thats only in there
thinking ... peoples brains wont centered & [they] see & want need
& Do see & say it as it would only best FOR THEM."*

•

Sitting poolside at the Sportsman's Lodge in North Hollywood's
Studio City, I find partial corroboration of Parfrey's judgments from
an unlikely source: Vince Bugliosi, who successfully prosecuted
Manson for conspiracy and seven counts of first-degree murder.

"When you think of Richard Speck or Jeffrey Dahmer," he says,
"you think of insanity. Then you lose interest. The mass-murderer
Charles Starkweather said words to this effect: 'No one's interested
in a crazy man.' People don't follow an insane person. They'll
follow an evil person, a man with abnormal values. Charlie's a self-
aggrandizing megalomaniac, and a sophisticated con man. But a
murderer? That's hard to say. There were 35 solved and unsolved
killings attributed to him, so he has an enormous preoccupation
with death. And look where he wound up—the Barker Ranch in
Death Valley—and there are three murders attributed to him out
there. I have no doubt he's capable of killing. But the record does
show he wasn't physically involved in the Tate-LaBianca murders."

Bugliosi is in an expansive mood after brunching with his New
York agent. After an unsuccessful 1974 bid for State Attorney
General, he has all but given up the practice of law for a hybrid
career as a co-author/self-simulacrum: Two books documenting his
cases led *The New York Times* Bestseller List before becoming TV
movies (in which he was portrayed by Richard Crenna). He was a
technical consultant for the unsuccessful Jack Webb series "The
D.A." (played by Robert Conrad), then appeared as himself in a
televised 1986 moot court, successfully prosecuting Lee Harvey
Oswald. Like everyone involved in the Tate-LaBianca case I speak
to, he seems to have aged in a vacuum: His body is limber and wiry

and his face is so identical to his 1969 photos his graying hair seems like the dye-job given some actor playing him in the 20-years-later scenes. Though he's lost none of the prosecutor's zeal for minutiae and subtle differences, and knows the details of the "Family" and the murders as well as anyone, he is clearly more fascinated with the idea of some unknown Manson than with the one he prosecuted. The details that stick in his mind, I notice, are intangible ones: lost facts of Manson's life, or the location of a house in Pasadena that Manson decided not to enter on the second night of killings. He is vexed by those he calls "Manson revisionists."

"It's become like some Kennedy-assassination thing," he says, reaching for my notebook and pen on the poolside table, "people with theories about the murders and Manson. It's been posited, for example, that Charlie visited the Tate house on Ciclo Drive, a few hours after the murders, to see for himself."

Bugliosi excitedly draws a rough map of the Belair street and marks the spots of the house, garage, and a back cabin with crosses and squares. "Look, you order a mass murder, and the reason you aren't at the scene is, you're insulating yourself from responsibility. Then you go back?" He makes a row of crosses up the street, showing a path of return, then fills the page with crosses, words, and stick-figures as he continues. I watch his doodling with some amazement. By the time he absentmindedly slides the notebook back across the table to me, he's finished a perfect companion piece to the street scene from *The Manson File*—though with words like "Motive" and "35 Murders" where Manson draws the animals "Egel" and "Coytoe," and crosses where Manson has some five dozen swastikas.

"Who would want to go back to the scene of a mass murder? If you're a Dahmer, and you want to fool around with body parts or something dumb like that? Maybe. But Charlie is extremely intelligent. It's always veiled, but he's very bright. When he's talking, for example, a lot of time it doesn't make any sense. Then it gets typed up and you see there's a complex, underlying message, that's full of riddles. Like his name: Charles Milles Manson. At some point, he changed the middle name to Willes. Why? So that, spoken a certain way, it becomes Charles' Will is Man's Son."

"What did he mean by that?"

"Who knows? But it's powerful. And Charlie had tremendous power in his circle of runaways and dropouts. He was a heavyweight in that world, it would be folly to dismiss that. Wherever he went, a congregation would form ... After the arrests, it was this power that really captured the imagination. It just seemed so bizarre to anyone outside his circle that this five-foot-two ex-con could dominate so easily. People are fascinated by murder, and the fact that celebrities were killed heightened the tension. But you know, I've talked about the murders countless times in the last 20 years and rarely, if ever, has anyone asked, 'How many times had Sharon Tate been stabbed?' No, there have been far more gruesome murders. It's the bizarre that draws people in."

As though to prove the point, Bugliosi calls several hours after I fall asleep that night, and begins talking as if in mid-sentence. "I wanted to warn you," he says, "about one of those 'Manson revisionists' I mentioned." I turn on my bedside lamp, flick through my notebook for my list of contacts, and try to guess whom he's talking about. "No, I'm not going to stoop so low as to mention this individual's name," he says emphatically. "I just don't want you to be deceived or anything ...

"And I just can't get that idea out of my mind," he says. "You know, about Charlie going back to Cielo Drive. It's a fascinating possibility, but it just doesn't make sense." He seems disturbed that a visit by Manson explains a number of unsolved details about the killings: a pair of unidentified eyeglasses found in the Tate living room, and differences in the crime scene left by the murderers and the one found the morning after. "If it's true though," Bugliosi adds with a chilled voice, "can you imagine what kind of monster you would have to be to go back to a house where you knew there'd be such horrible carnage?"

•

"I would Visit with you, but Im being punished cause Im to well known & that means Im always kept in Chains & under all the fear Yellow doubts & overall Bullshit."

•

In the photographs, Sharon Tate lies at the foot of a beige couch draped with a large, upside-down American flag, her legs tucked up awkwardly in front of her, wearing only underwear. Her eyes are open and staring at a blood-spattered carpet six inches away, and her lips are pursed unnaturally in the same direction, so that she seems to be smiling against her will. Her left arm, crossed over her breasts, covers all but one of five stab-wounds to her chest, and she looks still vulnerable after death, even though most of the blood in her body has settled to one side and to her forehead, causing that purplish tinge, known to coroners as "lividity," that makes a corpse so instantly recognizable. There's a razor-thin slash down her left cheek, which drew no blood, and a thick nylon rope wound twice around her neck, which leads across a yard of increasingly bloody carpet to another body, Jay Sebring, lying near a zebra rug by a fireplace. Unlike Tate's body, which is covered with an almost invisible patina of dried blood, the blue shirt, black-and-white pinstriped pants, and expensive black boots Sebring wears are caked with blood so much it's almost impossible to look at him—and the eye drifts back to the couch. For the first time, one notices the thin purple band beneath the rope on Tate's neck, indicating she had been garroted before dying, and that the fetal position of her body has obscured the fact that she is massively—more than eight months—pregnant.

In the four months between these murders and the indictments of Manson and five "Family" members, a German magazine had a standing offer of $100,000 for these photos, and for others even more gruesome: the morgue shots of Tate's houseguests on August 9, 1969, and the crime-scene Polaroids of Leno and Rosemary LaBianca, from the following night, stabbed with a bayonet and punctured with a carving fork and knife 67 times. The photos, which I'm looking at in the L.A. District Attorney's office, have since found a more utilitarian purpose in what Ed Sanders, author of *The Family*, calls the "prosecutorial performance art" of Stephen Kay, an assistant D.A. and former Manson prosecutor who exhibits them, with a slash-by-slash litany, at the parole hearings granted Manson and the actual killers those two nights: Susan "Sadie" Atkins, Leslie "Lulu" Van Houten, Patricia "Katie" Krenwinkel, and Charles "Tex" Watson, the former honor student and football letterman who delivered 90 per cent of the wounds.

"I'm the only one left," Kay tells me, "who still knows everything about the murders and the Family. These people like to minimize their individual participation, but they can't get away with any detail with me there." None of the 42 boards Kay has appeared before since 1978 has needed more than three hours' deliberation to deny parole, with Manson's hearings (there have been eight thus far) always proving the briefest. "Manson knows that he will never get out," Kay explains, "so why pretend he's innocent?"

•

"You've drugged me for years," Manson told his sixth parole board in 1986, reading a prepared statement through a pair of tiny spectacles, his long hair and immense beard peppered with gray, a swastika tattooed into the middle of his forehead, "... dragging me up and down prison hallways, laying my head on every chopping block you've got in this state, chained me, burnt me, but you cannot defeat me.... Before 1969, for over 20 years I suffered your prison cross. I give that to live, because I didn't know the difference. I forgive and it is in my will to forget. But for the last 15 years, there is no forgiveness. The IPCR is the green field with a red bull ... P.S.," he added with a big smile, "The United States started the Second World War."

"The references to chopping blocks and crosses," says Parfrey, "are Charlie's way of emphasizing the point. 'Drugged,' 'chained,' 'dragged' and 'burnt' aren't." Though diagnosed in 1982 as nothing more than "a psychiatric curiosity," half of Manson's last two decades have been spent under heavy medication in Vacaville, and all but three in solitary confinement, allowed out of his cell only in chains for exercise 10 hours a week. He has been transferred eight times from one maximum-security prison to another, while Watson, Van Houten, Atkins, Krenwinkel, and two other first-degree murderers in the "Family" remain in their original medium-security prisons. Watson, who is married, with three children, was baptized in a plastic laundry cart in the California Men's Colony at San Luis Obispo in 1976. He became an assistant to the chaplain, and speaks from the pulpit regularly. One of the star "regenerations" of Ray Hoekstra, the "Prison Chaplain" who began his work with Bonnie and Clyde's sidekick Floyd McDonald, Watson circulates a nationwide, tithing newsletter for his Abounding Love Ministries (ALMS), and has recently entered psychoanalysis.

In 1981, Susan Atkins (also converted by Chaplain Ray in 1976), married Donald Lee Laisure, a wealthy Texan with no discernible occupation who signs his name with a dollar sign for the S and drives a Cadillac with license plates reading FILTHY RICH. Her first marriage, it was his thirty-sixth. "These things just happen," says Laisure, who is now on his forty-fifth wife. "We spent a six-and-a-half-day honeymoon in a four-room apartment over the prison administrative office, equipped with a tiled bathroom, kitchen, and a color TV. I bought $360 of food for the stay, and we were supplied with a knife by the prison. The only problem was them floodlights every time you opened the drapes." They got into a fight, Laisure says, when he upset her "by commenting how pretty Bernadette Peters was. We were setting in the area between the kitchen and the living room, I was watching a TV show with Miss Peters, and Susan stabbed me with the knife, four inches below the rib cage. She meant to do me in, but she only glanced me with it. Drew a lot of blood, left a big scar, but the romanticism sure didn't stop. She apologized to me, then prayed quite a while. After that, it was non-stop for six days. And I'm 52 at the time."

During Manson's one period of relative liberty before returning to San Quentin in 1985 (he was allowed a guitar, tape-deck, and a work assignment in the prison chapel), he made a 90-minute tape of songs and ambient noises: toilets flushing, then a phone ringing for a minute until Manson cracks up the wing by yelling out, "I'll get it." His guitar and tape-deck were confiscated after the tape (smuggled out by a friend and sold under such names as "White Rasta" or "Charles Manson's Goodtime Gospel Hour") elicited tabloid headlines ("From Killer to Crooner") and started a series of death threats between various parties competing to market it as an album. He lost the job in the chapel when a hacksaw blade, home-made knife, 100 feet of nylon rope, and a mail-order catalogue for hot-air balloons were found in his cell. In Corcoran, he lives in a concrete cell with a concrete bed and footlocker, a window he can't look out of, and is granted one 45-minute meeting with the media every 90 days, manacled hand and foot, a privilege he usually refuses, for fear of being unable to defend himself if attacked outside his cell. In 1984 he suffered third-degree burns over 18 percent of his body when a 36-year-old Hare Krishna devotee, Jan Holmstrom (serving life for the shotgun slaying of his father), doused him with paint thinner and set him afire. Reportedly, Manson had asked Holmstrom to stop chanting.

•

"HERE HERE Heres a thought that may explain—Mom went to prison & left me alone—Dad Died in the WW II & I went in to the prison Boyschoals & reformschoals Homes & such & I learnt NOT to be there big people with the power over little people use them & to survive you must lern never to open up never trust & never let anyone with in & never go in to other webbs never go in the lifes or thoughts of others—Stay Center & survive git off Center your beet, hurt, misused."

•

Cincinnati hospital records show a No Name Maddox born to Kathleen Maddox, a 16-year-old unwed girl from Ashland, Kentucky, on November 12, 1934. Kathleen returned to Ashland and was married to a William Manson for two months in 1935, long enough to give the boy a name. The real father is said to have been Colonel Scott, a 24-year-old day-laborer at a nearby dam project, whom Kathleen later won a bastardy suit against. Manson, who writes that he remembers neither man, connects his paternity to prison and to World War II, which may or may not explain why he altered the X—which he'd cut into his forehead during the Tate-LaBianca trial—to a swastika.

Kathleen, whom Manson fondly recalls as "a flower child of the '30s," drank heavily and took up with a succession of men in towns along the Kentucky-Indiana-Ohio-West Virginia borders, often dumping him off with relatives or strangers for weeks at a time. (She once sold him to a childless barmaid in McMechen, West Virginia, for a pitcher of beer.) They were in Charleston in 1939 when Kathleen, arrested with her brother for the strong-arm robbery of a service station, was given five years in Moundsville State Prison. Charlie went to live with Kathleen's mother, then with an aunt and uncle in McMechen, up the street from the log cabin in which Sara Jane Moore, Gerald Ford's other would-be assassin, grew up. "I was very surprised," says Van Watson, a grocery store owner who sold candy to both Manson and Moore, "at how those two children turned out."

He rejoined his mother in 1942, and spent four years shuttling with her from one town, city, state, and "uncle" to another. She eventually remarried and settled in Indianapolis, and Charlie, 10 years old, began a new round of traveling, from foster homes to juvenile homes, then back with his mother, aunt, or grandmother. On a few happy occasions, he stayed with his favorite uncle, Jess, a moonshine-making hillbilly in Moorehead, Kentucky, who died either when his still exploded, as family legend runs, or "up in the nutwards of Kentucky," as Manson writes, c/o Blue, a letter read over the phone so quickly I can jot down only fragments: "I grew aware of ATWA because of Uncle Jess ... Grandma came down from Kentucky because she could see the ATWA dying in the hollers ... I seen the ocean dying up in Mendocino in '67 ... My water spirits are mad."

Jess seems to have died by 1947, as had Charlie's McMechen aunt and uncle. Kathleen, with no relatives left to send him to, pled hardship to an Indianapolis juvenile court, and he was placed in the Father Gibault Home for Boys, a boarding school in Terre Haute run by the Holy Cross Brothers—the beginning of 47 years spent (but for four periods of parole, totaling 61 months) in increasingly severe institutions. He stuck it out for close to a year at Father Gibault, then ran away to Indianapolis, convinced his mother would take him back. She took him back the next day, however, enraging Charlie, who escaped again and took to the road (at the age of 13) for the first of many times, sleeping in the woods outside Terre Haute or near train tracks, finally hopping a freight that took him the last of the 160 miles back to Indianapolis.

Not wanting to "stay where mother lived in sin" (as he later told juvenile authorities in Indianapolis), he slept in abandoned sheds by the railway or in alleys, until making a lucky find while stealing dinner from a grocery store: a cigar box under the cash register with over $100. He rented a room on skid row, bought some clothes, and for a few weeks was able to support himself by cleaning garbage cans, delivering Western Union messages, and stealing everything he could get his hands on. His inevitable arrest, for stealing a bicycle, made the Indianapolis front pages when a newly ordained Catholic priest, Rev. George Powers, took an interest in Charlie's extreme case and arranged both to have him profiled as a "model juvenile" and enrolled in Father Flanagan's Boys Town, near Omaha, Nebraska. "Almost everyone had rejected him," Rev. Powers remembers, "[though] all he ever did was steal food from grocery stores ... He was almost angelic-looking. Like an altar boy."

Charlie lasted either three or four days at Boys Town before running away with a kid from Peoria, Illinois, named Blackie Nielson. They stole a motor scooter, then a car they wrecked, robbed a grocery store and, he claims, a gambling casino at gunpoint, then made their way to Blackie's uncle, who sent them to work, burgling stores through skylights only they could fit through. Arrested on their third break-in, Charlie was sent back to the same juvenile hall in Indianapolis he'd left a month earlier, and he was on the front pages again the next morning, the "ringleader" of a gang of 30 boys he'd help escape with a pair of wire clippers stolen from the maintenance man. Arrested two hours later, trying to peer over the wheel of a stolen car, he became the youngest offender ever booked into the Indianapolis County Jail.

Though Charlie had broken a number of federal statutes, he was placed in a state reform school in Plainfield, the beginning of a three-year anal-sadistic nightmare. He tried to escape within the first half-hour, and was beaten senseless with a yard-long leather strap after roll call that evening. A week later he was gang-raped by four older inmates in the school dairy's feed-lot. Charlie avenged himself properly (he bashed one boy's head in with a three-pound metal bar late one night, then hid the bar under the covers of another, who was severely punished), but he had a reputation as a "joint punk" that he couldn't shake with two counselors. One, who had witnessed his rape, had a habit of pulling Charlie's pants down in front of other inmates and "lubing" him for their future delectation with a mixture of feed and tobacco juice; the other, an ex-Marine, made him run "jaw-lines"—either a gauntlet, run between two lines of the boys in his cottage, or a compulsory 25-foot sprint into the man's clenched fist.

Charlie ran away whenever he could. His eighteenth attempt, in February, 1951, took him as far as Beaver City, Utah, where he and two other boys were arrested for driving a stolen car across state lines. A federal violation, it kept him incarcerated in reformatories, training schools, and prisons in Washington, D.C., Virginia, and Ohio until six months after his nineteenth birthday.

Paroled out in May 1954, he managed to stay out of prison for 14 months. He returned to McMechen, and savored a few weeks as a non-inmate before going to work as a janitor, busboy, parking lot attendant, and groundskeeper. For a while he shoveled shit and fed the horses at Wheeling Downs. He married the first girl who'd have anything to do with him, a coal miner's daughter he met in a card room in Steubenville, Ohio, named Rosalie Willis, who wanted to go to California. Within a few months she was pregnant, and Manson, with no patience for debts, phone bills, or minimum-wage labor, went on a string of petty larcenies and car heists. He decided to honor Rosalie's wish to move to California after his delivery of a stolen Cadillac to Fort Lauderdale got him on the wrong side of a pair of local gangsters. He stole a 1951 Mercury, and he and Rosalie made a month-long crime spree of the drive out west, stopping in enough towns and cities along the way to gather a small nest-egg to set up housekeeping in L.A.

Arrested for driving the stolen Mercury 10 weeks later, he was given five years probation. Still facing a federal court date for the Cadillac he'd taken to Fort Lauderdale, he fled, leaving Rosalie, now well into her third trimester, in the care of his mother, who had moved to L.A. He managed to stay on the lam for six months before he was arrested, returned to L.A. and sentenced to 10 years in the Federal Penitentiary at Terminal Island, off San Pedro.

After 29 months, he came out a changed man. What little hope, love, fear, or vulnerability he had ever nurtured had ended when Rosalie ran off with a truck driver—taking their son—a year into his stretch. Manson, who had done time at Terminal Island with a leading Nevada pimp, drifted to Hollywood's Sunset Strip and began turning girls out. In the 19 months he stayed free, he seems to have "matured" into the Charles Manson the world would learn of 10 years later: endlessly adaptable, charismatic, and fearless. He was arrested for countless misdemeanors and felonies, including the Mann Act, but he always managed to influence some judge or court psychiatrist and walk with a probated sentence. By the time he reached Mexico City in March 1960, fleeing federal authorities in Laredo, Texas, for a second violation of the Mann Act, he was able to charm not only the local low-life but the Yaqui Indians of a nearby village out of a pouchful of mushrooms, a feat that earned him the attention of the *federales*, who returned him to Laredo.

The same judge who'd given him parole a year before ordered him to serve the remainder of his original 10-year sentence. Though he fought it for a year from the L.A. County Jail, Manson remained in prison for seven years, learning how to play guitar from a cell-mate named Alvin "Creepy" Karvis, the last surviving member of the Ma Barker Gang, and steeping himself in the Bible, Scientology, and the wisdom of Black Muslim and Native American prisoners, all of which he drew on heavily after his release. On the day he left Terminal Island, March 21, 1967, he told authorities that jail had become his home, and he begged them to let him stay in.

•

"I can be in a cell with what you think your you is & you will be truely alone ... My I is centered in & within over 45 years of prison halls. I call it puttin on faces, reflecting—Truth in every one comes from with in & there isnt much you can tell others. Most only here whats best for them to here."

•

It becomes increasingly tempting to believe Manson's mea non culpa—*I am only a mirror in whom people see their reflections*—with each admirer, "revisionist," and former friend, acquaintance, and prosecutor I speak to. Each seems to have his own Manson, dating with remarkable precision and self-reverentiality to the first encounter: Stephen Kay sees him, at parole hearings, "looking like a caged, vicious animal ... the same as when I saw him in 1970." Blue, who tells me she was a "cynical, objective person" when she met Manson in 1968—"chasing an illusion of adulthood, Ph.D., and some horrible job I already knew was corrupt"—found perfection in him, and eternal innocence as one of the two dozen or so children (Manson called them "young loves") of the "Family." Jerry Rubin, one of the first to visit Manson after his arrest, says he "fell in love with Charlie Manson the first time I saw his cherub face and sparkling eyes on TV." Jim Mason, a former George Lincoln Rockwell associate and founder of the Ohio-based Nazi splinter group, Universal Order, visited Manson in 1981, and found him "the result of a fortuitous genetic circumstance" that comes "once in a lifetime, like Hitler."

The Beach Boys' drummer, Dennis Wilson, took in Manson and a dozen young loves in his Sunset Boulevard mansion in the spring of 1968—"during that incredibly manic TM-Maharishi-serenity phase of his"—as Wilson's producer and friend Gregg Jakobson recalls. He called Manson "the Wizard," gave him free rein to his clothes, drugs, Rolls-Royce, and Ferrari, and included a reworked version of the Manson song, "Cease to Exist," on the Beach Boys' album *20/20*. Though Dennis recommended him in the same breath as the Maharishi to the rest of the band, his paranoid brother, Brian, locked himself in the bedroom of his purple Spanish-style house in Belair when Dennis brought Manson and a few girls over to record, then had his toilets disinfected several times, for fear of gonhorrea. The songs recorded that day, later released as *LIE* (the album's jacket features a well-known *Life* cover from 1969, with the *F* removed) are pure Manson: neither good nor bad, endlessly self-referential, and fascinating—once you grow accustomed to their dissonance.

I drive down to Laguna Beach to meet Jakobson, who was Manson's friend and philosophical confidante in 1968, and probably the only person who spent a significant amount of time with him while both cogent and "non-indoctrinated." One of the original L.A. beach animals (Zeppelin's "Black Dog" is very audible in the background when I call to arrange the interview), Jakobson tried for months to arrange financing and production for a documentary of Manson as an L.A. personality/happening. "If Charlie had come up 20 years later," he says, "with MTV, he would have been a natural. I never gave that much credibility to just his music, because his whole 'Helter Skelter,' Magical Mystery Tour trip was so visual, so much the experience." Jakobson became an important witness at the Tate-LaBianca trial, helping to establish the "Helter Skelter" theory, which provided not only a motive but what Bugliosi calls "Manson's symbolic fingerprint" at the LaBianca house: the words HEALTER SKELTER, which Patricia Krenwinkel misspelled, using Leno LaBianca's blood, on the refrigerator door.

"Charlie was a magic man," he says, "and in those days magic was allowed. Hanging out with him was an event, though you could only take so much of him, because he was always on, always on the move. I remember—and this is one of very few more or less conventional nights—we ended up on the Strip, at the Whiskey, with Dennis, Charlie, and a huge entourage. Some big show going on. Charlie hit the dance floor, and it wasn't but a minute till he'd cleared it. Don't forget, this is the Whiskey A-Go-Go in '68, and a pretty hardcore place. It's loud, it's happening, and nobody gives a shit about anything. But there's too much electricity coming off him. He's just humming, shooting sparks out of his eyes and his head."

"Was it good dancing?"

"Well, of course, *good* doesn't mean anything when it comes to Charlie. It was total freedom, and he was moving to the music, and if you'd want to define dance from the bottom up, that's not a bad place to start."

"What was it like talking with him?"

"Exactly the same. And his rap was solid. He had this charm of throwing ten things at you, and while you're still working on Number Three, he's at Seven, and getting physical about it. He'd bend down, pick up a handful of rocks and throw them in the air. They'd all come back to him, and he'd look at you and say, 'Throw it all away, and it'll come back to you.' There wasn't one thing Charlie wouldn't interpret for you, and he'd go out of his way to do it. One time, he was telling me about the end of everything, and I was saying, 'Charlie, you're full of shit, but we oughta film you and make some music.' He took me for a ride to one of the canyons, up at that end of the Valley where they were building 300 new houses or something. We drove up: new homes, new streets, new lights, not a soul there. And he stopped. Silence. He says, 'Where are we at? What does this make you think of?' It was like a graveyard. He said, 'Exactly, that's where we're heading. This is the future.'"

"Did you ever anticipate him getting violent?"

"No, though I remember once he held a gun to my head and said, 'What would you do if I pulled the trigger?' I said, 'Well I guess I'd die.' He really liked that, and just put it back in his belt."

"Weren't you afraid?"

"No, I really wasn't. And if I was and tried to fake it, Charlie would've seen through it, immediately. See, Charlie really believed what he believed in, he never faked it. His reality was bizarre, but so is prison and that's where Charlie came from. He was true to his conditioning: observe from a distance, through a glass wall, above barbed wire, and what comes out is strong ideology. He never learned that reality and ideology are two different things, and he was one of the few who can live with those two as one, like the Maharishi, Mother Theresa. One thing is for sure: Wherever you have a Mother Theresa, you'll also have a Charles Manson. I love them both. She brings tears to my eyes, and, strange as it sounds, I loved Charlie for pointing that gun at my head."

"What was he looking for?"

"I think he wanted some of that serenity. And I felt sorry for him, because I knew he could never get it. I wanted to put my arm around him, buy him a beer, take him down to watch the sunset, but he was never going to do that. You had the feeling that he couldn't afford it—to stop moving, charming, interpreting. He was into something that was not a static situation, with the girls and Tex. It was moving in a tight circle. At some point, that circle wasn't so nice anymore, and it started whipping, becoming really ec-centric. Charlie knew how to handle that, but those kids didn't.''

"When did it start getting nasty?"

"As I remember, a lot of it was about money. Not for money's sake, but Charlie was getting kind of survival-orientated, going back to his old ways, I imagine. Why, I don't know. He began wanting something—to prove his point, extend his sphere of influence. When me and Dennis first met him, he was so happy-go-lucky. He had his music, he had his big green bus, he had those girls, and with the girls, he had credibility, which was everything back then. But where he'd been writing about flies landing on his face, which was beautiful and very spontaneous, something else was driving him. I remember hearing about their creepy-crawling, where they'd go into strangers' houses and not take anything, just move things around. That's when I told Charlie, 'Man, you've gotta get out of here. Society is what it is. It's got some real strict parameters, and you're not a good member.' Charlie never really bought that. He'd nod his head and talk about him and the girls heading to the wide-open at Barker Ranch out in Death Valley, but I don't think he understood what society is, or anything about the heart culture."

Jakobson seems surprised when I tell him I've never heard the phrase "heart culture."

"You know, respect for the other person?" he asks. "Male-female? The spaces in between, planets revolving? Mother-love? It's nothing profound, just what you get from the mother, during your sponge-stage. I remember trying to talk to Charlie about this, about natural law, the order of the sun, planets revolving. He didn't even buy that. He had all these answers about the seven planes of existence aligning out in the desert and the holes matching up, so you could scoot through, the bottomless pit, and the underground river, all that Hopi legend stuff. The murders happened in L.A., and Charlie was an L.A. phenomenon, but it was fitting he wound up out there. It's one of the most extreme places on the globe, literally the lowest point of the United States. The more primitive you are, the lower you go, the easier it becomes to start making your ideology into your reality. This is what Hitler understood. You know, we look at Nazi Germany now and just see the Holocaust. Back then, those people were experiencing a great blossoming of humanity. Those are two sides of the same coin. That's a cliché, of course, but Charlie lived that cliché out, and he had that coin, so to speak, in his pocket. He just didn't know what to do with it."

•

"They always seem to End up blameing me, for being what They say—I was the phonie prophit befor I said four words."

•

Death Valley, as the crow flies, is only 170 miles from L.A., but it's one of those distances maps can't begin to measure. The first copse of Joshua trees and odorless sage welcome you, some 25 miles outside San Bernardino's city limits, to the sun-blackened gravel and red clay of the Mojave Desert. Road signs come every 15 miles, at best, advertisements vanish altogether, and the temperature rises a degree with every five miles. By the time you reach the Pinnacles, a series of conical mountains rising from the salt-flats that begin 125 miles out on Interstate 395, it's 121 degrees, and you feel a profound conviction in the worthlessness of all activity other than sitting utterly still. Various branches of the military have used this area as a heavy-ordnance target range and as a speed and endurance proving grounds since the 1950s; more recently, film crews like *Star Trek V*'s have come for extra-galactic locations. In the last three years, a new industry, the Ice Factory, has begun to flourish.

"There's an incredible stench when you cook methamphetamines," says Deborah DeRose, the public defender and parole lawyer for Susan Atkins who's driving us out. "In the Mojave, no one will smell it, no one'll bust you if they do smell it, and no jury'll convict you if they do bust you. I've got a D.A. friend in Victorville [a town in the Mojave's southwestern tip] who has the worst conviction record in history. People do not believe in cops out here."

"That's what drew Manson here in the first place," Bill Nelson chimes in from the back seat. "No one to stop him from killing."

Bill, an irrepressible, 52-year-old Orange County man, is easily the world's leading "Manson revisionist." An ordained minister and former Secret Service agent in the Nixon White House, he's devoted much of his last five years to an investigation of the Tate-LaBianca murders, culminating with the publication last fall of a vanity-press edition of his *Tex Watson: The Man, The Madness, The Manipulation.* Though Watson is his primary fascination, Bill keeps tabs on every "Family" member. He's been calling me for weeks, offering to let me "stake out Sandra Good's P.O. box with [him] this Saturday?" I can hear the pages of his File-A-Fax flip as he says, "How about Friday, from 1:15 to 3:45? We can tail Suzan LaBerge [the born-again daughter of the LaBianca's]. I know which aerobics class she goes to." Bill has a large Secret Service ring on his right ring finger—his own design, since taken up by many past and current agents. When his "Family" investigations get stymied, he tells me, all he has to do is "flash the ring and watch the doors open."

I've taken him up on his offer to go out to the Barker Ranch with a Mojave woman I'll call Onyx, a 40-something mother of five and former "Family" member who wants her name hidden, Bill tells me, to avoid further embarrassment with her neighbors. "Elf, her 17-year-old," he says, "already had to drop out of school last year because the kids were beating up on him for having 'the witch with the X on her face' for a mother."

As we pass the last of the Pinnacles and turn off 395 toward her town, Bill unsheathes a six-inch Buck hunting knife and puts it to his left cheek. "This is the knife Tex Watson used the first night of murders."

"How did you get it?"

"I bought it in a hardware store."

"I thought it was the knife Tex used."

"Nah, it's the same kind. He claims he was on so much speed he didn't know what he was doing. He knew exactly what he was doing! He gave Sharon Tate a slit down her cheek," Bill says, pulling the knife along his face with relish. "Like a cat with a mouse."

"Put the knife away," says Deborah at the wheel. She's had a lot of experience with Bill and his knives. "I don't wanna give this woman any ideas."

A brood of four of Onxy's kids are standing aimlessly outside the gate of the house, an old red-brick ranch stuccoed white with a half-foot coat of concrete—insulation against the heat. The garden is piled six feet deep with scrap metal. Elf, a tall, bony kid with stringy blonde hair that covers his eyes and a heavy green army jacket, hands Bill, who's been out here before, a list of the parts he needs to get his Yamaha 220 on the road: everything from clutch plates to twist grips, throttle cable, and O rings. His five-year-old brother is riding a home-made stingray that's half a foot too big for him up and down the gutted dirt road in front of the house. He keeps one foot on the pedal and taps the back wheel with his other, as a brake, which he tells me "Elf's too busy with his fucking Yamaha" to put on his bike.

Inside, there's a thick smell of mildew, and it's 50 degrees cooler, and dark. Onyx, a slender woman with white-blonde hair, sits on a couch with a daughter and a teenage girl from the neighborhood she's unofficially taken in, wearing Reeboks with colored laces, a black bodysuit, and a pouch strapped around her waist. In the yellow glare of a TV tuned to some cable station broadcasting a teletype of scripture and desert church events, she looks like a sepia-toned version of the dozens of photographs I've seen of her, not a day older. Under the sun, however, I see her face is deeply etched with frown and worry lines; as we pile into the back of Deborah's four-wheel jeep, I notice the X carved into the middle of her forehead. It's a startling sight, and I can't stop looking. In the intense desert heat it looks Biblical.

"Hey!" she screams at me, "you're crushing my fucking Gloria."

I smile foolishly for a few seconds, thinking what a weird day this is going to be, until she says, "Hey, get off," and reaches for the half of her waist pouch I'm sitting on and pulls out a cassette of *Gloria Estefan's Greatest Hits*. "No I don't want to lose you now," she sings as we drive out of town, looking at me out of the corner of her eye. "But if you're looking for God you have come to the right place, statistically speaking. There are 13 churches here, one for every .95 people." She sounds like Groucho Marx, but her look is full of dead-serious appraisal.

Deborah, who's also riveted by Onyx's forehead, asks what she tells her children about the past. "I tell 'em, 'Honey, your mom fell on a cookie cutter.'" Bill, sitting next to Deborah, starts roaring.

By the time we reach Ballarat, a two-building town that is the last stopover before the mountains separating the Mojave and Death Valley, I feel like I've gone through time travel into 1969. Onyx is a perfectly preserved specimen of a "type" I've long forgotten: completely present and out-there, talking in non-stop private clichés, new words, and two- and three-sided conversations in voices. Almost everything said conveys a faith in the undying newness of living in the moment—"in the Now," to quote Charlie—even though her presentation of past, present, and future happens mostly in snippets of mornings, afternoons, and evenings from 22 years ago.

I'm able to follow her epiphany until Ballarat, after which we head south along a rock road and hang a left up Golar Wash, a six-mile former waterfall/donkey trail that leads to Barker Ranch. I lose her during a conflation of memories of the "feral facial features" and the "species of the feces" suffered during an outbreak of dysentery at the ranch and a belladonna trip she and 10 others went on. "No recommend telache [the local Indian's word for deadly nightshade]," she says. "No good make pupil bigger than outside of eyelid. No, honest Injun," she says, her voice imitating an early-morning science-show host's. "It's true that it is not a good idea to make your muscles itch from the inside of the subcutaneous region, or, in any way, for you to make your chin go, Www-rrrhaann." She holds herself as if she's shivering. "I really didn't like it when those three men in homburgs and three-piece suits came either. And I just could not figure out what was in those briefcases. But as you can probably guess, I didn't really want to know."

The "Family" spent two significant periods of time out here: the late fall of 1968, when Manson fell in love with the remote and mystical peace of the desert, and two months in the early fall of 1969, after the Tate-LaBianca murders. They weren't under suspicion for Tate-LaBianca when they were arrested here in October—for torching a $30,000 piece of land-moving equipment used to cover up a nearby hot springs they loved—and they were due to be released on those arson charges when "Sadie" Atkins decided to shock her cellmates back in L.A. by gossiping about some murders she had committed for a man she loved named Charlie.

"Sexy Sadie, you broke the rules," Onyx is singing as we clear the top of Golar Wash and park in front of the ramshackle sprawl of Barker Ranch. "You laid it down for all to see-ee-ee-eeee." She seems disappointed by the bad state of repair the ranch is in. "Oh well, ground settles, concrete cracks, life goes on. We were happy here." The main room of the ranch-house is pretty much as it was left after two raids by local park rangers. Mattresses and an occasional piece of cheap furniture are strewn about, and some animal is rattling inside the oven. There are a few old hardcore porno photos hanging from the mantle above a fireplace, like a family album, and some graffiti of more recent vintage on a wall abutting a small room off to the side: 6/24/90 STILL LOYAL TO CHARLIE STEVE KEVIN MARK, and a pentagram with the words, JOHN & DON AUG 9TH '90 "TO SHARON."

I ask Onyx if any of the rumors of their involvement in black magic were true. "There was a lot of talkage," she says as we walk the quarter of a mile to Myers, a second ranch they often used but were never allowed to settle in. Bill has gone off with a Camcorder to film the ranch for an upcoming episode of "Geraldo." "Satan babble, Jesus babble. Hopi babble, Helter babble Skelter babble," Onyx says. "We talked scads of shit. But it was all a talkage, not a doage. Habla, habla, habla. Like with Squeaky. She was out here visiting in 1973 with Sandy. She knew how to get the bullet in the chamber, believe me. All she did with Ford in Sacramento was push everyone's parole back 20 years. Talkage."

"The murders were doage," says Deborah. "Weren't they?"

"Yes," she says. "That appears to have been a doage."

I ask about the one death Onyx was present for, of a sometime member named Zero, who died from a gunshot wound to the head in a house in Venice Beach, a month after the October arrests at Barker Ranch. Listed a suicide, it was generally posited that he was silenced by the "Family" as a possible leak to the murders. "Little Patty [a "Family" member] came out through the kitchen," Onyx remembers, "saying, 'Zero shot himself. Just like in the movies.' I went in and saw him sort of wake up, like from a bad dream, like he couldn't quite believe what was happening to him. I saw that look of, 'Oh, yeah,' and then he rolled over back into it. It was the same with the murders, I guess," she says. "Once you'd stepped in that door, you know, you're in. I came up to the car the night Katie and Lulu were heading out [for the the LaBianca murders] and asked them if I couldn't come along. They were my two best friends. They looked worried. 'Nah, we're just going out for a while.' 'You sure you don't need me to come with you?' 'Nah, we'll be fine.'"

"Did you know what they were going out for?"

"Hard to say. Hard to talk. Know's not the word. We were living something, not knowing it. What we knew we didn't have to talk about."

"Was it ideology?"

"Now you're talking," she says. "Habla, habla, habla."

"What were you living?"

"Damned if I know."

"What would you have done if you had gone to the LaBiancas?"

Onyx looks from side to side, says, "Guess I would have had to deal with it. Maybe reach into my bag of ideology, like Fritz the Cat." She points to the Myers Ranch, 100 yards ahead. "This was a kind of ultimate destination," she says. "For Charlie's ideology."

The Myers is a beautiful property, and a true oasis. Situated on a cold springs, the first water source I've seen for 50 miles, adorned with fig and eucalyptus trees, running showers, a swimming pool, and lush vegetation, it's also completely anomalous. It has the feel of a ranch in the Shenandoah Valley in the 1940s, though the expanse of Death Valley begins 50 yards from the eastern gate of the Ranch. Just above the house is a small canyon that could easily pass for a Kentucky "holler." Near a stand of closely planted fruit trees is a dense growth of eleven-foot reeds, which Onyx tells me they used to hose down for the "world's best kiddie slide," all the way from the ranch house down to the springs.

After two hours of listening to her monologues, I suddenly realize what's so weird about her: She has absolutely no sentiment. Everything she says and every story she tells has a twist with an emotional content, but the words stay hers, and the stories aren't shared or told to edify, impress, or whatever. Just manifested, as though under a glass bell. Climbing up the reeds, however, she begins to slip and grabs for my arm, and as she presses my forearm for a second, I can feel everything that's missing in her speech, like a surge of power from an outlet. She looks at me out of the corner of her eye as she lets go—the same appraising look as in the back of Deborah's truck—as if to see whether the immediacy of physical contact can also be found some other way. There isn't: I can't stop judging these people, and if I tried to fake it, as Jakobson said, they'd see through it, immediately.

"'Twenty years later," she says, "I still don't really know what happened, but we all really did love Charlie. He hit the magic peg, and he knew where it was, every time. I remember, during the trial, he'd come in looking different every day. Once, he came in like Don Ameche, his hair cut and slicked back, a little pencil moustache, and he got up on the defense table and started singing 'That Old Black Magic.' God, I was so proud of him."

She starts laughing. "It's so-o weird. I haven't thought about Charlie for ... months. But you're asking me these questions now," she says, looking at me directly—and accusatively—for the first time since I've met her. "And it's like I just saw him yesterday. Why are some people just like that?"

Once a Man, Twice a Child

The Tribulations and Trials of James Brown

Gus, the pasty-white, 300-pound cabbie driving me to the State Park Correctional Center outside Columbia, South Carolina, doesn't need to ask which of the 288 inmates I'm going to see. He just wants to know if I'm a writer or a lawyer. "Reason I ask," he says in his mellifluous, surprisingly feminine drawl, "if you a writer, I might just wait around for the return trip. James Brown don't see no more writers. They were coming down here by the busload till a few weeks ago, fans too, but they all went away empty-handed. That roly-poly preacher from New York seen to that."

I ask Gus if he means the Reverend Al Sharpton, whose agitation on behalf of James Brown and his recent troubles with the law made headlines down here last month. A former protegé (Brown "discovered" the preteen Reverend Al in St. Albans, Queens, in the mid-1960s), Sharpton brought the Tawana Brawley family for a celebrity visit with Brown after their angry pilgrimage to the Atlanta Democratic Convention last summer, then returned to South Carolina by himself a month ago to attend Brown's trial. Gus, who's been fairly taciturn the whole ride up, lets out with a riptide at Sharpton's name.

"That loud round mound of sound! He was standing on the courthouse steps in Aiken, day after the trial, holding onto Adrienne Brown and them ancient photographs of President Bush and Mr. Brown and him, talking racist verdicts, media circuses, and whatnot, making that bogus offer to serve James Brown's time for him. He was here in Columbia over Christmas too, holding his candlelight vigil in front of the prison with his lawyer buddy, Perry Mason, trying to stir up the ministers. They wouldn't give him the time of day. People here say that James Brown got his day in court, and more. Got to be every time you turned around, him and that wife is acting up. Time and again they let them off, time, time again he's shooting something up. People behaving like that—pistols, drugs, shotguns. Me and you'd have got all 30 years he was looking at, that's for sure."

Gus gets mollified as we coast past the rolling green lawns and maples hedging the State Park driveway and stop in front of what he calls the "nursing home." A jet of steam is coming out of the ventilation duct of a block-long hospital to the left; a tacky gift shop on our right is open, even though it's Super Bowl Sunday. Down a series of stone stairways strewn with ivy is the dirty red-brick prison, looking more like a 1940s-era subway station on the Grand Concourse than a penal institution.

"Still I feel for the man," Gus says as I get out. "'Cause it was the wife who drove him to it. Filing them charges for assaulting her, filing them divorce papers, saying his men planted them PCPs they bust her with all them times, setting fire to their hotel room. She done him in, that's for sure."

•

On December 17, 1988, an Aiken, South Carolina, judge sentenced James Brown, probably the most influential black musician of all time, to six years in prison for aggravated assault (reduced from two counts of assault with intent to kill) and for running a blue light (failing to stop for an officer's signal). Brown's targets, South Carolina police officers William Luckey and Ronald DeLaughter, had pulled him over 20 minutes into a two-state, 80-mph car chase that had begun outside the James Brown Enterprises office building in Augusta, Georgia, shortly after noon on September 24. Armed with a shotgun and allegedly under the influence, Brown had berated 40 people attending an insurance seminar in an adjoining building for using his rest rooms, then eluded two

Georgia police officers on the chase back to his estate in Beech Island, South Carolina. I've come down to watch his trial in Augusta—for the Georgia half of the chase and for a second arrest the following morning—at which Brown will be looking at 12 more years on nine charges: carrying a deadly weapon to a public gathering, carrying a weapon without a license, driving under the influence (PCP), assault, and related misdemeanors.

The Aiken trial was the fourth time in 12 months Brown has appeared before a South Carolina court on criminal charges, all, in one way or another, involving cars, PCP, or guns. Two 1987 arrests resulted in indictments for speeding, eluding arrest, and leaving the scene of an accident. On Easter Monday, 1988, he was arrested after allegedly beating his wife Adrienne with an iron pipe and emptying his pistol into her car's trunk as she tried to flee their house. (She eventually dropped the charges.) Six weeks later, he spent another night in an Aiken County jail before a $24,218 bond was posted on charges of assault (his wife again), possession of a pistol, PCP possession, running blue lights, and resisting arrest; he was given 30 months, probated to a concert benefiting local charities. The IRS, a 20-year nemesis, is suing him for $9 million in taxes, penalties, and interest—two years after he was forced to auction his Beech Island estate for back taxes. (Brown's Atlanta lawyer, Buddy Dallas, purchased the estate and now rents it back to him as a trustee for his two daughters from his second marriage.)

Though Brown has been indicted for more than 45 years worth of felonies and misdemeanors in the past year, local authorities say he could probably petition to have his current sentence commuted to a half-year spent in drug rehabilitation. Brown, however, resolutely maintains that he is being mistreated by the law, and says that he has no drug problem.

•

Mister Brown, as he insists on being called, has always been a law unto himself. After a childhood spent in a shack in a South Carolina woods, an Augusta brothel, then a series of reform schools and prisons, he emerged as one of the great, if at times more confusing, voices of righteousness in the '60s. Claimed and

rebuked by both sides of almost every issue of the decade, he was
clearly motivated by his own, innate sense of the law, an understanding he was able to express in two words: pride and power. At
a Black Power conference in 1967, Leroi Jones called him "our No.
1 black poet"; during the Memphis-to-Mississippi march in
support of James Meredith a year earlier, Stokely Carmichael
offended him with the label "the man most dangerous to the
Movement." In retrospect, both seem to have been correct: In
1968, Brown alienated the left by touring Vietnam; later that year
he terrified the right with "Say it Loud, I'm Black and I'm Proud."
After a coveted endorsement of Humphrey in 1968, he became a
far more active campaigner for Nixon's 1972 re-election.

Only the jukebox provided consensus: James Brown's singles hit
the top of the pop charts for more years than Elvis and the Beatles
combined, and though he never tried to cross over into the inte-
grated record-buying market he and Motown helped create, he
outperformed every act that did, hitting the charts 114 times
(Aretha Franklin had 84 hits, by way of comparison, Ray Charles
81 and the Temptations 76). Among the handful of performers
who arose unfiltered out of what was once openly called race
music, he was one of the few to escape death on the road, death by
overdose, death in prison, the living death of golden-oldie status,
or the retreat into the obscure immortality of gospel. Ten years .
before disco digitalized his beat, 20 before rappers appropriated
his hooks and screams and lyrics, he anticipated the future of black
music by stripping his sound to its rhythmic elements, blueprinting
Pan-African pop, a worldwide explosion against which the Beatles
and Stones are gradually being recognized as rather circumscribed,
Anglo phenomena. "Every time we landed in Africa," says Anne
Weston, who sang for the James Brown Revue from 1977 to 1981,
"you'd look down from a mile up and see the runway moving—
hundreds of thousands of people, literally, waiting for James
Brown's plane to land."

Brown's fight to retain control of the business of his own music
has been far less chronicled, though it was an idea he all but introduced to the industry. Well before Paisley Park and even Abbey

Road, he successfully sued for control of his master tapes (he kept them in a bag that never left his side), independently produced both himself and his sidemen, and for decades financed hundreds of recordings and ventures with his artist's and royalty earnings—occasionally fronting the entire budgets for projects like 1962's "Live at the Apollo," probably the most influential concert album in pop history.

Far too often, however, he borrowed from his labels against future earnings, a practice that cost dearly as earnings dropped off in the late 1970s. He now owes Polygram about $2 million, by one of his lawyer's estimates, and has little chance of repaying it: Michael Jackson (who auditioned for Motown's Berry Gordy 20 years ago by dancing to James Brown's "I Got the Feelin'") owns all publishing rights to Brown's songs (as well as the Beatles' and Little Richard's); and rappers, who sample him to death and pay homage in their music and interviews, refuse to pay him cash. Though money has clearly been at issue in his recent troubles, at 56, with little more than his current music to support him, Brown manages, somehow, to make it work: His "Living in America" hit #4 on the pop charts in 1984, and in 1988 only Sade's "Paradise" stopped him from topping the r&b charts for the eighteenth time.

•

When the first, relatively minor charges against Brown hit the wire services, there were predictable snickers about the pillar of black capitalism, the high-minded singer of "King Heroin," "Don't Be a Dropout," and "America is My Home," having misdemeanor troubles with the local authorities. After the Easter shooting of his wife's car (and the gruesome detail of the iron pipe) landed him onto the tabloid covers, however, the media began chronicling an endless string of marital incidents:

Adrienne files for divorce in March 1988, citing years of cruel treatment, showing a *National Enquirer* photographer bruises on her face and torso and bullet holes in their bedroom walls.

In April, Adrienne, arrested at Augusta's airport with eight grams of PCP, says it was planted by men hired by her husband to pressure her to drop her divorce suit.

In early May, Brown tells reporters that his wife set fire to his clothes in their hotel room in Bedford, New Hampshire, shortly after she is arraigned on charges of arson and PCP possession (seven ounces this time). "My wife's a real stinker," he tells an Augusta reporter when they return home. "She sets rooms on fire. She's a brat."

Four days later, Adrienne places an emergency call to the police, and Brown is captured a mile into a high-speed chase beginning at his driveway, which a green street sign proclaims—a la Graceland—JAMES BROWN BOULEVARD. "He was letting that Lincoln sail," says the Beech Island police captain. "We thought it was a B-17 coming out of that driveway." Brown claims his wife planted the seven grams of PCP he is arrested with.

Two days later, Adrienne is arrested at Augusta's airport for possession of eight ounces of PCP "The Godfather of Soul isn't what he pretends to be," she tells sheriff's deputies, again insisting she was set up. "He warns young people to stay off drugs, but he doesn't practice what he preaches to children. He's high on drugs, PCP, angel dust ..."

And on it went to court: indictments; bench warrants; missed court dates; a motion filed by Adrienne's lawyer to have her September 7, 1987 speeding, DUI (driving under the influence), and criminal trespass charges waived on grounds of diplomatic immunity (her husband, she stipulates, is the Ambassador of Soul); a suit filed by Adrienne's lawyer for $4,500 of legal fees incurred in making that motion; and then convictions—for weapons possession, PCP possession, resisting arrest, assault. The Browns, obviously under the strain of severe financial, domestic, health, career, and legal problems, were airing too many in public, and the media was waiting. "You know I love my wife," Brown assured a local reporter after one of his assault arrests. "I love you too, as a brother in friendship." Asked why Adrienne had made such serious accusations and set fire to his clothes, Brown, never one to waste words, summed it all up in four: "Love's a funny thing."

•

At the door of the prison, a gangly, red-haired guard in short sleeves and a handlebar mustache wants to know just where the hell I think I'm going. I explain I'm going to see James Brown, and he places a meaty hand around the entirety of my left elbow, and says, "No, you ain't neither." He gets a big kick out of the fact I've come all the way from New York, big enough to turn me around and lead me to a tiny guardhouse at the edge of the compound. One of his colleagues thinks that's too rich not to share with the lieutenant in the prison office.

Now on my second day in the New South, I'm surprised to see the lieutenant is a black man, and clearly in control of the prison, which he's quick to inform me is not a prison but a correctional facility. Stroking his salt-and-pepper mustache, he lists all the ordinances I've violated by coming as far as I have, then instructs the red-haired guard to escort me to my vehicle, making sure no one congregates with me in the meantime. At the top of the stairs, the guard begins explaining the fine points of maintaining security at such a correctional facility; he's a corrections officer, for example, not a guard; Mr. Brown is an inmate, not a prisoner; and I will certainly be placed in custody, he assures me, if apprehended at the facility again. I get a powerful, anomalous whiff of cosmetics as the guard lifts me a few paces to the side by my elbow and a chunky, raven-haired woman in a sable coat—Adrienne Brown—edges past. In her right hand is a plate of food under Saran Wrap, featuring a mammoth piece of coconut cake; tucked under her left arm is a huge, salon-style hairdryer, its long white nozzle whizzing through the ivy as she negotiates the steps on a pair of spike heels.

A cloying odor of Thai stick fills Gus's cab as I climb in the back, and he's giggling mischievously, stopping long enough to assure me the guard was just having some fun with me. He lapses into a strange fit of chuckling and coughing as we head to the airport; ten minutes later, he's still laughing so hard he can't get the roach of his joint lit. "Just thinking about that poor man," he apologizes, gunning the cab across a double yellow line onto the airport highway. "Checks into that nursing home for six years, and he still can't get away from his wife. Guess that's why they call 'em housekeepers," he guffaws, going 20 mph over the highway speed limit. "They always keep the house."

•

Whoever gave PCP the nickname "angel dust" was looking at the ephemera through the wrong end of the telescope. Phencyclidine, an animal tranquilizer, is a diabolic substance, attractive only to those interested in testing the extremes of physical and emotional experience—the limits, more specifically, of their control. Variously mislabeled a narcotic, hallucinogen, or psychotropic, PCP is known to produce psychotic reactions even in the smallest doses and cases of dust-induced homicide are legion.

"James Brown certainly never had a drug problem till he remarried," says Bob Patton, his tour and booking manager through the '60s and late '70s. "But he has one now. He's been smoking a joint or two of PCP a day, probably more the last year or so." Patton, like everyone I talk to who knows Brown well, insists he is not a violent or a high-strung man. "He is a paranoid man though, even without the drug. It was paranoia that was driving him on that chase. I think he was terrified. He had a gun, he was being chased by policemen across state lines, he was stoned out of his mind, and the police in South Carolina overreacted. How often does your average South Carolina policeman get a chance to pull a gun on James Brown, smash in his windows?"

Brown's singer Anne Weston also attributes the recent arrests "directly to PCP. Since the marriage to Adrienne, the drugs have been really bad, and I think he's been getting some awful stuff lately. I can't say when he started smoking, or how often. It was only onstage that you could tell when he was off, out of control, which is always a sure sign with James. Normally, he's totally in control. By 1981, when the Revue started heading downhill, it was clear he was slipping. I think his smoking then was recreational, and he could control it. Not anymore."

In a September 27 interview given in his Executive Park office to Linda Day, a staff writer for the *Augusta Chronicle-Herald*, Brown, his lower teeth missing and his cheeks Scotch-taped together below his chin (a home remedy for slack jaw after reconstructive surgery for a degenerative jaw disease), said he'd begun "substance control" treatment. Two days after twice being arrested DUI, Brown seemed out of control and still under the influence of something.

Asked about the shotgun-brandishing incident at the insurance seminar, for example, he replied: "I went to my gospel office, that I have, that I own. [Brown, too encumbered with IRS liens to own property, actually rents his office space.] Went to the gospel office and it was open, and they were using my rest rooms without saying, 'May I use it?' So then, I want to know, do I own something, or am I just kidding myself? I mean, what do I own here, or what do I control? I mean, do I control anything? Can't accept that. The last name is Brown ... Now, when I can't do that ... never do I want to exist anymore. A problem I have, you have problems ... We all have problems. Exactly why the Bible says to take the Sabbath Day to ask God's forgiveness of our problems and our sins, because we're human. We're not God. We're human. And he has saints down here that he designates for different programs. He called John, He called Job, He took Moses out of the bull—away from his sheep. He said, 'You must go.' He said, 'I can't go, I can't speak the language.' 'I will fix it so you can speak all the languages. But you will go.' But the Lord, who controls everything, knowing that he has the final say-so, He has the key to everyone, body, tongue, the devil, everybody, He did not take it upon His almighty power to rule. He called Aaron and the three wise men. Said, 'I need some help here. We have a roundtable discussion, like the United Nations.' Now God, who controls nothing before him, don't make the decision, how you gonna make that decision on me? I need help. I accept that. We all need help. Can we accept the ridiculing or the formalness? Go get you one. When I tell my Daddy I don't disagree, he get offended. Why? 'I'm your father.' I have my own mind. When you go to the rest room, I can be seated and you use it by yourself. When I go to the rest room, you can't go in there, so you be seated. When you eat I don't taste it. What you eat don't make me fat or lean. Independence is all I'm asking for. The word is spelled F-R-E-E-D-O-M. Nothing more I need to say. I rest my case. And I'm not going to say the devil made me do it. Stress made me do it. S-T-R-E-S-S! Emphasize it three times. S-T-R-E-S-S! S-T-R-E-S-S! One more time, S-T-R-E-S-S!"

Brown was more succinct when asked if he felt he owed the people of Augusta an apology. "I apologize," he said, "for the unawareness of what I was about. I apologize for the discomfort I caused you. I apologize for simply saying I love you. Just let me pass."

"James will talk like that from time to time," said Anne Weston. "It can be brilliant, poetic. You can only sit back and let him flow. But not like that. That's a very different James Brown. That's PCP talking."

I asked Bob Patton why a man like Brown would be attracted to PCP. "He's not attracted to it," Patton said. "He's addicted. He thinks it gives him power. James Brown has lost a lot of power."

•

Toccoa is a sleepy, once-pretty town lying in the foothills of the Blue Ridge Mountains in northern Georgia Except for a deserted, picturesque downtown that never modernized, there's not much to recommend it. A dusty travel brochure from the tourist office at the state line shows waterfalls and old Baptist churches and some quaint streets with white picket fences, but those are gone now, replaced by housing developments, desolate burger strips and malls with garbage blowing in the wind. Even the Baptist churches have been relocated into ugly, white-block two-story buildings abutting the chain stores in the malls.

In 1949, Brown was sentenced to a dilapidated reform school in Rome, Georgia, for stealing clothes out of a car in the middle of winter with three other boys. That school was condemned a year into his term, and Brown was transferred to the Boy's Industrial Institute, a disused paratrooper camp in Toccoa, where he served another year before his release. A local kid named Bobby Byrd, who'd gone out to the prison to trade gospel licks over the wire fence with the talented singer he'd heard about, got his mother to arrange parole in custody of a local Oldsmobile dealer, who gave Brown a job sweeping out his lot and waxing cars; a childless couple who ran the town barbershop took him in to live and to go to church with them. He sang in the choir, married a fellow chorister named Velma Warren, sired three children, and joined

Bobby Byrd in the Gospel Starlighters, the nucleus of the original Famous Flames. Mostly, he spent his days in Bill's Rendezvous, a tavern owned by a savvy woman named Delois Keith.

"James would practically open the place," Keith tells me, "so he could bang on the piano all day. He'd sweep out the place too, so he could bang on the piano some more. He had a beautiful gospel voice, but he was getting a taste for rhythm and blues, which is what happened at the Rendezvous at night. They'd been doing a little r&b when Little Richard came through with his band. It was at that point they decided spirituals was maybe a little too slow a path. Next time Richard came by here, James was running circles around him. He had people screaming, on the floor. Before long, they were touring. Every night a different place. It went on for years like that, till they finally moved on up to Macon, then up north after 'Please, Please, Please' made it so big in '56, even though the song didn't really have but the one word."

Guy Wilson, whom I've come to Toccoa to see, loaned Brown's band an old white station wagon they could "tour" in: one-nighters in bars within a 30-mile radius, occasionally venturing up to Macon, 70 miles away. A gentle man now in his late sixties, occasionally ephasiac from recent laser surgery for a brain tumor, he greets me at the door and seats me in his easy chair to watch the Super Bowl on his 25-inch TV.

"I was lucky I had insurance on that station wagon," he tells me at halftime, "'cause James was always a menace when it came to cars. That two-state chase was hardly the first of his car troubles. He lost his job at the car dealership when he totaled one of them on a joyride, and he had a ton of other wrecks. Almost lost his parole a couple of times. His son Teddy died in a car, too. But that was long after James had left Toccoa. He was back here for the funeral. They had to rent the second floor of a building just to put all the flowers that came in from the politicians and famous entertainers."

I ask Mr. Wilson if Brown came back often after he'd made it big. "All the time," he says. "This is where his family was, even if he and Velma'd broken up. James was first and last a family man. He was a proud man, and a good one, too, always handing out $10 bills every time he came around. See, when he first came to Toccoa he was a 20-year-old boy who'd been kicked out of Augusta—they wouldn't even let him go back and perform there. He'd lost what family he had, gone to prison. When he left Toccoa, he was a well-respected man. He left with his head held high, and always came back. Though maybe not so much since that last marriage."

Guy watches the second-half kickoff before continuing: "Only once or twice with the new wife. So, I was surprised when I heard James was in all that trouble, but not when I heard about the car stuff. It's like what they're always saying, right? 'Once a man, twice a child.'"

He walks me out to the car after the game, commiserating on my long drive ahead to Augusta. The temperature's dropped a good 20 degrees, but Guy, wearing only a thin cardigan over his shirt, seems to have one last thing he wants to say, but can't remember. "James never had any kind of luck in that town," he finally says. "He left there a poor boy and he came back a rich man. Time beat him back down, but he was on his way back to the top when all that trouble started up for him again. Still, I guess he should have known better, and it's true they let him off all them times. It's like what they say, right?" Guy winks at me when I start the car, apparently remembering what he's wanted to say: "The victim always returns to the scene of the crime."

•

Augusta is a three-hour drive from Toccoa along the South Carolina-Georgia border on Highway 17, an endless strip of road connecting towns with names testifying to their rural isolation: Black Well, Pignail, Lost Mountain. The only thing that holds this monotony of farmland and pine forest together is the radio, which is a veritable House of Music down here, built from the bottom up: gospel, bluegrass, jazz, and Delta blues filling the 80s on the dial, rockabilly, early Stones, and Broadway show tunes in the low 90s, everything from Vanilla Fudge to Simply Red for the rest of the dial, a few staticky stations playing rap and funk up at the top. Dotted throughout, of course, is country—the music Brown grew up hating as the sound "playing on the radio of every white man I ever worked for"—everything from Hoyt Axton's "Work your fingers to the bone/What do you get?/Bony fingers" to Loretta Lynn lamenting that "Success has made a failure of our home," to Hank Williams, Jr., bragging about how country boys can survive.

If you drive around these tidy, dirt-poor towns, you'll find your way into the black parts, and the only signs of life past nine p.m., a combination package store/bar, usually with more men standing outside than in, despite the weather, and invariably lit by some half-broken red neon logo. In the '50s and early '60s, these bars formed the Chitlin' Circuit, the subject of Brown's 1962 hit "Night Train": a 1000-mile swath of juke joints from Washington, D.C. to Macon to Jackson to Miami. In cars like Guy Wilson's station wagon, Brown put in tens of thousands of miles along roads like Highway 17 during the decade he and fellow travelers like Little Richard, Otis Redding, Little Willie John, Sam Cooke, Gladys Knight, etc., were inventing rhythm and blues. Brown eventually went his own musical way, working, stretching, and "scratching" every instrument (including his voice) to "get the funky job done," as he later put it, but for almost ten years his was one of the most powerful, versatile blues voices ever heard, screaming and crooning in coloratura range through songs like "Try Me," "Don't Let it Happen to Me," "You Got the Power," "Lost Someone."

On a line with Greenville, South Carolina, I pick up the legendary County Earl, "broadcasting way past my bedtime," and spend the next hour listening to his rare Bob Wills, Tennessee Plowboy, and Shorty Long singles, learning the best place to buy boiled peanuts on Highway 25 ("tell 'em Country Earl sent you and get an extra ounce for free"). At the Augusta Corporate Line, I begin to lose him while he's reading a letter from a reverend in Sky City, who says he's thinking about getting wed after all these years. Earl plays him a warning, George Jones and Tammy Wynette singing about life in the "Two-Story House" they could only dream of when young and poor: "I got my story," sings Tammy, "And I got mine," George responds, and they join for the refrain: "How sad it is we live in a two-story house."

A couple of stations up the dial, an Augusta deejay with an overripe sense of humor is playing some early singles with themes of confinement and bad love by way of announcing James Brown's trial tomorrow morning. The beauty and power of the voice turns the intended irony to sheer pathos:

> *I need no shackles to remind me*
> *I'm just a prisoner*
> *Don't let me be a prisoner*
> *You made me a prisoner*
> *When you made me love you.*

In 1970, the year after Governor Lester Maddox requested that he come down to help quell the riots in Augusta, James Brown returned to live here. He bought one of the biggest houses with one of the biggest yards on Walton Way, the town's Easy Street, and remained for over a decade on the edges of Old Town, Augusta's four-by-six block testimonial to the pleasures of Old Money, with its immense gingerbread houses and Lincolns and BMWs parked, unlocked, on its heavily landscaped avenues. "It got a little ugly when James bought the house," remembers Bobby Byrd, who moved to Augusta shortly after Brown. "A lot of talk going on ... petitions, some unfriendly offers to buy the house at twice what James paid. Gradually, though, the people in the houses on both sides started talking over the fence, you know how it is, coming over and getting him to sign records for their kids. I can't say, though, if James was ever really accepted in Augusta. I moved out after a few months myself."

Down the street from the old house is the Law Enforcement Center, which Brown has entered in markedly different ways over the years: in family court for divorce proceedings and custody battles with his second wife, Deedee; at the governor's request 10 years before.

The first visit came in 1949, two months after his arrest for stealing clothes from a car. Though Brown had escaped arrest the night of the crime, two officers were waiting the next day at his shoeshine stand on Broad Street. He outran them, ducking in and out of alleys he knew better, then returned, to elude them again. When he returned to the stand later that afternoon, a squad car was waiting, soon to be joined by others; after a short chase he was cornered in a blind alley and arrested at gunpoint by a majority of the Augusta police force. Still not sixteen, Brown, who later remembered these chases as a game, spent the difference in the Fifteenth Street Prison, and was tried as an adult. After 15 minutes before the bench, he was given eight to 16 years hard labor.

There are two men here, a county clerk downstairs and a bailiff, who go back far enough to remember George Haines, the solicitor who prosecuted the 16-year-old Brown. A grandiloquent orator with a passion for the maximum sentence, Haines had the habit of bringing a suitcase to court and announcing he'd leave town if the defendant were found not guilty, then standing at the exit door, suitcase in hand, while the judge pronounced sentence. Neither recalls Brown's trial, or if he got the suitcase treatment, but both remember feeling the irony of a show they saw in the early '60s, which ended with Brown—already "The Hardest Working Man in Show Business"—clutching a black suitcase with the words TRY ME stenciled in white across the front as he was dragged offstage "against his will" by members of his entourage.

The suitcase days are over, both for Brown and his prosecutors: With the windows open on this unseasonably warm day, one can hear the whoosh of tennis balls from a court on a higher level of the building, and State Court Solicitor Robert W. "Bo" Hunter III, conferring at the courtroom door with Brown's lawyers, Buddy Dallas and John W. "Bill" Weeks, looks like he stepped out of last week's episode of "L.A. Law." The absence of Al Sharpton, a sure sign Brown will plead out and not ask for a jury, is one of two topics of discussion among the press seated in the first few rows of the gallery, the other being the wording of an ambiguously dated "EXCLUSIVE INTERVIEW: BROWN BEHIND BARS" in this morning's USA Today. Buried at the end is a fantastic quote: "I'm the Einstein of Sound, the Napoleon of the Stage. I can still dance three times faster than anyone else—and I can keep it up for two hours. I can roll out of my bed and sing. I am James Brown, twenty-four hours a day, and they can't take that away."

I notice a tiny woman in her mid-seventies with a striking resemblance to James Brown in the back of the courtroom, paying close attention to the proceedings, and go introduce myself. "I'm James's mother," she tells me, then writes her address in Bamberg, South Carolina—very carefully—inviting me to visit any time. "Now, though," she says with a familiar, cleft-chin smile, "I have to keep an eye out for my boy."

James Brown is #1 on the docket today, the list of his charges taking up a third of the first page of the court calendar. I watch the 20 or so five-minute DUI and speeding trials that go on while his is temporarily adjourned: Each man, head bowed, stands before Justice Hamrick while one of the six Assistant D.A.s, rising from the prosecutor's desk, cites previous arrests, notes the defendant has decided to waive his right to a trial by jury, then recommends sentence. The judge calls each defendant by name only once: "Mr. Snopes, don't drink and drive," before coming to what increasingly seems like the sole point of the proceedings: "How is the defendant disposed today for the payment of fine?" To Justice Hamrick's embarrassment, Mr. Snopes, a short, acne-scarred man in his mid-30s, wearing jeans that barely make it to the top of his white socks, a heavily starched white shirt, and a clip-on tie, pulls out a wad of fives and tens and begins counting his way toward $350 before the bailiff can lead him to the jury bench to sign his Plea and Waiver along with the other defendants.

Adrienne Brown, accompanied by a lawyer, makes her appearance in the courtroom, and a battery of TV cameras, tape recorders, and cameras loaded with 3200 ASA film start rolling and clicking. A pretty, stocky 38-year-old woman with a hard-earned reputation for being high-strung, she seems regal today: A two-inch diamond broach glinting on the lapel of her camel-colored, mink-trimmed skirt suit, she endures her bench trial without wasting a word or gesture. Listening carefully while her lawyer and Assistant D.A. itemize her pleas and waivers to the DUI, speeding, and criminal trespass charges arising from her 1987 arrest, she examines her three-inch nails while the two men attest to their personal knowledge of her law-abiding nature, of which the prosecution seems far more well-versed: The influence she had been driving under, he explains, was simply the "high end of the therapeutic level of butalbitol," a painkiller prescribed following a hysterectomy and colon surgery; and "that little criminal trespass charge" (incurred when she took a nail file to the back of the police on the way to jail) is estimated at "about $75 worth of upholstery damage to the vehicle," and hardly worth prosecuting. She gets off lightly: a $650 fine, limited attendance at the DUI course, $75 restitution for the squad car. As she's led to the emptied jury box to fill out her paperwork, the cameras and tape recorders are shut off, and one of the younger reporters is sent to ask her A.D.A. how to spell butalbitol.

Everything is switched back on a minute later when James Brown enters the courtroom, looking like the negative of a Matthew Brady portrait of a plantation owner: a black three-piece suit with epaulettes and wide lapels, black bowtie knotted loosely under the collar of a maroon silk shirt, black patent leather shoes gleaming under the camera lights, a huge, immaculately coiffed shock of processed hair framing his head. Standing casually before Justice Hamrick, flanked by lawyers for both sides, holding a pair of zippered black leather racing gloves behind his back, he looks far less like an imprisoned man than a Sunday motorist who's impatient to get back outside to his Excalibur. He clearly is not having an easy time countenancing his presence here: While the charges are read and pleas announced—guilty to everything except handgun possession (dropped for lack of evidence) and *no lo contendre* to the drug charge—he shakes his head, a slow, stereotype motion he keeps up as Solicitor Hunter advises the court that the State wants only some period of incarceration and as Buddy Dallas talks briefly and dreamily about his intimacy with the defendant, followed by a few exculpatory remarks about "this old shotgun Mr. Brown clearly never intended to threaten anybody with." The headshaking stops when his South Carolina lawyer, Bill Weeks, begins to speak for Brown, which he does with conviction: "Sometimes it takes a knock on the head before you get someone's attention," he tells Hamrick. "Well, South Carolina certainly gave him a knock on the head, Your Honor. Very honestly, I think they laid a heavy hammer on him."

Adrienne, her head turned away from the proceedings, looks out of the corner of her eyes when Brown is asked if he'd like to say anything on his own behalf. In an almost inaudible rasp, he tells the judge that it hurts, especially for a man of his beginnings, to appear in court this way. Not even the most sensitive tape recorder in the room picks up the remainder of his speech, however, and he becomes intelligible only as he concludes: "My life has always been a model, and I just don't feel good about it at all ... I hope this is behind us."

There is some disappointment among reporters hoping for an encore of the melodrama that accompanied the South Carolina trial: Brown telling the D.A. he loved him, then attempting to take the Fifth after agreeing to testify; the judge admonishing Adrienne, sitting in the gallery, for "prejudicing the interests of the defendant" by whispering loudly and making gestures; the testimony of a young man who'd driven 200 miles to tell the court that "God has set this man on the earth ... as an example for all men to follow"; and surprise testimony from the court bailiff, a former evangelist, who asked to take the stand and tell the court that God Himself had placed him in the court to meet a "star like James Brown": "If Satan throws us out," the bailiff testified, "God will take us back."

The Augusta sentence is read off quickly: Amounting to six and a half years, it's to be served concurrently, but for the additional six months, with his South Carolina time. The sentence, as lenient as could be hoped for, seems to disgust Brown. Leaning against the railing of the judge's bench with one hand, the other held statesmanlike at his hip, he looks over a shoulder to scowl at the entire court, giving the D.A. bench and the gallery an "I've wasted enough time in this place" hate-look before pivoting smoothly on one heel and gliding out the door.

•

James Brown's father brought him from South Carolina to Augusta in 1938, at the age of five, and for 10 years he lived in various relatives' houses in what is still, in less than polite society, called the Terry—short for Negro Territory—a 130-block range of closed businesses and ancient one- and two-story houses that run the gamut from abjectly poor to uninhabitable. Until the age of nine, he lived in a bar/whorehouse at 944 Twiggs Street, owned by his aunt, Honey Washington, a fearless woman who ran her establishment with open contempt for the Augusta police, who extorted her on a monthly basis and closed her down almost as frequently.

On Twiggs Street, a desolate, barracks-like 1940s-era housing project stands where 944 used to be. Mrs. Nunnally, an aproned woman who comes to the door of one of the well-scrubbed, dilapidated houses across the street, remembers Honey, but little about James Brown. "He was just one of those kids, you know the kind, sort of lives on the street. Especially after the police closed up Honey's place for good in the '40s. My husband," she says, nodding disgustedly down the street at a wiry man dragging a tar bucket up to the house, "can tell you about James Brown. I think they were in prison together or something. Finally, I get all the war stories confused."

"Back in '48," Robert Nunnally tells me reluctantly, leaning against the one unbroken spot of his peeling wooden fence as he lights up the last of his Pall Malls, "me and James were in prison together, that's true." With his hair processed slick, his 57-year-old body pure muscle and tar stains after 30 years as a roofer, Nunnally could easily play the doppelgänger in a film about Brown: Though they came from the same street, the path of Brown's life led him far away, if by force at first, and Nunnally seems more than a little bitter about the course his own life has taken. "I can't tell you much more about him, because he's been on the road," he says. "I just stayed here."

Nunnally gets angry when I ask if he was one of the kids who got caught stealing clothes from a car on Broad Street with James Brown. "I never stole a damn thing in my life. No, what happened with me," he says remorselessly, "is I shot a man when I was 16. But I stayed in the Fifteenth Street Prison—it was a state prison then—digging ditches, working behind the dragline. James got moved away, and I didn't see him for 20 years."

I ask if he remembers Brown before the arrests. "Sure I do. And it's true he was a thief, seemed to always have half his body under the hood of someone's car. But look around," he says, nodding at the empty blocks leading off Twiggs Street. "Nothing's changed around here since then. James wasn't stealing for pleasure. And he wasn't no violent man. That's why I can't understand those assault charges."

"Have you seen much of Brown in the last few years?"

"All the time," Nunnally says proudly. "James comes around regularly, handing out $20 bills. At least until he got arrested. That's why he moved back to Augusta. Here's where he comes from, where his family was, where his people are. Here on Twiggs," he says, marking the spot by grinding his cigarette underfoot. "And by the bars on Ninth Street. Not on no goddamn Walton Way."

•

"You have to remember that the events Brown is taking all this heat for happened in the space of one hour," Bill Weeks tells me outside the courthouse in Aiken, South Carolina. "And it was a freakish hour—as in a 'freak accident.'"

A six-ten, soft-spoken man who chooses his words precisely and well, Weeks fills me in on the details of the chase, most of which somehow never came out in the trials or news reports. Later that day, I clock the route, a 10-mile stretch of city, suburban, and interstate road passing 11 housing complexes, six large shopping malls, 11 small ones, 12 Baptist churches, 13 gas stations, 11 car lots, 19 burger joints, 15 fried chicken stands, and three weapons shops.

Brown, carrying his shotgun, entered the insurance seminar in the Executive Park building at 12:20 p.m. and asked to use the microphone. "He was sweating, his hair was messed up," says Dory Gonzales, a woman sitting in the first row. "His shirt was open, his T-shirt was exposed. He was not making sense." Brown demanded to be told who'd been using his rest rooms. Learning it was a licensing seminar, he also asked how to get a driver's license (his had been suspended). "I thought that if I answered one of those questions wrong," said Jerri Phillips, who was conducting the seminar, "he was going to kill me and everyone else...." A Columbia County sheriff named Gilbert Lopez, attending the seminar, claims to have been more amazed than frightened. He says he initially failed to react as a peace officer because he "couldn't believe somebody would come into a room with 40 people with a shotgun. It seemed to me he was not in his right mind."

Brown asked two women to accompany him to the rest room, leaving the shotgun behind in the insurance seminar. Lopez went out to his car to get his .45, and was walking back toward the building when he saw Brown come out the front door, holding his shotgun. "I didn't want to approach him," Lopez said. "I figured someone might get hurt." Brown got into his red-and-white Ford pickup, Lopez got into his car, and Brown followed him out of the parking lot. A police car came toward the building, flashing its lights. Brown made a U-turn, drove back to the building, stopped, and took his truck out of gear. When the police car, driven by a Lieutenant Overstreet, pulled up behind him, Brown took off, the tires of his pickup screeching as he turned onto Claussen Road. He made a left on Washington Street and raced three miles to Interstate 20, with Overstreet hot in pursuit.

"After all this stuff happened that I don't know verbatim what happened," Brown said in his interview four days later, "God said, 'Boy, go home.' I got in my truck and I tried to go home. Then the police began to chase me. They would literally not let me go home, where I just wanted to close the gates, lock the door, and don't come out till the next day."

"I know James was high at this point," says Bobby Byrd. "And I'm sure he was probably figuring that, once he got into South Carolina, he could find his way along the back roads, which he knows better than anybody. He really didn't know what he was doing. But in his mind, if I know James, he was heading home."

A mile onto Interstate 20, Brown stopped a second time for Overstreet. When the policeman pulled over and got out of the car, however, Brown took off again. He was up to 80 mph as he drove past the 25-foot-high SOUTH CAROLINA WELCOMES YOU sign, and back up to 60 mph 100 yards after negotiating the S-curve ramp of the Martindale Road exit in North Augusta, South Carolina.

Seeing the flashing lights of Officer Ronald DeLaughter's car at a hastily set-up road-block half a minute later, Brown floored it, again getting up to 80 mph before he saw the second blue light, of Officer William Luckey's car, and pulled into the lot of an abandoned filling station across from the Exxon at Martindale and Atomic Roads.

The Exxon attendant says he didn't see what happened across the street, so there's only the testimony of Brown and the two policemen to go on. While DeLaughter began questioning Brown at the window of his truck, Luckey tried to open the passenger door, which was locked. "I was getting ready to get out," Brown testified at the Aiken trial, "when he [Luckey] started beating on the door and the window ... glass went everywhere, and I knew he was enraged."

Luckey says he jumped away from the truck when he saw a shotgun in the passenger set—strange testimony from an officer responding to a call about an armed suspect. The truck bolted backward a foot as Brown got it in gear and gunned it forward; Luckey claims Brown was trying to run him down. As Brown pumped it, DeLaughter, Luckey, and two other officers who'd arrived on the scene began firing—some 25 rounds, 18 of which connected: two hit the truck's gas tank, others punctured the front tires, and five more from the rear blew out the back tires and window. "I was scared to death," Brown later said. "I went to Vietnam, and I was never that frightened."

By the time Brown reached the Fifth Street Bridge, leading across the Savannah River back into Augusta, his tires were nonexistent, he had eight squad cars behind him, and his truck was doing 30 mph, flat out. He got off the highway onto Walton Way, four blocks up from his old house, then looped around and headed back four blocks.

The victim always returns to the scene of the crime: Two long avenue blocks up from his old shoeshine stand, Brown made a right onto Broad Street, then headed through Old Town, sparks shooting from the rims he'd been driving on for almost a mile. He skidded and careened past the mayor's house on Third Street, and managed somehow to keep control of the truck as he finally made it across East Boundary Street and back into the Terry.

Once a man, twice a child. Forty years after Brown had baited police three times to chase him through the back alleys of Augusta, he was doing it again. With 14 cars now flashing blue lights behind him, he made two rights and kept going for almost a mile, down to less than 10 mph, until his brakes locked and the truck skidded across the street. He landed in a shallow ditch, facing backwards, a little more than half a mile from Twiggs Road.

At the deputy's office in Augusta, Brown, carrying $7,978 in cash (a normal amount for him), bailed himself out for $4,100 and waived extradition. He was driven to Aiken, booked again, given blood and urine tests, and then bailed out by his attorneys at 10 p.m. for $21,268. Four hours later, he was back in the bars along Ninth Street in Augusta, handing out money and buying drinks. At 7:25 in the morning, his Lincoln Continental was spotted weaving on the road five blocks down from Ninth Street. Brown, behind the wheel, "just had his hands up in the air while he was driving down the street," said the arresting officer, T.J. Taylor. "He was incoherent and couldn't hold his balance." Taken to University Hospital, he was tested positive for PCP.

●

I see something bizarre at the last intersection in Aiken, heading out to see Brown's mother: Two flatbeds hauling the halves of a white, two-story prefab house are waiting side by side for the light to change. As they turn left, I catch a glimpse of the interior of one side of the house—dining room, kitchen (major appliances already in place), patio, and a pine stairway leading up to a master bedroom. White curtains are blowing in the windows of the living room, second bedroom, and bath on the second trailer. The two halves come within inches of each other a hundred yards down the road as the drivers pull level and start talking out the windows; downshifting, I start thinking about George and Tammy, and James and Adrienne, as I follow the bifurcated house down the highway at 30 mph. It finally turns right onto the red-dirt drive of a

210 \ No Success Like Failure

former plantation site.

Barnwell County, in which James Brown was born in 1933, is plantation country, with historical markers and red-dirt drives dotting the roadside every mile or so. Prefabs or run-down farmhouses sit dejectedly on the once-magnificent front lawns of most of the sites, more often than not next to a 20-foot, FOR SALE – NO RESTRICTIONS sign, spelling the end, 127 years after abolition, of white plutocracy in the rural South. Off a similar red-dirt road, I find an enclave of similar houses on the outskirts of the town of Bamberg, situated at the edge of a thick, intensely pungent pine forest; a polished Silver Shadow Mercedes in one driveway tells me which house is Mrs. Brown's.

"I had to leave James when he was four, you know," she says apologetically, pouring coffee at the kitchen table. A pair of jays are cawing loudly from a birdhouse nailed to a tree in the backyard, and she tells them to shut up. "We were living out in those woods, because that's what James' father's work was, pulling turpentine out of those trees. One thing about him that never changed, though: He couldn't sit still. Even when he was a baby, he was always crawling out of the house, eating dirt, always eating dirt. One time he ate so much dirt I had to take him to the doctor to get it all out of him. See, he had to stay with his father when we parted, because I was going to New York, to work in the factories, and I couldn't care for him. I didn't see him for over 20 years, until I went to the Apollo Theater, and waited on that line around the block. After the show his people brought him to see me and my two sisters on the third floor of the Theresa Hotel, above the Apollo. I turned it into a game, to see if James could tell which of us was his mother. He knew right away."

I tell her the resemblance is uncanny, and she thanks me. "Even then James was always moving. One place one night, another the next. He's still like that. Gotta keep moving, gotta keep moving. Now how's he going to make it, sitting in a cell all that time?" She shakes her head, raising three fingers. "Three weeks is all I give him. Three weeks to think about what he did. Then I want him to come out and behave, like he's been doing all these years."

•

"Aaaa-aaahhh," James Brown is screaming into the telephone in his Executive Park office in Augusta, 27 months later. "Listen, what I want you to do is, you talk to them all. Say that James Brown said such things have got to be said. Don't ask. Demand. Use the name."

Even with two closed doors and 20 feet between his office and the reception area I'm sitting in, I can hear, if not understand, every word of his rather amazing end of a string of phone calls: a sing-song, gravelly rush of clauses and impulses built, as often as not, around the words James Brown. He says them more like some compound noun, *Jamebrown*, than his name: "We love you," he's telling someone else a minute later, "and you know it too. And James Brown and you's good down the line. And the government'll underwrite it, 'cause the President, the judge, the governor, the whatnot's a friend of James Brown. Aaaa-aaahhh."

It's a nasty, breezeless day outside, even by Augusta's swampy standards. An intense noonday sun and 95 percent humidity has reduced everyone in the office complex to short sleeves and facial handkerchiefs and a New York photographer, who shot Brown on a makeshift dance-floor in the parking lot, to a dizzied dehydration. In the corner office of the adjacent white stucco building, the one Brown entered with a shotgun, a salesman's seminar for a floor-cleaning product is under way: one huge, profusely sweating man with his shirt wide open, lecturing two others. A drowsy temp receptionist in front of me answers the phones: "Top Notch II, a James Brown Affiliate, Home of the Godfather of Soul, may I help you?" as his publicist and chauffeur remind me never to call him James—"It's Mister Brown." Lest I forget, there's a mammoth circular statue of welded brass and steel hanging on the densely lacquered paneled wall that Brown's Faulknerian stream is wafting through. It's a very strange object, indiscernible from up close; standing a good 15 feet away, I can make out what seems like James Brown's profile on an oversize Roman coin—a four-foot head of hair framing the noble forehead, high cheekbone and foot-long granite jaw. The face looks exactly like Elvis Presley's.

"Bless you for that," says the voice behind the wall. "Bless your heart." Then comes the scream: "Aaaa-aaahhh. 'Cause you know we are working on getting the hope factor back into this, and it is a long haul." Click.

More calls follow about this "hope factor," which I can feel burning through the lacquer. Now 59, Brown is releasing a new album and a boxed set of his hits; plugging a bizarre, propagandistic documentary of his life (narrated by Dick Cavett) and a pay-per-view concert in Los Angeles (promoted by boxing impresario Butch Lewis); he also has a tour of half the world penciled in, and plans for resurrecting the careers of every singer, dancer, and athlete of his generation who, like him, refuses to go gently into retirement. There's a strange, temporal parallax going on in this office: The names coming through the wall could fill a new volume of the *Whatever Became Of* series; back at the Augusta Sheraton, over a dozen, incredibly trendy-looking media people from four countries are waiting their chance to photograph and interview him.

In the sleepy towns of the pine barrens of South Carolina and across the Georgia border, *sightings* of James Brown have been reported in the past year: emerging at the Quikshop from his silver 1985 Lincoln Continental, its sales tags, for some reason, still on the window; at gas stations, wearing a self-designed, emerald-green pinstriped suit with his name stitched on the pocket. These sightings, of course, are simply the locals' phrase—half-venerating/half-mocking—for the return of Brown, confined to two counties by the terms of his work-release: going home on his fortnightly furloughs, and to and from his work with the disadvantaged of Aiken and Barnwell counties: everything from counseling students at Jack's Beauty College in a local shopping mall to picnicking with senior citizens. Brown was considered a model prisoner; he made headlines twice, unwittingly, during his term: An eccentric, emeritus South Carolina judge had him summoned to his court to sign autographs for his friends, after which Secret Service (i.e., tax) agents searched Brown's cell, allegedly because Brown had signed for the judge on a play $100 bill bearing his own likeness. (In the cell, they found $48,000 in cash and certified checks.) Granted parole in February 1991, he flew immediately to Los Angeles for cosmetic surgery: permanent eyeliner tattooed on his lids, and a new set of eyebrows. "I got tired of waking up without them," he told a reporter from *People*.

When Brown appears at the reception area door, asking, "This all right for the photo shoot?" my eyes blink reflexively, as if undergoing a sighting. He looks like an apparition: form-fitting black jacket and pants with tight vents and black-thread inlay, a silk magenta shirt open to the sternum, alligator boots tipped in silver on the toe and heel, a jet-black ascot lying like fleur de lys on his massive barrel chest. He has a diamond ring on each hand, a solid-gold watch with a complicated, sea-green face on his wrist, a foot-long, collapsible Afro pick, makeup sponge, and a ring with over 100 keys in his hands, and the most amazing head of hair I've ever seen—fried, dyed, and laid to the side. Standing in the dark hallway, he seems to be glowing—perhaps because every eye-level inch of the hallway is lined with gold records.

I suddenly remember he's talking to me. "You look beautiful."

"Yeah," he nods tautologically, heading back to his office, where he changes into a green suit. "I'll be with you in a little while."

•

"I'm at the height of my career now," Brown tells me. "I had to go to prison for them to realize that all of America has got to get behind James Brown. Rest of the world already knew it."

Proclamations like this punctuate the general silence as we glide along the outskirts of Augusta in his 25-foot Lincoln Continental limo, getting rubbernecked by every driver and pedestrian we pass. It's just past three p.m., and school has let out. On a corner outside an elementary school, a traffic-warden's whistle falls out of her mouth as we stop at the light, and 50 or so kids under three feet tall, holding hands, are squealing as they cross the street. Brown takes it all in from the rear of the limo, his chin held meditatively in one hand; he reminds me from time to time that he doesn't want to discuss his troubles, though I haven't mentioned them. "Keep it positive," he says under his breath, several times, like a refrain from one of his songs. When Brown finally starts talking, I notice that

214 \ No Success Like Failure

this is a small tic of his: a series of beleaguered, Popeye-like phrases that fall like backbeats against the groove of his set-speeches: "Wore me to death," "Keep it going," "You can have this day." Long after parting with him, I realize this is a subtle, perplexing form of control. For the moment, I just feel perplexed, and Brown seems to like it like that. "You're quiet and respectful," he says. "You'll get a lot more out of an entertainer like me that way."

When I ask my first question: "Why do you have a six-year-old car with the sales tags still on?" he says, "Can you believe it? Lincoln dealer said he didn't have any others to sell me. That's a vintage model, only 2,500 made. I got another Lincoln, that's an '86, only 24,000 miles on. I still got the truck they shot up, and"— he mutters himself to a sudden halt: "Keep it positive."

I ask what it's like driving his 1964 Excalibur, which was also parked out in the Executive Park lot.

"Oh man, you got to remind yourself all the time in that car. Time was, I'd open it up to 150 without a thought. Now I won't do but ... Man, you're itching to get me talking about that, aren't you. Listen, the whole truth's going to come out"—he drops an ominous pause before adding: "someday. But I'm not into that now. If the kids of this country wanna get hostile, let 'em do it for themselves. Not in my name. I want to get their good minds, bring the hope factor back."

"What do you mean by 'hope factor?'"

"Simple. Put them in a groove to think good, stay in school, stay off drugs. Why get in trouble, when you can get like Smokey the Bear? Prevention! And I'm not Moses, or an impresario, but I gotta take the position of a Moses, if I'm gonna help."

"What position do you mean?"

"Leadership," he says. Suddenly he's shouting: "TAKE 'EM DOWN FROM THE BULLRUSHES. Brought 'em a long way already. I didn't finish seventh grade, but I'm a PHENOMENON, and that's raw talent. RAW ENERGY. Because the things I say, I didn't read them out in a book. When it comes from within, I got one of the most fantastic minds in the world. But, if you're like me, you believe in God. I don't believe my mind turns all this over. I believe God gives me this, gives me extra mind. See, it's just like the music," he finishes with a huge, rhetorical smile. "Come from God."

•

Within a half-hour of meeting Brown, I've learned to accept these global/biblical self-pronouncements as items of fact. He utters them so blithely, and the numbers are there to back him up: "Four years ago," he shrugs his shoulders, "I played behind the Berlin Wall, to 200,000 people. Michael Jackson was on the west side and he had 40,000. Whitney Houston was 90 miles further up, and she didn't have but 8,000 ...

"They just gave up on me," is how he sees the long eclipse of his career. "Because my stuff was too complicated. They took what they could"—his voice goes up an octave as he minces out, "littttle pieces. The simplest rhythms for their disco, here and there with their samplers. Never the whole funk. They couldn't. I hid it in too many places. See, you can take any line, any scream, or drumbeat you want from me, but you cannot take the funk. It's an experience, what you learn along the way. I just took the gospel and jazz," he concludes with another shrug of the shoulders, "and did a great thing there."

I tell Brown I've never really understood what funk is and he screams, "Aaaa-aaahhh, I love you for that," and puts his hand on my forearm. "You know what I'm gonna do though? When I leave, I'm gonna do like Einstein, and put together a little thing for their hearts, a manual on how to put the funk together. See, you play chords like"—Brown sings me a sweet, 16-note vamp, then taps it out on my forearm. "But you still gotta get the feel of the dances today." He sings the riff again, but with a stiff, stentorian rhythm, his voice sounding like a frog croak. "But that's different from"— he sings it again, with the sweet music back in as he taps out a double-time shuffle that accents each note twice.

"Those are polyrhythms?" I ask.

"That," he gives me a crocodile grin, "is the pocket. P-O-C-K-E-T. Right where you want it. Get it in the pocket"—he grabs my forearm and squeezes it tenderly—"and it's all the same."

I try to ask another question, and he howls: "GET IT IN THE POCKET. It's just like when I'm sitting in the church and getting it in the pocket, you're gonna faint and you're gonna jump up and you're gonna jump down. You don't know where or when or why the Holy Ghost hit you but you are gonna jump up and down.

"But tell me," he gauges the darkness of my sun-tanned forearm with his jeweled fingers, "you're Afro-American, aren't you?"

Thinking he's just flattering me, I say nothing. "Down here," he says, looking out the window as we cruise through the downtown toward the Savannah River, "believe me, you're Afro-American."

•

As we walk along Augusta's newly gentrified waterfront, the entire populace seems to converge on us. Blacks approach Brown reverently, and as Mister Brown. An elderly woman comes up for a hug and starts crying as she tells Brown that she lost her son in the Gulf War. Whites call out Brown's name with an easy familiarity. "Well, I'll be damned," says a man in a short-sleeved shirt, coming up to pump his hand. "If it isn't James Brown. Glad to see you, James."

We climb a hill by the river toward the Sixth Street railroad trestle, where the photographer sets up for a shoot away from the crowd. A faint smell of creosote on the railroad ties gets Brown talking under his breath dreamily. I pick up the word "barefooted" and ask what he means. "We used to come up here to look for the good coal," he says. "Train coal, which would burn twice: as coal, then as coke, which you could cook on. It looks exactly the same here," he says, balancing himself on the rails as he smiles for the camera, "only now I got shoes. Then it was barefooted."

He repeats the word three times—a sotto-voce field holler as he raises a fist at the photographer's request, louder the second time, flashing a peace sign, then with a big smile and a scream: "Bare … foot … ed. Mind over matter. Had no mind, so it just didn't matter."

I point to our right, the Fifth Street Bridge, where he buck-danced for quarters as an eight-year-old, and which he crossed on the return to Augusta during his chase. Brown steps off the rail and wags his finger, saying "Keep it positive." He looks at the woods of

South Carolina, across the river. "We used to go hunting at night," he says. "For something I don't want to talk about, much less eat. Possum. Terrible. See, when you shoot something wild," he says, "you got to string it."

Brown points to the back of his thigh and draws a hand across it, like a karate chop. "Cut that string in the back of the leg, or it's too gamey, and the critter'll seize up on you. I didn't learn that till I didn't have to eat possum anymore," he says, flashing me that crocodile grin one more time as he heads back to the limo. "Too late then."

The Big Think
The Black and White World of Chess Mania

If you want to ruin a happy man, a Yiddish proverb runs, teach him how to play chess.

Outside the Penta Hotel's Georgian Room, site of the New York Open Tournament, a half-dozen masters and international masters in their mid-thirties stand by a seven-by-twenty foot crosstable of the top-rated players, talking politics, modems, Derrida, anything but chess. Filled with acronyms and intellectual minutiae, unspeakably cynical, superior, and entre nous, their conversation sounds like the minutes of a MENSA meeting, c. 1968, though laced with the turgid, acid bonhomie one finds only in chess circles. I know a few—they argue politics and literature and obscure grandmasters of the 1920s and '30s for hours in a cafe near the Chess Shop on Thompson Street—but most are strangers, living in university towns upstate and across the country. Fifteen years ago, they were all studying political science and ancient Greek together at NYU, living for chess and nothing but.

A fellow traveler steps out of the Georgian Room after a quick mauling by the Romanian grandmaster Mihai Suba. "Chess?" he asks, sidling over to a laptop PC he's patched into a phone jack the hotel has stupidly left free. He calls a computer bulletin board in Santa Cruz, $15/hour, plus long-distance charges, and scrolls down a list of subject entries on the expensive, dark-blue screen.

"Semiotics?" he asks the guys. "Sexuality? Sports? Who the fuck plays chess anymore?"

By way of contradiction, the doors of the Georgian Room fly open and Ben Feingold comes barreling out, his agile bulk bursting through his perennial ALL AMERICAN CHESS TEAM jacket and his WORLD CHESS FESTIVAL T-shirt, twirling a white pawn between his thumb and ring finger like a Colt revolver. Chess players' ages are often impossible to gauge. With his slight mustache and his oily hair hanging over never-fully-open eyes, Ben looks like some incurable 30-year-old, living in the black-and-white world of chess obsession; he's actually only 16, and one of the great natural talents to come up in the last few years: I spent an afternoon last winter watching him trade insults and play blitz (in which each player gets five minutes for the entire game) with a grandmaster in St. John, New Brunswick. During one endgame, the words "Mate in eleven" came up in his nonstop patter, while sacrificing a rook for a bishop; 11 moves and 10 seconds later, when this actually happened, the former World Champion Mikhail Tal, also watching the game, said, "I saw the sacrifice and also the mate, but how do you count to eleven so fast?" Ben looked at him as though he were an idiot.

He's looking at me now in the same way. "You wanna know about life?" he asks me in his lazy, high-pitched bellow. "Where do I know you from anyway? The Manhattan [Chess Club]? St. John? There are five things in life. There's chess"—he points to the Georgian Room behind us; "there's chess"—jutting a huge thumb toward the Grand Ballroom, where over 1000 amateurs are competing for $80,000 in prizes; "there's chess"—he waves disgustedly past the Grand Ballroom to the St. Louis Room, where a dozen or so hustlers and "customers" are playing for $2, $5, or $10 a game; "there's chess"—he flutters a hand tentatively toward his older friends huddled around the PC (i.e., the social pleasures of chess); "and, five, there's Judith Polgar. Hey," he calls out to his friends, leaving me behind without further ceremony, "can you believe that little fucking Polgar got an IM [International Master] norm?"

•

At Board 327 in the Grand Ballroom, under the pleasing glow of old chandeliers, I await the arrival of Calderon, my first-round opponent, a little blissed from the 2000 mgs. of L-Tryptophan that got me early to bed last night, thrilled to be in a room with over 1000 people who've never heard of sun-dried tomatoes, Jacques Lacan, or Agnes B. My neighbor on 326, a computer engineer from Quebec who stutters indifferently in French or English, is arguing the merits of digital chess clocks with a handsome, blond-haired systems analyst from Chelsea on 328, a divorcé from Chelsea who feels his wife was probably right to have left him for the man she did, and can't immediately recall what street he lives on when I ask.

Mr. Calderon arrives—not the scarf-wearing Catalan I've been expecting, but a 50-year-old Filipino with thick, brown-tinted aviator glasses who whispers into his hands while he calculates. I spend my first eight moves grinning like Caliban: my three center pawns bask in a pool of soft white light on the fourth rank, lines open for my pieces, poised to destroy this idiot with the temerity to play the Polish Defense against me. He moves a pawn to c5, I develop my knight; he pushes his queen pawn and out comes my bishop, threatening his queen—all seen long before—and soon, I'm beginning to suspect, Mr. Calderon will have to be resigning.

He slams his bishop down on b4 and says "Check" in an ugly voice. As I nose my knight up to c3 to interpose, an alarm goes off. His bishop move, I suddenly see, has created an escape square for his king on f8, which means that when I shuttle my queen to h5 next move and put him in check I won't be mating him or picking up his rook on h8 after all. In fact, all I've done is lost a rook. I look at my hand, glowing sickly white as it lets go of the knight, then realize that if I'd at least put this piece on d2 instead of c3, I could've forced his bishop to take, and gotten my queen on a better square. But I've already let go, the move is made, and I'm completely busted, the first of over 1000 people to lose. In a kind of dream state, I watch my hand open as it reaches across the board to resign to Mr. Calderon.

•

Fifty paces away from the disclaimers and monomaniacs, Judith

222 \ No Success Like Failure

Polgar sits like Caesar at Board 17 inside the Georgian Room, her mind moving upon silence. I study her through a telephoto lens—her light hair tied back severely from her bone-white face, her hands cupped over her eyes so that nothing is seen but the board. Her eyes are doing the "calculation dance:" a steady, impassive scanning movement from square to square that gives them a heavy, inhuman quality, for they no longer look at anything but simply follow the mind thinking through them. Every 30 seconds, a line of calculation run through, she blinks, sneers up at the mob that invariably forms around her game, then tightens the visor of her hands over her forehead and goes back into it. Beside the chess clock to the right of her board, atop a paperback of Yuri Averbakh's *Pawn Endings*, is a three-inch brown bear that's come with her from Budapest, facing forward, so it can watch the game. Judith, 11 years old, doesn't understand what psychic murder that bear must be on her opponent.

After 20 minutes she emerges from what Bobby Fischer used to call a "big think" and reaches for a knight on d4. Her hand begins to shake wildly until she clamps her little fingers on its head and slides it to f5. These tremors can happen to the most seasoned grandmasters on critical moves, I've noticed, and to anyone coming out of a big think, this conversion of a half-hour of entirely abstract and exalted existence into one paltry movement of a piece of plastic over a few inches. She seems to have done it right. Her 13-year-old sister/fellow prodigy Sofia comes over, glances at the position, gives Judith one of their *Village of the Damned* smiles, then skips off to see how their 19-year-old sister, Szuza, is doing on Board Seven.

•

Going up Sixth Avenue on a packed #7 bus, I'm aware of wanting to murder Mr. Calderon and the more unpleasant sensation that the ads on the bus are reaching me: that the Real People in the Winston ad do have Real Taste, that my morning was shit because I didn't have la mas cafe. It's only after cashing a paycheck in a midtown bank, half an hour later, that I realize how much this defeat has fractured me, and how much I've forgotten the Real Game of Chess: two voices calling my name as I'm leaving the bank, the teller and the *guard, informing me I've left my $910 in cash at the window, next to my wallet and pocket chess set.*

●

In the St. Louis Room you pay as much for the floor show as for the privilege of losing a few bucks over the board.

Hank (names changed here to protect the writer) is on a roll this year, massaging out-of-towner masochism and the desire for a "good Broadway show" for $10 a game. His early-Open third-person routines ("Look what this leper's doing to the Hank," "Give to the Hank the Hank's due, you fucking sleaze") has given way to fecal classics, now that his name is properly advertised. The board becomes an anal-erotic minefield:

"Do I smell ... a caca in little asswipe's jammies?" he asks a Colorado golden boy currently losing the plane fare home. "Yes," taunts Hank, "look what the turd's gone and done on f6," his beefy finger shaking with disgust in front of a bishop his opponent, for no good reason, has just moved there. Hank sniffs the air above the bishop for added effect, and the finger moves like a divining rod to a pawn on h7. "And how, may I ask, is this poo-poo, this vile little black waste product, hoping to survive the royal ... flush?"—he peashoots the pawn into the young man's chest, then slams his queen down on the square.

Yiannis, a walking Greek chorus of scatological antiphony, is making money on side bets this afternoon, having stayed up till six this morning with a customer of his own. To ensure his wagers, he sits next to the kid, howling today's neologism, *Caca-poo-poo,* repeatedly into his ear from point-blank range, alternating with bellows of "Yes, I'm sick, I have a paranoia mycropsis," and "Very sexually played, Hank baby" with the Hank's every other move. The kid, who's probably never imagined human beings could behave this way, seems to be toying with the idea of belting one or both of them, which seems like a pretty good idea to me. Finally, he just breaks down into strange, whimpering laughter and reaches into his wallet for a pair of $10s.

●

I began playing serious tournament chess six years ago, after a partic-

*ularly nasty break-up, and quickly found myself in good company.
The chess clubs and tournament halls of the world abound with
escapees from life's uglier dictates—either for the nonce or as part of
the lifetime plan. So quickly, for these pensioners, the disenfran-
chised, the romantically disappointed, 52 weeks become 64 squares,
humanity narrows to the strange camaraderie of chessplayers, and
society to the limited, accountable solace of chessmen. It's a testimony to the richness of chess how precisely all value and wisdom
translate into the game's impenetrable logic, how each game recapitu-
lates the mistakes of the life that you're avoiding by playing chess:
From an opening teeming with intent and possibility and complica-
tions, a plan is conceived, put into action, and then a hundred things
start going wrong: An unimportant square, for which no provision
has been made, has become critical, a rook that should have made it
to e1 is still on a1. "Life," like the man says, "is what happens to you
while you're busy making other plans."*

•

By the age of 10, Bobby Fischer had mastered enough Russian,
German, Spanish, Dutch, and Serbo-Croatian to find his way
through the polyglot sprawl of chess literature, a necessity a quick
spin around the Georgian Room will confirm. Now in the last day
of the Open, the once-quiet hall has become a kibbitzing Tower of
Babel, a low hum of Russian, English, French, Romanian, the
weird, hard consonants of Hungarian, Spanish, Icelandic,
Hebrew, Tagalog.

The lingua franca of any real tournament hall is Russian: Forty
per cent of the top players here were Russian-born and raised, and
at least half of the 200 or so people who can make a living playing
chess in the United States were born there. "In Soviet Union," the
emigré grandmaster Dmitry Gurevic explains to me, "100 percent
of budget is for military, 10 percent for chess. When you emigrate
you gain 100 percent freedom, and you lose 10 percent chess."

This has become obvious at the Open: The heretofore unknown
Vassily Ivanchuk, a Raskolnikovian 18-year-old who stares beseech-
ingly at the ceiling throughout his games while he calculates, is
basking in his 15 minutes of fame after winning the $20,000 first

prize in the international tournament held before the Open. The Soviet machine has been stamping out talents like Ivanchuk for 40 years. He clinched first place with a seventh-round demolition of Boris Gulko, a prematurely grey cause-celebre refusenik/ex-prodigy who spent 10 years in hunger strikes and exile to obtain release papers for himself and his wife; behind him on Board Two sat his former countryman Vadimir Tukmakov, behind Tukmakov the ex-prodigy Alexandr Cernin, earning his share of third-place money by squeezing a torturous endgame out of the Soviet defector Igor Ivanov.

•

Ivanov is probably the most peaceable man ever to move a chess piece, but a successful one nonetheless. Sweetness is an occupational liability in a chessplayer: Chess is a struggle for dominion between two people. Ivanov, who will not be dominated, has no wish to ruin anyone. He simply wants to make enough money to cover the plane to Montreal, and maybe something to live on as well. When I first started playing, I went up to him once in the Chess Shop on Thompson Street and challenged him to a game. I think he liked me, for he taught me a strange lesson. After winning two hard-fought games from him, I looked up, my head reeling with disbelief, to see him smiling at me, one of the most humorous smiles I've ever seen. Then he got up and walked away.

•

In the last round, Ivanov is playing the 22-year-old emigre grandmaster Maxim Dlugy for all the marbles. Dlugy, one of the up-and-coming superstars, is too well-prepared theoretically for Ivanov to beat in a straightforward grandmaster game, and Ivanov throws a wrench into the opening, angling to take Dlugy "out of the book" (of known opening theory) and into terra incognita. By his 15th move, it's becoming clear his probing has worked. What he's seen are two tricky knight maneuvers: The first is an exchange of pawns on e5, where he recaptures with a pawn instead of the knight, contrary to normal procedure in such positions, the second a knight's tour from f6 to a5, whereby he wins a pawn, and with it the game and $10,000. Nothing visionary, a simple game—except, of course, for the two grandmasters sitting next to me in the audience who were convinced Ivanov was "busted," "ruined," and "hopeless" after 12 moves.

•

"Chess," the philosopher/world champion Emanuel Lasker once said, "like life, is a fight for truth." To lose a game of chess, if one has devoted a part of one's life to finding truth over the board, is to lose a mini-series of one's life, which is an outrage, and to lose truth, which is unbearable. In the remaining seven rounds, I come to the board galvanized to take back what I've lost, no longer charmed by the misfits but wanting their blood, which I can taste in the back of my throat. In my gut before each game, the butterflies of nervousness and aggression are at war. "Anyone who can make a friend of that awful feeling," Boris Spassky once said, "is a dangerous opponent."

But for now it's a beautiful spring day. In the pocket park on 53rd Street and Fifth, I set up the position of my debacle on my pocket set, piecing ways out of Calderon's little trap, each winning position that I reach only telling me more about the loss. I become aware of a shadow over the board and look behind me: One of the old men who spend their days in the park is analyzing the position. He asks me if I'd like to play with him, and I tell him I'd like nothing more.

•

On my way out of the Penta, I see Ivanov celebrating by himself at the bar. I ask him if he remembers the day we played a couple of games in the Village, and he says No, he must have been drunk or something. I ask about his most famous victory, over then World Champion Anatoly Karpov, which helped earn him an invitation to a tournament abroad, and the chance to defect. A few sheets to the wind, Ivanov tells me his life story instead.

"I was born in Leningrad and I spent in Leningrad 30 years of my life, or 31. I was invited to Moscow, and after two years in Moscow, I left the country forever."

Why Moscow?

"I wanted to leave, somehow, but in the Soviet Union it's not available, you can't just apply for passport and go. Chess was only possibility. In Moscow, I could talk to Communist Part chiefs, authorized people. But only two things worked. I gave money to some people."

And the other?

"I promised to give some more. After two years they let me go. A tournament in Cuba. They didn't know my plans when they took my dirty money. I was playing a game with them, you can call it a dirty game. They can say I was a bad person, but for me it was a different kind of game. If I say I want to go, maybe I go to Siberia. I was never ashamed what I did to those people.

"At the airport I heard the plane was stopping in Canada. But I wasn't prepared for this! To make such a decision in six hours! I didn't have any money, any languages, just some ideas about Canada I heard on my radio late at night in Moscow. I was crazy then, 33 years old. Christ was 33 when he was crucified, so I figured, What the hell?"

How old were you when you ... ?

"I started to play chess at five; maybe I had some talent. But I didn't play seriously until I was 14. My mother wanted me to play music. Cello. My poor mother. When she died I forgot cello."

You don't seem very ambitious?

"Me? I'm 41. I want peace in my life. But it's not very easy to find it without money. I'm very happy that the airplane stops in Canada. In Europe, I'd have to play more. I played a lot in the U.S. when I first came, to pay my bills. I don't play very much now, maybe I don't live as well as before. Maybe I'm even less ambitious. This is your question, yes? I survive."

Do you love chess?

"Chess? It a nice game. Maybe it is a little boring?" He finishes his vodka, gives that incredible smile again, and orders another. "I really hated the cello," he says.